IN TUNE
WITH
AMERICA

OTHER BOOKS OF INTEREST FROM MARQUETTE BOOKS & DEMERS BOOKS

Norma Sawyers-Kurtz, *How to Cope with the Loss of Your Child: A Guide for Grieving Parents* (2010). ISBN: 978-0-9816002-5-3

John V. Wylie, *Diagnosing and Treating Mental Illness: A Guide for Physicians, Nurses, Patients and Their Families* (2010). ISBN: 978-0-9816002-6-0

Eric G. Stephan and R. Wayne Pace, *7 Secrets of a Successful, Tranquil Life: A Guide for People Who Want to Get Out of Hyperdrive* (2010). ISBN 978-0-9816002-7-7

John Wheeler, *Last Man Out: Memoirs of the Last Associated Press Reporter Castro Kicked Out of Cuba in the 1960s* (2009). ISBN: 978-0-9816002-0-8

Tom Graves, *Crossroads: The Life and Afterlife of Blues Legend Robert Johnson* (2009). ISBN: 978-0-9816002-1-5

Charles J. Merrill, *Colom of Catalonia: Origins of Christopher Columbus Revealed* (2009). ISBN 978-0-9816002-2-2

John W. Cones, *Introduction to the Motion Picture Industry: A Guide for Students, Filmmakers and Scholars* (2009). ISBN: 978-0-922993-90-1 (paper)

John Schulz, *Please Don't Do That! The Pocket Guide to Good Writing* (2008). ISBN: 978-0-922993-87-1 (booklet)

John W. Cones, *Dictionary of Film Finance and Distribution: A Guide for Independent Filmmakers* (2008). ISBN: 978-0-922993-93-2 (cloth); 978-0-922993-94-9 (paper)

Hazel Dicken-Garcia and Giovanna Dell'Orto, *Hated Ideas and the American Civil War Press* (2008). ISBN: 978-0-922993-88-8 (paper); 978-0-922993-89-5 (cloth)

Tomasz Pludowski (ed.), *How the World's News Media Reacted to 9/11: Essays from Around the Globe* (2007). ISBN: 978-0-922993-66-6 (paper)

Jami A. Fullerton and Alice G. Kendrick, *Advertising's War on Terrorism: The Story of the U.S. State Department's Shared Values Initiative Program* (2006). ISBN: 0-922993-43-2 (cloth); 0-922993-44-0 (paper)

Stephen D. Cooper, *Watching the Watchdog: Bloggers as the Fifth Estate* (2006). ISBN: 0-922993-46-7 (cloth); 0-922993-47-5 (paper)

Ralph D. Berenger (ed.), *Cybermedia Go to War: Role of Alternative Media During the 2003 Iraq War* (2006). ISBN: 0-922993-24-6 (paper)

David Demers, *Dictionary of Mass Communication: A Guide for Students, Scholars and Professionals* (2005). ISBN: 0-922993-35-1 (cloth); 0-922993-25-4 (paper)

Ralph D. Berenger (ed.), *Global Media Go to War: Role of Entertainment and News During the 2003 Iraq War* (2004). ISBN: 0-922993-10-6

Melvin L. DeFleur and Margaret H. DeFleur, *Learning to Hate Americans: How U.S. Media Shape Negative Attitudes Among Teenagers in Twelve Countries* (2003). ISBN: 0-922993-05-X

IN TUNE
WITH
AMERICA

Our History
in Song

George R. Nethercutt, Jr.
With Tom M. McArthur

MARQUETTE BOOKS SPOKANE, WA

PRINTED IN THE UNITED STATES OF AMERICA
by Thomson-Shore, Dexter, Michigan

LIBRARY OF CONGRESS CONTROL NUMBER
2010924011

ISBN FOR THIS HARDCOVER EDITION
978-0-9826597-0-0

Cover Jacket Design by Jane Floyd of JF Design
Interior design by Marquette Books

Published by

MARQUETTE BOOKS
3107 East 62nd Avenue
Spokane, Washington 99223
509-443-7057 (voice) • 509-448-2191 (fax)
books@marquettebooks.org • www.MarquetteBooks.org

THIS BOOK IS DEDICATED TO
THE THREE MOST IMPORTANT
WOMEN IN MY LIFE

My wife, Mary Beth,
who has lived my dreams with love

My mother, Nancy S. Nethercutt,
who always believed in me

My daughter, Meredith,
who is heroic to me

CONTENTS

A WELCOME FROM THE AUTHORS

*I*n *Tune with America.*

This is a history book. This is not a history book. Actually, it's a love story. May we explain?

Too often, books we describe as "history books" are uninviting — especially college textbooks. They look at history in such detail that readers are overwhelmed with seemingly irrelevant dates, obscure facts and ancient figures that most of us don't know or find hard to remember. Yet, the United States — the representative republic that is our homeland — is a rich mixture of outstanding and interesting people and leaders spanning over two centuries. Their collective contributions over generations — to a society that values freedom above all — are worthy of our attention as citizens.

Ours is a story of struggle, heartbreak, triumph and growth. It is a story all Americans should know and love because it is a story about us. And knowing our story makes us all better Americans and helps us more deeply love our country — better prepared to value all that America provides us, to defend it, preserve it and make sure our children, and their grandchildren, do, too.

Being "in tune with America" has an extra dimension in this book, not just knowing about our country, but more. It adds a twist to knowing our story — a musical twist. Since 1776, the year the United States declared independence from Great Britain, there have been moments when patriotic Americans put their thoughts to rhyme and music, in song, to express what they felt, and sometimes saw, as witnesses to history. They describe — in music — their emotions: fear, sadness, joy and sometimes resolve, as history unfolds before their eyes. Through music they record their impressions of events, policies, injustices and victories. They were "in tune" with the significant and memorable events of their era.

When Richmond, the Confederate capital, fell to Union forces in April 1865, ending our nation's bloodiest conflict — the Civil War — the man whose leadership had preserved the nation, President Abraham Lincoln, asked a military band to play a song. It was not a song of triumph over enemies, for Lincoln referred to the Confederates as "our friends across the river." It was not a song of war or destruction. President Lincoln asked the band to play "Dixie," the tune that stood for the secessionist South through four long and bloody years. It was now America's song. And with that one musical gesture, President Lincoln tried to set the nation on a road to healing that, tragically, he would not live to see. This is but one dramatic example of how music has been intertwined with the fate of our nation — dating back even to the days before there was a United States, when we were merely colonies of the British Empire.

Songs are the poetry of American history. Knowing the stories of the music of an era helps us know the story of our country and the many eras through which it has emerged — that story is our national story. If you are a citizen, whether born or naturalized here, this is your story, too — and every American, regardless of ethnic background or heritage, should know it.

Written as a resource for Fellows of the George Nethercutt Foundation (www.nethercuttfoundation.org), this volume reflects a fundamental truth that our country — as President Lincoln put it

— is a nation conceived in liberty and dedicated to the proposition that all men are created equal. Knowing America's story and understanding liberty's history is important to our national citizenship — it gives us a solid basis upon which to judge current events, assess essential leadership qualities and possess a fundamental knowledge of American democracy as history unfolds before our eyes.

English attorney Frederick Weatherly (who wrote the lyrics for the classic "Danny Boy") writes in 1926,

> We may listen to the noblest sermons. We may study the deepest philosophy. We may be elevated by the loftiest speeches. We may read the brightest pages of history. And yet none appeal to us with quite the same appeal as song and story. Is it not perhaps that all the rest appeal to the intellect and need mental powers which only the few possess? But song and story appeal to the heart. From the heart they come and to the heart they go.

We live in a time when too many Americans have forgotten — or are not taught — how the United States came to exist, or the relevance and importance of America's founding documents. The Constitution, Declaration of Independence, landmark laws and society-changing Supreme Court decisions seem somehow "irrelevant" to the busy lives we lead. But they make our country what it is — the greatest democracy in history. To be unfamiliar with America's story is to diminish why and how the United States became free and makes us ignorant about those who fought to make it so.

So, this is an overview of the story of our national family, without hyphens or qualifiers, but illustrated and punctuated by musical selections. More than dates and facts, this book helps bring to life through music the drama that enriches who we are — as a nation and as a people.

E Pluribus Unum — from many we are one. This is our motto and this is our story of freedom. We are simply Americans. Enjoy a noteworthy story about us and the freedoms we enjoy.

It is something to sing about!

GEORGE R. NETHERCUTT, JR.
TOM M. MCARTHUR
Spokane, Washington

CHAPTER 1

THE AMERICAN REVOLUTION

For Independence We All Now Agree

You say you want a revolution
Well you know
We all want to change the world

John Lennon
"Revolution"
The Beatles
1968

The Beatles record "Revolution" in July of 1968. It is a raucous song. The world, at the time, is filled with tension. In America, large groups of citizens demonstrate for civil rights and protest against a war in Vietnam; France is jarred by riots for regime change. In writing the song, John Lennon says he is "painting in sound a picture of revolution."

Revolution. The word comes from Latin: *revolvo*, a turn around. When an engine turns around, it is measured in revolutions per minute (RPM). When a political system turns around, it is often measured in great loss of human lives and property. A revolution, in the political sense, is a fundamental change in power: One group takes power; one group loses.

Revolutions occur repeatedly throughout human history — they are usually radical and extreme. There is a wide variance in how they happen, how long they last and why they erupt. Regardless, revolutions bring change, whether in politics, cultural standards, economies or leadership. Throughout the past three centuries, we witnessed the French Revolution in 1789; the Russian Revolution in 1917; and the Chinese Revolutions in 1927 and 1949. The Castro Revolution in Cuba has lasted from 1959 to the present day. In modern times, revolutions occur in nations of Latin America, the Middle East and Africa. Looking back, there is usually some evidence of dissatisfaction, unrest or inequity from which full-scale revolutions develop.

The American Revolutionary War or the American War of Independence — from which the United States of America is born — occurs from 1775 to 1783. It is a revolt against British colonization and control of North America. And the struggle is illustrated in many songs, including J.W. Hewlings "American Hearts of Oak," written in 1775.

Come rouse up my lads, and join this great cause
In defence of your liberty, your property, and laws!
'Tis to honor we call you, stand up for your right,
And ne'er let our foes say, we are put to the flight.
For so just is our cause, and so valiant our men,
We always are ready, steady boys, steady;
We'll fight for our freedom again and again
The Scotch politicians have laid a deep scheme,
By invading America to bring Charlie in;

And if the Scotch mist's not remov'd from the throne,
The crown's not worth wearing, the kingdom's undone.

J.W. Hewlings
"American Hearts of Oak"
1775

For our country, revolution officially starts the American story. The England of the mid-17th century is a nation of pomp and circumstance — a regal, monarchical and aristocratic society that is exceedingly formal and at times oppressively restrictive. Its colonies have global reach. Americans today have such an abundance of freedom that we find it hard to fathom having been controlled by a government a continent far away. It is not hard to understand that the Founders of the United States of America widely envisioned a new existence, one living beyond the unnatural state of English domination.

Yet the genesis for America's love of freedom and independence and the seeds of revolution are first the establishment of Jamestown Settlement in Virginia in 1607, and then the migration in 1620 of a small group of religious separatists from England on a ship christened The Mayflower. These Pilgrims are seeking religious freedom and independence from Great Britain and the Anglican Church to which unchallenged allegiance is owed. They decide to pull up stakes and leave the only country they know for an arduous trip across the Atlantic Ocean to an uncertain destiny. Determination marks their launch to the New World. With 102 passengers and crew on board, The Mayflower's departure from Southampton, England, on September 16, 1620, is both sorrowful and sobering. Ocean travel for sixty-six days proves harrowing. Upon arrival at what is now Cape Cod, Massachusetts, forty-one of the ship's passengers sign the Mayflower Compact, a document that serves as the first majoritarian model for self-government, a social contract by which the Plymouth settlers agree to be bound in the governing of their affairs. It is a significant step toward independence.

The Compact does two things: It affirms the settlers' colonization of this new land and establishes a form of self-governance to which they pledge their allegiance. The Compact is undertaken "for the Glory of God and advancement of the Christian Faith." Its co-equal purpose is the advancement of the "Honour of our King and Country." Its importance is not so much that the settlers represent England, but that they are establishing, in writing, the principles of self-governance and the foundation for the constitutional democracy that will last for centuries.

Between the early 1600s and the mid-1700s, colonization of the new land continues. A look back lets us now see the commitment to independence. Thirteen original colonies are established, principally on the northeastern and southeastern coasts. They are Delaware, Pennsylvania, New Jersey, Georgia, Connecticut, Massachusetts, Maryland, South Carolina, New Hampshire, Virginia, New York, North Carolina and Rhode Island. By 1775, the original group of several hundred settlers has grown to almost 2.4 million. Each of the colonies is connected by the common thread of commitment to independence, individual freedom and adventure. Facing disease, hardships posed by long distance from England, the challenges of natural resource use, relationships with Native Americans and the novelty of self-governance, the settlers personify extraordinary self-reliance and bravery and a seriousness of purpose in the name of liberty. By now, a generation of independent spirit has been established.

Colonial conditions and attitudes have also changed dramatically. Anger at Britain's growing repression in the colonies reaches a boiling point. Taxes levied from Mother England are deemed excessive. British control of colonial settlements is so strict and dogmatic in recent years that the colonists yearn even more for independence. The colonists have elected a Continental Congress — representatives who convene as a legislative group to make decisions for all thirteen colonies.

So, in 1776, the foundation has been laid and the stage is set for a revolution. The colonial leaders who step forward to found this new country believe in the new concept of government — freedom and self-government — that they have practiced since the Mayflower Compact was signed. They recognize the importance of individual rights to the success of any central state. They embrace the concept of representative government — electing public leaders to represent their interests.

They also have a model for a new government — it is fashioned after the *Magna Carta* (Latin for "Great Charter"), widely viewed as one of the most important documents in the history of democracy. It is a foundational document for the colonists — it leads them to the U.S. Constitution and a "people-based" government.[1]

With this background, the American Revolution is under way. Its lofty purposes are self-government and liberty, with a clear dedication to the individual. Philosopher John Locke writes that "the state is a vehicle for protecting the natural rights of man, and if it cannot, the people have every right to rise up and rebel." Self-governance concepts are understood by the colonists in the 1770s as fundamental, self-evident truths, worthy of protection, and worthy of revolt.

The right of rebellion accepted by the colonists of the late 18th century leads them to action against King George III. That action is war.

Hark, hark, the sound of war is heard,
And we must all attend;
Take up our arms and go with speed
Our country to defend.

Benjamin Dearborn
"War Song"
1776

Many of the songs of the American Revolution are calls to arms, encouraging actions to stem a tide or fight a battle. Dr. Jonathan Mitchell Sewall of New Hampshire is a colonial Loyalist (even those loyal to the King want independence) who writes a song called "On Independence" in 1776. Despite the heritage of the Loyalists, the song reflects their deep devotion to their common cause and their unwavering conviction that the independence of their fledgling colonies justifies rebellion.

Come all you brave soldiers, both valiant and free,
It's for Independence we all now agree;
Let us gird on our swords, and prepare to defend,
Our liberty, property, ourselves and our friends.

In a cause that's so righteous, come let us agree,
and from hostile invaders set America free,
the cause is so glorious we need not to fear,
but from merciless tyrants we'll set ourselves clear.

Heaven's blessing attending us, no tyrant shall say
That Americans e'er to such monsters gave way,
But fighting we'll die in America's cause,
Before we'll submit to tyrannical laws.

Dr. Jonathan Mitchell Sewall
"On Independence"
1776

The lyrics of Dr. Sewall's song reflect the priorities of the colonists on the eve of the American Revolution and the intangibles by which they are driven. The word "Heaven" is mentioned six times in Sewall's song; the words "independence," "liberty" and "free" are mentioned seven times. These words are the hallmarks of America's beginning and will sustain the new nation through future challenges.

In 1774, Thomas Jefferson, a thirty-one-year-old political philosopher and Virginia state legislator, writes his first published work, "A Summary View of the Rights of British America." It is a lengthy counter to the Coercive Acts[2] passed by the British Parliament that year. Jefferson asserts that the British have no authority to govern the American colonists. To the contrary, the colonists have the natural right to govern themselves. Jefferson's paper articulates a theoretical framework for the concepts behind the American Revolution. It is this framework that defines Jefferson as a thoughtful architect of American independence, well equipped to help draft the Declaration of Independence two years later in 1776.

In addition to the enumeration of specific complaints against King George III, the Declaration of Independence passed by the Continental Congress carries the frightening assurance that the signers pledge "our lives, our fortunes and our sacred honor" to the great cause they are bound to undertake.

For the American colonies to wage war against the British Empire in 1776 is analogous to a high school team lining up against the pros. But the American colonists have leadership and resolve — two essential ingredients for victory. A bloody and tragic seven-year war is waged in all thirteen colonies. Thousands are killed; thousands more are wounded. Dramatic battles won and lost produce American leaders and heroes who earn the privilege of serving in war and in the peace they ultimately achieve.

America and England sign the Treaty of Paris in 1783, ending British rule in all thirteen colonies. What comes of seven years of fighting is a new nation that adopts a constitutional democracy and establishes a legal system that protects individual rights, guarantees due process of law, affirms states' rights, and ensures the construction of a governmental system that will serve the people's needs and desires. But the democracy earned by war and separation develops slowly. The Continental Congress commences work on a governing document, beginning in May 1787. Colonial independence evolves into national unity — delicately.

After five months of Congressional debate, the Constitution is adopted by Congress on September 17, 1787. Thirteen years after the Continental Congress adopts the Declaration of Independence and two years after adopting the Constitution at Philadelphia, Pennsylvania, the new government under the Constitution begins operations on March 4, 1789. All thirteen states ratify the

Constitution by May 29, 1790. The Constitution balances the equities of individual rights with national order, and balances the rights of states with the necessity of having a unified central government. It has sectional balance that acknowledges the economic and social realities of the South as different from the values of the northern colonies. Generations later those Southern traditions will be balanced with the social and economic values of the nation as a whole.

The year 1789 also marks the year that "Hail, Columbia" becomes the nation's new unofficial anthem. It is composed and adopted for the inauguration of George Washington, the nation's first president and the most famous soldier of the Revolutionary War. Written by violinist and musician Philip Phile, it is titled "The President's March." The song's lyrics are written by Joseph Hopkinson nine years later.[3]

The song, "Hail, Columbia" celebrates America, reveres its new president and exalts patriotism and freedom. The chorus strikes a consistent message after the opening stanza:

Hail Columbia, happy land!
Hail, ye heroes, heav'n-born band
Who fought and bled in freedom's cause,
Who fought and bled in freedom's cause,
And when the storm of war was gone
Enjoy'd the peace their valor won.
Let independence be our boast, ever mindful what it cost;
Ever grateful for the prize, let its altar reach the skies.

CHORUS
Firm, united let us be,
Rally round our liberty,
As a band of brothers joined,
Peace and safety we shall find.

Philip Phile, lyrics by Joseph Hopkinson — 1798
"Hail, Columbia"
1789

This song, now the U.S. Vice President's official song, remains the unofficial national anthem until 1931, when the "Star Spangled Banner" officially replaces it. Both anthems have common themes. They extol the virtue of America, record the real-time feelings of nationalism at a significant point in history and are timeless as Americans salute the achievements and virtues of freedom and liberty.

The liberty and freedom of the day are reflected in the Constitution, which sets out procedures for governing the nation — and the people. The new nation needs structure and certainty, but less than the British model. Too little government can frustrate national cohesion. The Constitution does something else. It outlines the rights and obligations of Americans, and the American government, one to the other — rights that protect the individual through the Bill of Rights, and the nation. It will be the national constitution with the longest history of any in the world.

It divides the national government into three co-equal branches — the Legislative, Executive and Judicial Branches. By design, the Legislative Branch is the largest elected branch: It has sixty-four members (now 435) in the U.S. House of Representatives, and twenty-six Senators (now 100), two Senators per state, regardless of a state's population. The Judicial Branch consists of the U.S. District (Federal) Courts, U.S. Circuit Courts of Appeal and the U.S. Supreme Court. There are now nine Justices of the U.S. Supreme Court, but there were only five in 1789, six in 1802, eight in 1837, ten in 1861, back to six in 1866, eight in 1869 and nine from 1871 to the present. The Executive Branch of the federal government consists of one U.S. President, and a Cabinet Secretary for each federal Cabinet agency.

The Supreme Court is the smallest branch of the government, but arguably the most important. With lifetime appointments, its purpose and role is defined by Article 78 of the Federalist Papers, written by Alexander Hamilton.[4] It is not until the decision of *Marbury v. Madison*, establishing in 1801 the Court's right of judicial review, that the Court gains a foothold in American government.

The Founders learn that independence is a complicated, evolutionary process, one filled with self-interest and national interest, selfishness and self-consciousness, and with narrowness and simultaneous magnanimity. America is not easily described, even from its beginnings. But the nation is resilient; it survives intact with the solid principles of its founding, and the revolution, in place and understood.

Through generations of immigrants, with varied backgrounds and history, through world wars and minor conflicts, the United States withstands any major overhaul that threatens its existence. Its principles, institutions, system of justice and politics are designed to withstand the passage of time. Its consistency exists because American leaders build on a set of accepted ideals through successive generations. The principles of democracy in the Declaration of Independence and the United States Constitution are timeless principles that assure all Americans of life, liberty and the pursuit of happiness. Read them again and again — they affirm our basic freedoms, even though those freedoms evolve over time to adjust to modern circumstances. (See Appendices B & C)

We have many tangible reminders of the intangible principle of freedom. The greatest of these is, perhaps, the Statue of Liberty — a gift from the people of France to the United States in 1886 to represent the friendship established between the two countries during the American Revolution. "Liberty enlightening the world," the statue's official title, captures Libertas, ancient Rome's goddess of freedom from slavery, oppression, and tyranny. Her raised right foot is on the move. This symbol of Liberty and Freedom is not standing still or at attention. She is moving forward, as Lady Liberty's left foot tramples broken shackles at her feet, in symbolism of the United States' wish to be free from oppression and tyranny. The seven spikes on the crown epitomize the Seven Seas and seven continents. Her torch signifies enlightenment. The tablet in her hand represents knowledge and shows the date of the United States Declaration of Independence, in Roman numerals, July IV, MDCCLXXVI (July 4, 1776).

Smaller reminders of freedom may be found on bumper stickers many people have on their cars today: "freedom isn't free," "land of the free because of the brave," and "these colors do not run." They are crafted as slogans based on an American record of sacrifice and commitment, by men and women who loved the United States, from the founding revolution to today.

The American Revolution ends with a freedom-loving population in a new land, a charter governing the relationships of the nation and its citizens and a dream that democracy and representative government will endure — that the independence and liberties fought for will be sustainable.

It is an American dream.

CHAPTER 2

A NATION DEVELOPS

Sweet Freedom's Song

"Oh say, does that Star Spangled Banner yet wave,
O'er the land of the free and the home of the brave?"

Francis Scott Key
"The Star Spangled Banner"
1814

While each of the sovereign states struggles with what it is to be in the 1800s, the United States struggles with its own identity crisis. Starting in 1803, as the United States under President Thomas Jefferson makes the Louisiana Purchase and doubles the size of the country, the President ignites a national curiosity to explore what lies to the west. A few weeks after the purchase, Jefferson asks Congress for an appropriation of $2,500 for an expedition to find a Northwest Passage to the Pacific Ocean. He selects his good friend, Captain Meriwether Lewis, a hunter and outdoorsman originally from Virginia and Georgia, to lead it, and writes him:

> The object of your mission is to explore the Missouri River and
> such principal stream of it as by its course and communication
> with the waters of the Pacific Ocean whether the Columbia,

Oregon, Colorado or any other river may offer the most direct
and practicable water communication across this continent for
the purposes of commerce.

Lewis asks William Clark, a seasoned soldier originally from
Virginia and Kentucky, and later, a Missouri territorial governor,
to share the leadership of the journey with him. The "Corps of
Discovery," as it comes to be called, includes forty-two people —
including Clark's slave, York, and a Shoshone Indian woman,
Sacajawea. The expedition sets out from Camp Dubois (Hartford,
Illinois, today) on May 14, 1804. On December 3, 1805, Clark writes
"Ocian [sic] in view! O! The Joy!"

While the Lewis and Clark expedition tells Jefferson that a
Northwest Passage across the United States does not exist, it
presents him with 140 maps of North America and describes 100
species of animals and nearly 200 plants previously unknown to
science. The new knowledge about the Northwest's geography,
natural resources and native inhabitants sparks American interest
in the West and strengthens the nation's claim to the area.

The Revolutionary War does not put aside conflict between the
United States and Great Britain. In fact, it simmers for thirty years,
during which time the United States makes no real investment in its
armed forces. Notwithstanding this, the Congress of the United
States of America approves a Declaration of War against Great
Britain on June 18, 1812, officially beginning the War of 1812 — the
first war of our new nation. The United States has 6,000 men in
uniform and sixteen Navy vessels at the time. Great Britain has a
quarter-million men in uniform and 600 Navy vessels.

The cause of the war stems from British interference on the
high seas with American vessels seeking to pass through
international waters to pursue global trade opportunities. It is the

second time the United States engages the British militarily since the American Revolution in 1776. England and France are in a continuous state of European war since 1793. Britain wants to stop the expansion efforts of Napoleon I and that conflict threatens to draw in other nations, including the United States, that want to stay neutral.

Starting in 1807, America faces the British action of impressment, which is the seizing of American vessels and seamen on the open seas for service in the British Navy. Looking for British deserters who sail under the American flag, the British create a crisis in 1813 by firing on an American ship, the Chesapeake, a few miles off the American coast, demanding to search her for British subjects. The Chesapeake refuses to be boarded, and the British vessel, the Leopard, fires on her, killing American sailors. President James Madison orders the British out of American waters, and the British apologize for the attack. But the British continue seizing American ships, as Britain's ongoing war with France intensifies. British harassment of American ships at sea and France's aggression in its war with Britain are eventually too much for American leaders. Trade relations are suffering, and Americans are blaming the British.

Continually taunting the United States, the British begin a naval blockade of the Chesapeake and Delaware Bays and later, on August 24, 1814, invade Washington, D.C., with 3,500 British troops. They storm and set fire to the Capitol, the Navy Yard and the White House, destroying each as they sweep through America's capital city.

This act of aggression by the British, attacking and destroying the institutions of government of the new United States, is not only offensive to the American system, but also frightening to its citizens. It is a time of fearful uncertainty. What will happen next?

Will the American nation have a short life, only to be terminated by the empire from which it broke free late in the last century? James Madison succeeds Thomas Jefferson as President in 1809, but Jefferson has left his mark of statesmanship on the nation.

As a Founding Father and principal author of the Declaration of Independence, Jefferson is the country's third president, succeeding John Adams. He serves as Secretary of State for President George Washington and Vice President to President John Adams and is experienced as a Virginia legislator, Governor, and Minister to France. He is a learned man and an intellectual, well-read and prominent among the leaders of his day. His presidency is a success: The Louisiana Purchase is transacted with France in 1803 for $15 million and the Lewis and Clark expedition, commissioned by Jefferson, continues from 1804-1806.

The Louisiana Purchase is likely the most significant historical event of the early 1800s. It doubles the land mass of the United States, with thirteen separate states carved from this massive area — states that expand the country from east to west, opening a new area of exploration, lifestyle and open spaces. Jefferson's actions imbue the United States with an undeniable national identity and enable it to withstand British threats to American sovereignty.

The War of 1812 is an expansive one, involving Canada on the north and threats of conflict that stretch along the entire eastern seaboard of the United States. After the British sack the capital in 1814, forcing President Madison to flee the White House to safety on the eve of the assault, the attention of the nation turns to the prominent port of entry and trade headquarters — Baltimore, Maryland — America's next important battlefield. The mighty British Navy amasses ships outside the harbor, readying for an attack. It dwarfs the American Navy, and its manpower vastly outnumbers American fighting men. The British blockade of U.S.

ports along the Atlantic seaboard is complete. The blockade has a severe economic impact on American commerce, and as Americans weary of the war, James Madison becomes increasingly unpopular.

Fort McHenry guards the Port of Baltimore, one of the Atlantic harbors vital to U.S. commerce and trade. Shaped like a five-pointed star and named after James McHenry, President George Washington's Secretary of War, the port is an attractive target for the British. Defeating the Americans here would open a wound that could cripple American resistance to British control over the region.

The date is September 3, 1814. A thirty-five-year-old Maryland attorney, Francis Scott Key, and Col. John Stuart Skinner board the HMS Minden flying a flag of truce. Key is an amateur poet educated at St. John's College at Annapolis. Skinner, a twenty-five-year-old lawyer, is a prisoner-of-war exchange officer commissioned by President Madison to negotiate the release of American prisoners. They carefully sail out beyond Baltimore Harbor to meet with British officers to negotiate the release of a popular Maryland physician, Dr. William Beanes, who was captured by the British and held hostage. The two climb aboard the British flagship and negotiate with British officers for Beanes' release. The British agree to release all three Americans, first on a British ship, then on their own vessel, but forbid the trio from returning to Baltimore, convinced the Americans now know British strength and plans for attack.

In the early morning of September 13, 1814, the British attack on Baltimore Harbor begins. British Navy vessels launch cannon fire at Fort McHenry for twenty-five straight hours at a range of two miles. The American defenders fire back. Both sides have inaccurate weapons, so few casualties occur. Francis Scott Key is offshore, with Skinner and Beanes, witnessing the battle. All through the day of September 13 and into the night, the three helplessly watch the fighting from a distance, not knowing who is winning. But as the smoke of battle clears on the early morning of September 14, they look toward Fort McHenry and see the American flag flying, with fifteen stars and fifteen stripes, all red, white and blue, symbolizing the American resolve to prevail in battle.[5] They know the fight has ended. The British are not able to take Fort McHenry. The Americans successfully defend Baltimore Harbor! As Skinner, Beanes and Key exult and make their way back to Baltimore, Key scrawls this poem on the back of a letter in his pocket, which later is set to music:

O' say can you see by the dawn's early light
What so proudly we hailed at the twilight's last gleaming.
Whose broad stripes and bright stars through the perilous fight,
O'er the ramparts we watched were so gallantly streaming.
And the rockets red glare, the bombs bursting in air,
Gave proof through the night that our flag was still there.
Oh say, does that star-spangled banner yet wave
O'er the land of the free and the home of the brave?

On the shore, dimly seen through the mists of the deep,
Where the foe's haughty host in dread silence reposes,
What is that which the breeze, o'er the towering steep,
As it fitfully blows, half conceals, half discloses?
Now it catches the gleam of the morning's first beam,
In full glory reflected now shines on the stream:
'Tis the star-spangled banner! Oh long may it wave
O'er the land of the free and the home of the brave!

And where is that band who so vauntingly swore
That the havoc of war and the battle's confusion,
A home and a country should leave us no more!
Their blood has washed out their foul footsteps' pollution.
No refuge could save the hireling and slave
From the terror of flight, or the gloom of the grave:
And the star-spangled banner in triumph doth wave
O'er the land of the free and the home of the brave!

O! thus be it ever, when freemen shall stand
Between their loved home and the war's desolation!
Blest with victory and peace, may the heav'n rescued land
Praise the Power that hath made and preserved us a nation.
Then conquer we must, when our cause it is just,
And this be our motto: 'In God is our trust.'
And the star-spangled banner in triumph shall wave
O'er the land of the free and the home of the brave!

Francis Scott Key
"The Star Spangled Banner"/The Defence of Fort McHenry
1814

Key shows the poem to Skinner and decides to publish his work six days later in *The Baltimore Patriot* with the title "The Defence of Fort McHenry." The words are adapted to the rhyming style of an English drinking song titled "To Anacreon in Heaven." The song becomes so popular that it is recognized by the U.S. Navy in 1889 as a proper song to accompany the raising of the American Flag. In 1916, the song's prominence grows as President Woodrow Wilson orders it played at numerous military and official occasions. One-hundred-seventeen years will pass before that song, renamed

"The Star Spangled Banner," becomes, by law, America's National Anthem. President Herbert Hoover signs that law on March 31, 1931. Now sung before all major government convocations, sporting events and countless other public assemblies, the song is a noteworthy part of the American story, composed by an eyewitness to history and revered by generations who pay tribute to all that the American flag symbolizes and the words that affirm our love for the United States, the "land of the free and the home of the brave."

The War of 1812 is fought over a period of three years with battles along coastal states from Canada to Louisiana. As the British grow weary of their twenty-two-year war with France, they also lose decisive battles with the United States. The War of 1812 ends in 1814 with the signing of the Treaty of Ghent peace agreement between the United States and Britain. But the important message of the war is that the United States is a country capable of fighting to defend its interests. Even though the Treaty of Ghent is signed on December 24, 1814, news of the peace accord doesn't reach the United States for two months. Oblivious to these developments, the British amass army and navy forces for travel to New Orleans for a last-ditch military assault on the American port there, still hoping to defeat the United States.

President James Madison orders Army Major General Andrew Jackson to defend the city of New Orleans against the massive British forces assembling there. His foe is led by Sir Edward Parkenham, an English aristocrat and war hero renowned for his defeat of Napoleon's forces at Leipzig, Germany. Jackson is a rough-hewn fighter from Tennessee. The British have 8,000 troops; the Americans, 5,000. It is now January 1815. An epic battle stage is set. Parkenham's soldiers are highly trained and battle-tested; Jackson's men are mostly militiamen from Kentucky and Tennessee.

Parkenham launches his attack on January 8. Jackson's forces fight fiercely and kill or wound 2,000 British troops in the first twenty-five minutes. Jackson is fearless and aggressive. Parkenham quits the attack and withdraws, never to resume the fighting. Ten days later, the British forces withdraw. The Battle of New Orleans is the greatest battle of the war, delivering a resounding victory to the United States. With this battle, the fighting is truly over, and the Americans are victorious. The signed Treaty of Ghent reaches the United States by February 11, 1815, and, days later, is ratified by the U.S. Senate.

Over a century later, high school principal and history teacher Jimmy Driftwood writes a song about the Battle of New Orleans to help his students learn about this pivotal event in American history. The song "Battle of New Orleans" is set to a popular fiddle tune of the day ("The 8th of January") and earns Driftwood a Grammy Award for Song of the Year in 1959; it earns Johnny Horton a Grammy Award for Best Country and Western Performance for his recording of it.

FIRST AND LAST VERSES

Well, in eighteen and fourteen we took a little trip
along with Colonel Jackson down the mighty Mississip.
We took a little bacon and we took a little beans,
And we caught the bloody British near the town of New Orleans.

We fired our guns and the British kept a'comin.
There wasn't nigh as many as there was a while ago.
We fired once more and they began to runnin'
down the Mississippi to the Gulf of Mexico.

Well, they ran through the briars
and they ran through the brambles
And they ran through the bushes where a rabbit couldn't go.
They ran so fast the hounds couldn't catch 'em
down the Mississippi to the Gulf of Mexico.

We fired our guns and the British kept a'comin.
But there wasn't nigh as many as there was a while ago.
We fired once more and they began to runnin'
down the Mississippi to the Gulf of Mexico.

Lyrics by James Morris (Jimmy Driftwood)
"Battle of New Orleans"
1958

This pivotal victory exalts President Madison and launches the political career of Andrew Jackson, who is elected President in 1828. It also reinforces the indisputable stamina and commitment of the American nation. At a time when the nation is frightened for its existence and survival, Jackson's victory at the Battle of New Orleans restores a sense of equality among nations. The United States' defenses are strong, and the nation is unafraid of foreign threats; it can defend itself against the strongest of world powers.

Turning inward is now the nation's focus as America looks westward for expansion. But the expansion doesn't occur without the establishment by the United States of standards for her dealings in foreign/international affairs.

James Monroe is the 5th President of the United States, serving from 1817-1825. A Virginian, he serves the United States with distinction, first as a major in the Army, a Minister to Great Britain and France, Virginia's U.S. Senator, twice Governor of Virginia,

Secretary of War and Secretary of State. He comes to the presidency fully experienced and knowledgeable about foreign affairs and government. He is an Anti-Federalist (favoring a smaller central government) and loves his country. And the people of America love him; he is elected twice with little opposition. Under his presidency, Florida, Mississippi, Illinois, Alabama, Missouri and Maine achieve statehood — Missouri as a slave state and Maine, a free state.

On December 2, 1823, Monroe presents to Congress a proclamation that will establish international ground rules for foreign nations dealing with the United States. President Monroe declares this time of expansion, with the growth and development of southern states, an "Era of Good Feelings." Monroe sends a clear message to European countries: The United States will not engage in European conflicts nor stand for any colonization by European nations in the hemisphere, particularly Latin America. It is a bold declaration, one that will be listed as a great achievement for Monroe. Known as the Monroe Doctrine, its impact will be lasting. It stakes an unequivocal claim for United States territory and sovereignty. Having seen victory in the War of 1812, the United States is emboldened to issue a peremptory challenge to those foreign countries that might test the nation's resolve to defend itself and preserve its identity.

Andrew Jackson assumes the presidency in 1829, after the one-term presidency of John Quincy Adams, our 6th president, who defeated Jackson for the presidency in 1824. A veteran of the Revolutionary War in which he fought at age thirteen, Jackson has known starvation, hardship, assault by British officers, tragic family loss (he is orphaned as a teenager) and has been a prisoner of war. Educated as a lawyer, and settled in Tennessee, Jackson is a master of many trades: a rugged trial lawyer, a merchant, a builder and a merciless fighting military officer. He enjoys the nickname "Old

Hickory," because he never backs away from a fight. Jackson is elected as a U.S. Representative and later, a Senator. In 1824 Jackson is nominated for President against John Quincy Adams. He loses that election, but goes on to win the presidency in 1828.

Jackson is the quintessential Democratic Party leader as the 7th U.S. President. Called a "jackass" by one of his opponents, Jackson relishes the nickname, and the fighting donkey becomes the long-standing symbol of the Democratic Party. He comes to office as a populist, able to grasp the problems and challenges of ordinary Americans. He is the first President to open the White House to the public after his inauguration. Doing so almost proves a serious mistake, as rowdy citizens find the food and drink there too much to resist and, in their revelry, do damage to the White House.

But there is one constituent group to which Jackson has an aversion — the American Indian. During his presidency, Jackson takes cruel and expedient steps to relocate Indians as the United States grows and Americans move westward. The issue is important to his campaigns for President in both 1824 and 1828. The Cherokees appear to be the tribe most acutely affected by Jackson's signing of the Indian Removal Act of 1830. Indian removal from states in the South to Illinois and Oklahoma will affect close to 50,000 Indians involving five major tribes. The forced relocation of the Cherokees, which results in the "Trail of Tears," rivals the inhumane treatment of slaves during the pre-Civil War history of the United States. In fact, slaves of African heritage affiliated with the Cherokee and Choctaw tribes join the forced march of the Indians, reflecting the kinship of aggrieved peoples of the times. For a person like Andrew Jackson, who suffers hardships in his life and deals with oppression and loss, his views and actions toward Indians run in stark contrast to his instinctive sensitivity to the poor and oppressed, and to the philosophy of his political party.

This removal is referred to as one of the dark periods of American history and constitutes a blight on the nation's movement westward. Modern Americans lament the internment treatment of the Japanese at the outset of World War II, but lamentations are equally deserved for Indians whose lives and livelihoods are destroyed by a public policy of the early 1800s that by any standard is inhumane and beneath the values of freedom and liberty envisioned by the Founders and memorialized in the U.S. Constitution.

Jackson faces two more historical crises during his presidency — one economic and one structural. The economic crisis involves Jackson's objection to the Second Bank of the United States. The First Bank of the United States is created in 1791 as a vehicle to fund the cost of the Revolutionary War. The Bank had been the creation of Alexander Hamilton, the brilliant Treasury Secretary for President Washington. It is a quasi-governmental creation, intended as a stable source of backing for government funds. It also represents a symbol of the debate between those who seek a strong federal government and those who oppose it. The First Bank's twenty-year charter expires in 1811. It is the subject of the famous Supreme Court case *McCulloch v. Maryland.*[6]

After the expensive War of 1812, the country faces an economic dilemma — charter a new national bank with greater government involvement in the nation's economic affairs, or struggle to pay off war debts without currency stability and endure a significant post-war inflation. The Second Bank is chartered for twenty years under the presidency of James Madison in 1816, but Jackson is convinced it is corruptly operated and does not meet the needs of what he sees as the "agriculture republic." He undertakes to revoke its charter, arguing that it is controlled by foreign interests and too centralized and elitist. In 1832, Jackson vetoes the recharter and withdraws U.S. funds from the bank. The result is chaos in the financial sector, leading to the Panic of 1837, numerous bank failures and a deep economic depression.

The other crisis is structural and has a serious impact on the United States for the next thirty years. It involves the "nullification" crisis, more commonly known as the secession crisis that Jackson desperately wants to avoid. Jackson loves the country — the union — and wants to preserve it at all costs. He fights foreigners to preserve it. He suffers personal injury and heartache over its existence. He rises to the highest levels of government service and is revered and respected by his countrymen. It is no surprise that, having shed blood to form America, he will surely shed blood to preserve the nation and all of its significant components: states, regions, peoples and sectional strife.

The crisis begins in 1828, when Congress passes, and President John Quincy Adams signs, protective tariff legislation greatly restricting the import of goods from Europe. The tariffs are imposed because after the War of 1812, European nations can bring cheap goods into the United States for less than the same goods and materials can be made in the United States. While the tariff legislation favors the northeastern states, it disadvantages southern states because they have to pay higher prices for goods made in the North and are restricted from exporting goods made in the South to the British. South Carolina is so distressed that it suggests possible secession from the Union. That challenge is made directly within the Jackson Administration.

Jackson's Vice President is John C. Calhoun of South Carolina. Calhoun loves his state and region and loves the liberty afforded by the United States — perhaps loves liberty above union. The situation makes for a classic loyalty conflict and a moral dilemma — does Calhoun support President Jackson and the administration he serves, or does he support his region, his state and his conscience? Calhoun believes his beloved state has the right to "nullify" the tariff law. In fact, it has the right to declare void ANY federal law that goes against a state's interests in violation of the Constitution. South Carolina considers an "Exposition and Protest," a lengthy document attributed to Calhoun, which lays out the argument for secession and the state's right to nullify the tariff legislation. Even though the Exposition is not adopted by South Carolina as state law, it so outrages President Jackson that he threatens the state with military action. While Jackson loves the South, he loves the union more. Calhoun's love of his state compels him to resign as Vice President and return home to become a U.S. Senator from South Carolina, aligning with the secessionist movement.

During America's first fifty-five years, the presidencies of George Washington, John Adams, Thomas Jefferson, James Madison, James Monroe, John Quincy Adams, and Andrew Jackson are all faced with the challenges of war, domestic unrest, territorial acquisition and boundary establishment, and constitutional uncertainty. But the principles of democracy and representative government guide the new nation through the perils of growth and the passage of time. While the Union is temporarily preserved after the War of 1812, the stage is set for the crisis that will become the greatest source of death and nationalism for Americans that U.S. history will know — the Civil War.

It is now 1831. A twenty-three-year-old student at Andover Theological Seminary in Andover, Massachusetts, undertakes a project to set some lyrics to music, heard in Muzio Clementi's Symphony No. 3; he is Samuel Francis Smith, a prominent Baptist minister:

My country, 'tis of thee,
Sweet land of liberty,
Of thee I sing;
Land where my fathers died,
Land of the pilgrim's pride,
from every mountainside,
Let freedom ring!

My native country, thee,
Land of the noble free,
thy name I love;
I love thy rocks and rills,
Thy woods and templed hills;
My heart with rapture thrills,
like that above.

Let music swell the breeze,
And ring from all the trees
Sweet freedom's song;
Let mortal tongues awake;
Let all that breathe partake;
Let rocks their silence break,
The sound prolong.

Our father's God to Thee,
Author of liberty,
To Thee we sing.
Long may our land be bright,
With freedom's holy light,

Protect us by Thy might,
Great God our King.

Samuel Francis Smith
"My Country 'Tis of Thee"/"America"
1831

This song, "My Country 'Tis of Thee," also known as "America," is first performed on July 4, 1831, in Boston as part of an Independence Day celebration. It becomes and remains a beloved hymn celebrating a nation under God.

But the issue of slavery and statehood persists, and on this day in Virginia, as "America" is being sung 550 miles away in Boston, another action in the name of God is being planned but under less celebratory circumstances. In the aftermath of the Missouri Compromise, the growth of America continues unabated with the nagging issue of slavery ever-present. Nat Turner is now a thirty-one-year-old, deeply religious black man, born into slavery in Virginia with only a first name. Acting on a "vision from God," Nat Turner (his master's last name) has received instructions from God to slay his enemies; he plans the rebellion for July 4, 1831. It is delayed until August 21, when Nat and his fellow slaves go on a rampage to kill white people indiscriminately, using knives, hatchets and other quiet instruments of assault and murder. It is called "Nat Turner's Rebellion." It results in the death of sixty whites. Although the rebellion is quelled within forty-eight hours, Turner escapes, but is later captured, tried and executed on November 5, 1831. But the Nat Turner legacy further raises the fear level for both black and white; the white slave owners fear any future uprisings — the slaves fear retribution and mistreatment by whites. The Turner Revolt results in the most casualties of any slave rebellion in the South. It is another dark chapter in the history of slavery, both for the white America of 1831 and the black America that has killed in the name of freedom.

The next decade brings conflict and change. The Texas war for independence in 1835-36 is another form of rebellion in the South that creates a national adjustment. It affects the configuration of the nation and its relations with its neighbor to the south — Mexico. From 1810-1821, Mexico is fighting for its independence from Spain. August 24, 1821, brings success in the signing of the Treaty of Cordoba, ending three centuries of Spanish ownership of Mexico. But it is not until 1836 that Spain fully recognizes Mexican independence. Mexico consists of nineteen states and four territories; Spanish Texas becomes a state inhabited by more Americans than Mexicans. The years 1835-36 are marked by unrest between the Mexican government and the inhabitants of the area later known as Texas. Fighting breaks out between the Americans, led by Stephen Austin and, later, General Sam Houston, and the Mexicans, led by President Santa Anna, as the Americans try to free themselves from the oppressive control of the Mexican government. The Mexican Army suffers high casualties as it tries to overwhelm the Alamo, a fortress near present-day San Antonio. Even though all Americans, including the legendary James Bowie and Davy Crockett, are killed, Santa Anna suffers defeat when he moves on to the Battle of San Jacinto. Legend and some history have it that Santa Anna is defeated because he is romantically occupied by the "Yellow Rose of Texas," Emily D. West, a "mulatto" woman, and is unprepared for Houston's assault. The lyrics of the song (now the Texas state song) originated as a minstrel version from 1836 that is revised by Mitch Miller in 1955:

FIRST OF SIX VERSES

There's a yellow rose of Texas, that I am going to see,
Nobody else could miss her, not half as much as me.
She cried so when I left her, it like to broke my heart,
And if I ever find her, we nevermore will part.

Charles H. Brown by J.K., composer/author unknown
"Yellow Rose of Texas"
1858

The Battle of San Jacinto results in Texas' independence from Mexico, as provided for in the Treaty of Velasco. Santa Anna is captured, but spared, in the deal for Texas independence in May 1836. As Texas is admitted to the United States in 1845, Sam Houston becomes a U.S. Senator and then Governor of Texas; he is recognized as the Father of Texas. But Texas independence and statehood will not end the conflict with Mexico. The War with Mexico results in the establishment of modern-day California and New Mexico, both claimed by the United States. The Rio Grande River is and remains the boundary between Mexico and the United States.

As the 19th century unfolds, the belief that the United States is divinely ordained includes an expectation of expansion from the Atlantic Ocean to the Pacific Ocean, across the entire North American continent. This belief — that American expansion is obvious ("manifest") and certain ("destiny") — becomes known as Manifest Destiny, a phrase coined by journalist John L. O'Sullivan in 1845. The result includes the exploration and settlement of what will be the states of Washington and Oregon. The belief is used to sweep aboriginal people out of the way as the nation expands. After hearing the reports of Lewis and Clark, President Jefferson believes it will take 100 generations to populate the land they explore. Americans do it in four.

The doctrine of Manifest Destiny is used to justify the Mexican-American War of 1846-48, which will lead to a western expansion that will involve slavery, economic growth and the definition of expanded statehood. It will nearly lead to the destruction of the Union. During this period, a crisis develops that will be forever remembered by all Americans as the Civil War. It is a period and an event that will create and destroy great leaders, define forever the true meaning of freedom and independence, and test the courage and resolve of a nation less than a century old either to remain as one democracy or splinter into two lesser nations.

It is the greatest test the United States will ever face.

CHAPTER 3

THE AMERICAN CIVIL WAR

Ring with the Harmonies of Liberty

Imagine being a slave. A master can buy you, sell you, use you as property and separate you from your family. Plantation slaves work from dawn until dusk, unless injured or ill, and are whipped for breaking the master's rules or running away. Little is spent to feed, clothe or house them and few ever learn to read or write. Personal stories are instead preserved within and expressed through music and singing, which provide a common bond. The songs are often sung in the round at a campfire, with one voice calling and a group answering. The songs are a source of relaxation, a stimulus to courage and a tie to heaven.

The world's slave trade flourishes for 300 years starting in the 16th century. Twelve million Africans are shipped to the Americas during this time, most to Brazil. An estimated 645,000 are shipped to what will be the United States.

African slavery begins in Colonial America in the summer of 1619. The Dutch ship, The White Lion, comes ashore at Old Point Comfort (Fort Monroe, Virginia, today) with twenty enslaved Africans won in a battle with a Spanish ship bound for Mexico. The Dutch ship needs repairs and supplies; the colonists need able-bodied workers. The human cargo is traded. The dangerous practice of human trafficking begins — dangerous for the slave and dangerous for the social system that will dominate American politics for the next two centuries. In reality, the practice of slavery will continue here until passage of the 13th Amendment to the United States Constitution in 1865 — 246 years later. A century later, a man with African heritage will be born who later becomes the 44th President of the United States. Every one of the thirteen original American colonies practices slavery during the British colonial period.

British America

Colony	Year Founded	Founded by
Virginia	1607	London Company
Massachusetts	1620	Puritans
New Hampshire	1623	John Wheelwright
Maryland	1634	Lord Baltimore
Connecticut	1635	Thomas Hooker
Rhode Island	1636	Roger Williams
Delaware	1638	Peter Minuit and New Sweden Company
North Carolina	1653	Virginians
South Carolina	1663	Eight Nobles with a Royal Charter from Charles II
New Jersey	1664	Lord Berkeley and Sir George Carteret
New York	1664	Duke of York
Pennsylvania	1682	William Penn
Georgia	1732	James Edward Oglethorpe

In the North, slaves are primarily house servants; in the South, slaves work on farms and plantations growing rice, tobacco and cotton. Slaves are not recognized as human beings, but rather as property. Even the United States Constitution (Article I, Section 2), under consideration in 1787 in Philadelphia, contains language stating that "three-fifths of all other Persons" (slaves) shall be counted in state populations. Laws of the day offer no recognition of slave marriages and offer no protection to keep slave families together. Our first president, George Washington — a Virginian — inherits ten slaves when he turns eleven.

Washington, though, takes a remarkable stand for his day. At his Mount Vernon estate, he adamantly refuses to sell any of his slaves or break up their families. As president, in 1789, he signs the first federal civil rights law that prohibits slavery in all territories held by America at the time and in any new state that joins the Union.

> I never mean ... to possess another slave by purchase; it being among my first wishes to see some plan adopted, by which slavery in this Country may be abolished by slow, sure and imperceptible degrees," Washington writes to a friend after the Revolutionary War. To another friend, he writes, "There is not a man living who wishes more sincerely than I do to see some plan adopted for the abolition of slavery.

The adoption of a true national policy of anti-slavery must wait beyond the ratification of the U.S. Constitution in 1789, the turn of the next century and the service of fifteen successive presidents over eighty-six years. Most such presidents will have had southern roots.

Between the American Revolution and the American Civil War, as the nation expands westward, the cultivation of cotton and the institution of slavery are growth industries. But as time passes and the nation grows, sentiment also grows for the belief that slavery is a social evil. Near the end of his life, George Washington loses his stomach for slavery. In his Last Will and Testament,

Washington includes a provision that emancipates his more than 300 slaves upon the death of his wife. By 1804, all of the northern states pass emancipation acts.

But slavery does not end. It becomes an institution in the South, making slave life a fact of southern life. The southern colonies develop an economy based on the labor-intensive production of cotton. A culture of slavery, therefore, flourishes in the South. The northern colonies develop an industrial-based economy. A culture of manufacturing, therefore, flourishes in the North.

In these early years of our country, slaves gather in secret to sing "camp songs" or "corn ditties." These gatherings provide an opportunity to socialize and hear news from other plantations. The songs evolve into spirituals in which slaves sing of faith and hope.

Some slaves escape to the North, risking their lives if caught. Many make the journey on the Underground Railroad — not really a railroad, but a network of secret operations that use railroad jargon: slaves are "passengers," and those who help them are "conductors." The people who escort refugees to freedom jeopardize their lives and property, too, whether white or black. Many "Negro Spirituals" tell the story of the journey.

When the Sun comes back
And the first quail calls
Follow the Drinking Gourd.
For the old man is a-waiting for to carry you to freedom
If you follow the Drinking Gourd.

The riverbank makes a very good road.
The dead trees will show you the way.
Left foot, peg foot, traveling on,
Follow the Drinking Gourd.

The river ends between two hills
Follow the Drinking Gourd.
There's another river on the other side
Follow the Drinking Gourd.

When the great big river meets the little river
Follow the Drinking Gourd.
For the old man is a-waiting for to carry you to freedom
If you follow the drinking gourd.

Composer unknown
"Follow the Drinking Gourd"
1800s

This song advises the slave to begin his or her journey to the North in late winter, when the days are noticeably longer and when birds begin singing again, a signal that spring is approaching. The journey will take a year. About the time the slave needs to cross the Ohio River, it will still be winter in the north, and the frozen river is easily crossed. The "gourd" is the Big Dipper (Ursa Major) that points the way. On the journey, whatever the time of year, the surest way to avoid bloodhounds and bounty hunters trying to catch you is to leave no tracks, to wade in the water.

Wade in the water (children)
Wade in the water
Wade in the water
God's gonna trouble the water

If you don't believe I've been redeemed
God's gonna trouble the water
I want you to follow him on down to Jordan stream
(I said) My God's gonna trouble the water
You know chilly water is dark and cold
(I know my) God's gonna trouble the water
You know it chills my body but not my soul
(I said my) God's gonna trouble the water

(Come on let's) wade in the water
Wade in the water (children)
Wade in the water
God's gonna trouble the water

Composer unknown
"Wade in the Water"
1800s

The Underground Railroad has a rich history; it is an epic story of hardship, danger, courage, sacrifice and morality, all for the greater cause of abolishing a practice that is dividing a nation. As slaves escape the shackles of slavery and move in the night to freedom, a new movement to freedom is created that undermines institutional slavery in the South. It stretches across the states of

Illinois, Indiana, Kentucky, Ohio and Virginia and extends north through Pennsylvania, New Jersey and New York, all the way to Michigan and the old Canada West. It is a sixty-year movement that leads up to national crisis — the Civil War. But it produces the emancipation of tens of thousands of enslaved Americans and a new birth of freedom and equality that changes the nation and renews its purpose.

At the time of the War of 1812, American free and slave states are in balance:

1776-1812

Slave	Year	Free	Year
Delaware	1787	New Jersey (Slave until 1804)	1787
Georgia	1788	Pennsylvania	1787
Maryland	1788	Connecticut	1788
South Carolina	1788	Massachusetts	1788
Virginia	1788	New Hampshire	1788
North Carolina	1789	New York (Slave until 1799)	1788
Kentucky	1792	Rhode Island	1790
Tennessee	1796	Vermont	1791
Louisiana	1812	Ohio	1803

Controversy over whether Missouri should be admitted as a slave state results in the Missouri Compromise in 1820. The Missouri Compromise allows slavery in the proposed state of Missouri but prohibits it elsewhere in the former Louisiana Territory north of the 36th parallel. That same year, President Thomas Jefferson — a slaveholder — writes of slavery: "We have the wolf by the ear and we can neither hold him nor safely let him go. Justice is in one scale and self-preservation in the other."[7]

As the Mexican-American War (1846-1848) brings the issues of territory and slavery to a boiling point, the Compromise of 1850 is enacted — a collection of five laws that attempts to balance the interests of the slave states of the South and the free states of the North. It admits California as a Free State and New Mexico (modern Arizona and Nevada) as a state subject to "popular sovereignty." The District of Columbia would have no slave trade, with Texas giving up for compensation part of its western land to New Mexico, and all states agreeing to return runaway slaves regardless of the legality of slavery within a state. The Compromise is not perfect, but it postpones the simmering issue of secession and civil war.

The Compromise of 1850 preserves the Union, but only for a decade. In 1854, both the Missouri Compromise and the Compromise of 1850 are nullified by the Kansas-Nebraska Act, calling for "popular sovereignty" in the territories (code words for allowing slavery). This law divides the nation and points it toward civil war. It also makes way for the admission of two new states, forces railroad expansion in the northern tier of the United States and opens the door for the perpetuation of slavery. A divisive development, it wipes out the progress toward peaceful coexistence between the southern and northern states and between the abolitionists and the advocates. It illustrates the attempts by lawmakers to find middle ground between slavery and anti-slavery forces. The free economy of the North allows its states to industrialize while the South clings to its tradition of using slave labor to produce cash crops. In 1860, the North has more miles of railroad, more expansive steel production, more modern factories and more people — all of which allow it to be better prepared to supply, equip and man an army that will ultimately be victorious.

The U.S. census of 1860 shows about four million slaves in a population of about twelve million people in the fifteen states in which slavery is legal. At the time, blacks are one-third of the total population in the South. In the North, blacks make up two percent of the population.

Between the War of 1812 and the American Civil War, the federal government of the United States struggles to keep the Union together. It does this by balancing the number of free and slave states, admitting new ones mostly in pairs:

1812-1860

SLAVE	DATE	FREE	DATE
Mississippi	1817	Indiana	1816
Alabama	1819	Illinois	1818
Missouri	1821	Maine	1820
Arkansas	1836	Michigan	1837
Florida	1845	Iowa	1846
Texas	1845	Wisconsin	1848
		California	1850
Kansas	(blocked)	Minnesota	1858
		Oregon	1859
		Kansas	1861

Citing a threat to states' rights, eleven states take an extraordinary and dangerous route. They secede from the Union, forming the Confederate States of America (CSA) — seven states before April 12, 1861, a beginning point of the war: South Carolina, December 20, 1860; Mississippi, January 9, 1861; Florida, January 10, 1861; Alabama, January 11, 1861; Georgia, January 19, 1861; Louisiana, January 26, 1861; Texas, February 1, 1861 — and four after the war begins: Arkansas, May 6, 1861; Virginia, April 17, 1861; Tennessee, May 7, 1861; and North Carolina, May 20, 1861. (West Virginia secedes from Virginia in 1863 and joins the Union.)

The actionable start of the Civil War occurs on April 12, 1861, in South Carolina at Fort Sumter, an offshore federal fortress outside of Charleston. Confederates attack the fort, built after the War of 1812, five days after South Carolina secedes from the Union and thirty-nine days after Abraham Lincoln's second inauguration as President. This is an attack on the government of the United States by Americans, and represents the beginning of a dark and difficult period in American history. The fort is eventually taken by the Confederates, and its takeover is symbolic of the seriousness of the split in the Union — disunity after only eighty-five years of national unity.

The Confederate States of America (CSA) has its own leadership. Its president, Jefferson Davis, establishes a capital city in Richmond, Virginia. On March 21, 1861, CSA Vice President Alexander Stephens declares in Savannah, Georgia, that the new government's "cornerstone rests upon the great truth that the Negro is not equal to the white man; that slavery subordination to the superior race is his natural and normal condition. This, our new government, is the first, in the history of the world, based upon this great physical, philosophical and moral truth."

Two weeks after Jefferson Davis becomes president of the CSA, on March 4, 1861, Abraham Lincoln becomes president of the United States. He is the 16th President. Born in Kentucky, self-educated, and later a lawyer and Illinois legislator, he serves only one term in Congress before being elected president. Awkward and rangy, but articulate and intelligent, Lincoln is moderate and enlightened on the issue of slavery, challenging the slave power of the South as being unhealthy for the nation. His views are articulated for public consumption in his run for the U.S. Senate in 1858 against Senator Stephen Douglas, author of the Kansas-Nebraska Act. They engage in seven public debates throughout

Illinois. Douglas ends up being chosen for the Senate by the Illinois state legislature, but Lincoln's reputation as a brilliant speaker is established and equips him to become a legitimate candidate for the presidency two years later. On November 6, 1860, Lincoln defeats three other candidates, including Democrat Stephen Douglas, and is elected the first Republican president in the nation's history. In his inaugural address on the East Portico of the Capitol, President Lincoln concludes his speech, saying:

> In your hands, my dissatisfied fellow-countrymen, and not in mine, is the momentous issue of civil war. The Government will not assail you. You can have no conflict without being yourselves the aggressors. You have no oath registered in heaven to destroy the Government, while I shall have the most solemn one to "preserve, protect, and defend" it.
>
> I am loath to close. We are not enemies, but friends. We must not be enemies. Though passion may have strained, it must not break our bonds of affection. The mystic chords of memory, stretching from every battlefield and patriot grave to every living heart and hearthstone all over this broad land, will yet swell the chorus of the Union, when again touched, as surely they will be, by the better angels of our nature.

In the audience that day is a well-known actor — John Wilkes Booth — who will take the life of President Lincoln shortly after his second inauguration, at the end of the Civil War.

When Fort Sumter is attacked at the beginning of the Civil War, President Lincoln offers General Robert E. Lee command of the Federal Army. Lee demurs, considering himself a citizen of Virginia first, the United States second. When Virginia announces its secession from the Union, Lee resigns his commission in the

Union Army and takes command of the armed forces of the State of Virginia (later the Army of Northern Virginia).

The early years of the war do not go well for the Union. On September 22, 1862, President Lincoln signs an executive order known as the Emancipation Proclamation (see Appendix F), which declares the freedom of all slaves in any state of the Confederate States of America. The proclamation is widely attacked as freeing only the slaves over whom the Union has no power. In a larger sense, however, the proclamation commits the Union to ending slavery. As news of the proclamation spreads through the South, large numbers of slaves escape across Union lines. At the close of the war, many slaves are free, but it is not until ratification of the 13th Amendment to the United States Constitution on December 18, 1865, that the institution of slavery is officially abolished.

The most significant battle of the American Civil War is fought in and around the small Pennsylvania town of Gettysburg, July 1-3, 1863. The battle is the high-water mark for the Confederacy. In three days of fighting, there are 58,000 casualties on both sides — the largest of any battle in the war. (For historical perspective, there were 58,226 American casualties in the entire Vietnam War.) That fall, President Lincoln travels to Gettysburg to dedicate a cemetery to the fallen, and to rededicate the Union to the war effort. His "Gettysburg Address," delivered in just over two minutes, is regarded as the greatest speech in American history. These words are carved into the south wall of the interior of the Lincoln Memorial, built in 1922, in Washington, D.C.

> Four score and seven years ago our fathers brought forth on this continent a new nation, conceived in Liberty, and dedicated to the proposition that all men are created equal.
>
> Now we are engaged in a great civil war, testing whether that nation, or any nation, so conceived and so dedicated, can

long endure. We are met on a great battle-field of that war. We have come to dedicate a portion of that field, as a final resting place for those who here gave their lives that that nation might live. It is altogether fitting and proper that we should do this.

But, in a larger sense, we can not dedicate — we can not consecrate, we can not hallow — this ground. The brave men, living and dead, who struggled here, have consecrated it, far above our poor power to add or detract. The world will little note, nor long remember what we say here, but it can never forget what they did here. It is for us the living, rather, to be dedicated here to the unfinished work which they who fought here have thus far so nobly advanced. It is rather for us to be here dedicated to the great task remaining before us — that from these honored dead we take increased devotion to that cause for which they gave the last full measure of devotion — that we here highly resolve that these dead shall not have died in vain — that this nation, under God, shall have a new birth of freedom — and that government of the people, by the people, for the people, shall not perish from the earth.

Remarks of President Abraham Lincoln
Delivered at the Soldiers' National Cemetery
Gettysburg, Pennsylvania
November 19, 1863

The antebellum song, "Lorena," becomes a favorite of both blue-uniformed (USA) and gray-uniformed (CSA) soldiers during the American Civil War, who think of their wives and sweethearts back home when they hear it. A Confederate officer pins the South's defeat to the song. He sees his men become so homesick upon hearing the mournful ballad that, he reasons, they lose their will to fight.

FIRST AND LAST STANZAS

The years creep slowly by, Lorena,
The snow is on the grass again;
The sun's low down the sky, Lorena,
The frost gleams where the flowers have been;
But the heart throbs on as warmly now,
As when the summer days were nigh;
Oh! the sun can never dip so low,
Adown affection's cloudless sky. ...

It matters little now, Lorena,
The past — is in the eternal past;
Our heads will soon lie down, Lorena,
Life's tide is ebbing out so fast;
There is a future — Oh, thank God —
Of life this is so small a part,
'Tis dust to dust beneath the sod,
But there, up there, 'tis heart to heart.

Rev. Henry DeLafayette Webster
"Lorena"
1858

The Civil War ends on April 9, 1865, when CSA General Robert E. Lee surrenders the Army of Northern Virginia to Union General Ulysses S. Grant in the parlor of the home of Wilmer McLean, in the village of Appomattox Court House, Virginia. In Appomattox Court House (formerly Clover Hill), McLean is asked by Confederate Col. Charles Marshall on behalf of General Lee, if McLean's house can be used as a meeting place for Lee and General Grant to meet to discuss the terms of surrender of the Confederate Army, and an end of the Civil War. The two generals meet at McLean's country home at 1:30 p.m. on April 9, 1865, in a historic moment of Confederate surrender that will affect the nation's course toward internal peace and reconciliation.

While the nightmare of war is over, the national bad dream lingers as President Lincoln is assassinated five days later, April 14, 1865, and the struggle for southern state integration begins.

Lee is demonized as a turncoat (wearing the colors of the other side); his farm is appropriated by the federal government that sets out to use it as a military cemetery. Union General Montgomery Meigs renders Lee's home (Arlington House) uninhabitable should he ever attempt to return. A burial vault containing the remains of 1,800 casualties of the Battle of Bull Run (called the Battle of Manassas by the CSA) is the first monument to Union dead erected under Meigs' orders. At war's end, 16,000 graves crowd Lee's former home.

Today, Arlington House — across the Potomac River from Washington, D.C. — and its grounds are known as Arlington National Cemetery. Nearly 300,000 people are interred in its more than 600 acres, veterans and military casualties from every one of our nation's wars, from the American Revolutionary War to the present conflicts in Afghanistan and Iraq. The grave sites of President and Mrs. John F. Kennedy (with an eternal flame), the Tomb of the Unknowns and the U.S. Marine Corps Memorial ("Iwo Jima Memorial") are among the most visited places at Arlington National Cemetery.

The Virginia General Assembly passes House Joint Resolution 728 on February 24, 2007, acknowledging "with profound regret the involuntary servitude of Africans and the exploitation of Native Americans, and call for reconciliation among all Virginians." Virginia is the first of the fifty United States to apologize for American slavery. The United States House of Representatives passes a resolution apologizing for American slavery on July 30, 2008.

At the inauguration of President Barack Obama on January 20, 2009, Rev. Joseph Lowery uses the third stanza of a Negro spiritual, known as the Negro National Anthem, to begin his benediction:

Lift ev'ry voice and sing,
'Til earth and heaven ring,
Ring with the harmonies of Liberty;
Let our rejoicing rise
High as the listening skies,
Let it resound loud as the rolling sea.
Sing a song full of the faith that the dark past has taught us,
Sing a song full of the hope that the present has brought us;
Facing the rising sun of our new day begun,
Let us march on 'til victory is won.

Lyrics: James Weldon Johnson
Music: John Rosamond Johnson
"Lift Ev'ry Voice and Sing"
1900

On April 14, 1865, John Wilkes Booth shoots Abraham Lincoln with a single shot to the head while the President attends a play at Ford's Theatre, a short carriage ride from the White House. Booth, a committed Confederate, believes Lincoln to be a traitor and expects to be hailed as a hero for Lincoln's assassination. Instead, Booth is branded a traitor; Lincoln becomes a martyr in the war against slavery. Twelve days later, Booth and several companions are hunted down for their assault on Lincoln and Secretary of State William H. Seward. Booth is shot and killed. His co-conspirators are tried, convicted and hanged nearly three months after the assassination.

The degree of change imposed upon the United States by the Civil War and Lincoln's assassination — both shocking events — is so profound that the nation's foundation and future are uncertain. The war is over, but the nation's war wounds remain, and are slow to heal.

The Civil War marks Lincoln, many historians believe, as America's greatest president, not only because he held the Union together, but also because his presidency marks a milestone in human relations: the affirmation of the equality guaranteed by the United States Constitution and the establishment of an American ideal of human justice that will change attitudes and policies in the nation for generations. Lincoln's gift to American history of beautifully spoken and written words will be memorialized across the American landscape.

Besides representing the greatest loss of American life in wartime history (over one million casualties, including over 600,000 soldiers), the Civil War is a sad drama of human cruelty, philosophical and sectional division, the illumination of presidential greatness and numerous incidents of battle-led heroism. But the greatest lesson is that the Union withstands the challenges of the times and fights a heartbreaking civil war to become a nation of people that embraces an indivisible United States. These sentiments are memorialized and set to music in the following songs:

Mine eyes have seen the glory of the coming of the Lord
He is trampling out the vintage
where the grapes of wrath are stored;
He hath loosed the fateful lightning of His terrible swift sword:
His truth is marching on.

Glory, glory, halleluiah,
Glory, glory, halleluiah,
Glory, glory, halleluiah,
His truth is marching on.

William Steffe
"Battle Hymn of the Republic"
1855

I wish I was in de land ob cotton,
Old times dar am not forgotten;
Look away! Look away! Look away, Dixie Land.
In Dixie Land whar I was born in,
Early on one frosty morning,
Look away! Look away! Look away! Dixie Land.

Daniel Decatur Emmett
"Dixie Land"
1855

When Johnny comes marching home again
Hurrah! Hurrah!
We'll give him a hearty welcome then
Hurrah! Hurrah!

The men will cheer and the boys will shout
The ladies they will all turn out
And we'll all feel gay
When Johnny comes marching home.

Henry Tolman
"When Johnny Comes Marching Home Again"
1863

While the Union prevails in the Civil War, President Lincoln and General U.S. Grant believe the South deserves to maintain its dignity. It is a tribute to both men's character that they share a moderate view of dealing with the South after the war. A period of reconstruction prevails at Lincoln's behest with the knowledge that the spoils of war should not include further punishment of the South so that integration is left impossible. It is further evidence that Lincoln treasures the perpetuation of the Union; the granting to certain Confederates of limited amnesty testifies to his sense of fair play. The implementation of Republican principles (representative government, fiscal recovery, free enterprise) testifies to Lincoln's vision for a unified United States, in every way possible, so that the American experiment in democracy would continue.

While Lincoln does not live to see his vision of reconstruction take hold, his spirit and legacy inspire those who come after and write the next chapter of American history, approaching a new century with excitement and innovation that becomes an American hallmark.

CHAPTER 4

RECONSTRUCTION IN AMERICA
And the Skies Are Not Cloudy All Day

One of the invaluable compensations of the late Rebellion is the highly instructive disclosure it made of the true source of danger to republican government. Whatever may be tolerated in monarchical and despotic governments, no republic is safe that tolerates a privileged class, or denies to any of its citizens equal rights and equal means to maintain them. What was theory before the war has been made fact by the war.

Under the title "Reconstruction," Frederick Douglass writes these words — with typical 19th century flourish — in an article that is published in *Atlantic Monthly* magazine in 1866. Douglass, born a slave, joins a national conversation on how best to bind the nation's wounds in a way that will forever change the verb of our country from the plural "the United States are" to the singular "the United States is." Near the end of the article, Douglass writes:

The policy that emancipated and armed the negro — now seen to have been wise and proper by the dullest — was not certainly more sternly demanded than is now the policy of enfranchisement. If with the negro was success in war and without him failure, so in peace it will be found that the nation must fall or flourish with the negro.

But it will be another hundred years before the United States fully embraces civil rights.

When something is reconstructed, there is an underlying assumption that something is broken or is in need of repair. When considering the word as it relates to the United States after the Civil War, the American landscape, both social and physical, needs to be rebuilt. The process of reconstruction of a broken nation marks the United States as a beneficent country, as future world wars would affirm. It is the correctness of rebuilding a post-Civil War national union that sets the American standard for post-war foreign policy, a policy of offering human assistance to the vanquished by the victors, particularly after World War I and World War II.

The United States is, in 1865, a fractured country. The 13th Amendment is ratified on December 6, 1865. While it officially ends slavery, declaring in Section 1, "Neither slavery nor involuntary servitude, except as a punishment for crime whereof the party shall have been duly convicted, shall exist within the United States, or any place subject to their jurisdiction," American attitudes about race relations will be mixed, and uncertain.

The two executive orders President Lincoln signs in 1862 and 1863 that officially emancipate slaves (the Emancipation Proclamation) become fully integrated into the Constitution and American consciousness with the adoption of the 13th Amendment after the cessation of domestic Civil War hostilities. It is an affirmative effort to reunite the nation and reconcile the unavoidable progress needed to ultimately reach the literal language of Constitutional expectation — that all men are created equal. It is a difficult struggle for Americans touched by the Civil War to forgive and forget. But it is a necessary struggle. A way must be found to bring southern states, blacks, bitter southerners and vindictive northerners and the Congress together to preserve Lincoln's dream of national unity.

Lincoln's Vice President, Andrew Johnson of Tennessee, constitutionally succeeds to the presidency after Lincoln's assassination (Article II, Section 1). Like Lincoln, he wants to speed reconstruction, to rebuild the nation into a new, integrated United States, and readmit the southern secessionist states to the Union. His is an assertive, aggressive presidency that rankles Congress as Johnson tries to use his war powers to implement his post-war domestic policies. In a dramatic show of constitutional checks and balances, Congress rejects presidential authority on reconstruction matters and asserts its legislative prerogative. The issues are complex and political: the proper role of the Confederate states, the citizenship of freedmen, the role of those who fought against the Union, the voting rights of all who were subject to post-Civil War state integration and the balance of domestic power. These conflicts test the dynamism of the Constitution and come to a head in the Congressional elections of 1866.

Republicans gain a greater majority in Congress and undertake the ultimate challenge to any president — impeachment. The Republican majority in Congress so opposes President Johnson's policies that it moves, for the first time in history, to use the Constitution's Article I, Sections 2,3 impeachment process against President Johnson because of his repeated attempts to dominate Reconstruction policy. The basis for impeachment is the Tenure in Office Act of 1867, which Johnson vetoes because it gives Congress authority to override personnel appointments and removals by Johnson. The trial, the first impeachment in history, lasts for three months, and Johnson is acquitted by one vote in the Senate. He emerges diminished.

The balance of power shifts to the Congress for Reconstruction policy, making the implementation of voting rights, state integration and Confederate suffrage slower. The result is a temporary loss of voting rights for those loyal to the Confederacy. The issue of black-white race relations continues to be a source of conflict during and after Reconstruction, from 1866-1900. It seems that the nation, struggling to unify, is touched by a case of the "blues."

A.A. Chapman publishes a song in 1871 that captures an American sentiment that will be sung for more than 100 years:

Oh, ain't I got the blues!
My sadness you'd excuse,
If you knew like me, what 'tis to have
Such a terrible fit of the blues.

A.A. Chapman
"Oh, Ain't I Got the Blues"
1871

Reconstruction constitutes a period of social integration that finds its roots in the U.S. Constitution. The 14th Amendment, ratified on July 9, 1868, becomes the most significant constitutionally based amendment in history. Its adoption has wide-ranging human rights importance for America's future. Its most compelling provisions expressly affirm the concept of representative government and prohibit states from abridging the rights of United States citizens without due process of law. It implements the concept of equal protection of law for all citizens, but the nation's definition of equal only includes white men over the age of twenty-one. Such a limitation spawns movements for civil rights that affect women and blacks in America, a struggle that will evolve until passage of women's suffrage and black equality decades ahead in time. But the 14th Amendment will be the vehicle to fully secure such rights. In 1870, the ratification of the 15th Amendment occurs on February 3, eliminating racial restrictions on the right to vote. Two years later, the women's movement to vote begins, but it is not settled and is led by suffragette Susan B. Anthony, for whom a dollar coin will be named in the next century.

The last twenty-five years of the 1800s are a time of social progress, business progress and modernization of life for forty million Americans. The Rockefeller family dynasty begins with the incorporation of the Standard Oil Company; Alexander Graham Bell invents the telephone; Thomas Alva Edison invents the phonograph and the electric light; the nation migrates further westward into the Rocky Mountain West; and P.T. Barnum creates the Three Ring Circus. "Modernization" and "innovation" are the most important words of this period as America discovers a new era of invention and the nation lurches toward the 20th century.

As Americans move westward before the start of the new century, their music reflects the times. President Lincoln's signature on the Homestead Act of 1862 results in the development of the Midwestern United States. In Kansas, Dr. Brewster M. Higley writes a poem at his residence in Smith County, a locale that will be affected by westward expansion. Homesteaded in 1871, Smith County grows like other Midwestern regions in a farm belt that will produce generations of rich corn and wheat crops. But it is the wide-open spaces that likely draw Dr. Higley there. He publishes a poem in 1873 about this far north, mid-state Kansas farm region that he makes his home. It is remembered and sung in the next century in movies, plays and cartoons by figures as diverse as Cary Grant and Porky Pig and will eventually be known as the unofficial anthem of the American West. Now the "land of visionary enchantment" that Lewis and Clark wrote of nearly seventy years before is flung open and becomes the land of opportunity. The idyllic West will soon only exist in songs like "Home on the Range," which is commercially recorded for the first time by Vernon Dalhart in 1927.

FIRST STANZA AND A CHORUS
Oh, give me a home where the Buffalo roam,
Where the Deer and the Antelope play;
Where seldom is heard a discouraging word,
And the sky is not cloudy all day.

CHORUS
A home! A home!
Where the Deer and the Antelope play,
Where seldom is heard a discouraging word,
And the sky is not clouded all day.

Brewster M. Higley
"Home on the Range"
1873

The song goes through two more iterations, one in 1904 by William and Mary Goodwin and another in 1910 by John A.

Lomax, where the words in the popular version of the chorus will remain into the next century:

CHORUS

Home, home on the range
Where the deer and the antelope play;
Where seldom is heard a discouraging word,
And the skies are not cloudy all day.

President Franklin Roosevelt later declares "Home on the Range" his favorite song in 1932. It is the official song of the state of Kansas.

By 1870, all eleven southern states that had formed the backbone of the Confederacy are "readmitted" to representation in Congress and reconciliation is underway. That reconciliation includes the election of black Americans to public office. By the 1876 elections, 633 blacks are elected in those eleven states (Alabama, Arkansas, Florida, Georgia, Louisiana, Mississippi, North Carolina, South Carolina, Tennessee, Texas and Virginia). Black education is on the increase, but racial integration will not come for decades. Although the Constitution is color blind, society is not. Political party splits among regions become the dominant political reality, and those splits are racially motivated. American race relations come to a head by 1890 as white legislators erect barriers to black voting practices, and poor whites are equally disenfranchised, creating a populist movement and a Populist political party that will last in variable forms for over a century.

Even though more than 100 years have passed since America has been under the control of a king, a new form of royalty emerges in the late 1800s and early in the new century. It ushers into American consciousness a new genre of music. It is called ragtime. Its "King" is Scott Joplin.

Minstrel shows offering black singers and dancers had been present throughout the Reconstruction era. The post-slavery emergence of Joplin breathes new life into the black entertainment world and allows the showcasing of black performers, paving the way for big-city entertainment throughout the United States, but particularly in the northern states. Born of an ex-slave father and a free mother, Scott Joplin personifies ragtime with his piano talents and syncopated rhythms, which are pleasing to ears of all colors and the hearts of all music-loving listeners. His music does not need words — it has rhythm and that is enough. Joplin's "The Great Crusch Collision" (commemorating the head-on crash of two trains in Texas in 1896) and "The Entertainer" (made popular in the movie "The Sting" in 1973) are typical ragtime piano compositions that will memorialize Scott Joplin in the music world and afford Joplin the opportunity to act as a mentor for black entertainers who will follow in his footsteps. Joplin's timeless "Maple Leaf Rag" is recorded on the banjo and other instruments starting in 1908.

The outlet for ragtime and minstrel shows is a new genre of variety entertainment called vaudeville — as much a creation of time as technology. Electricity, the "ghost servant," settles into urban areas and breathes life into horseless streetcars, automatic fans and incandescent light bulbs, which conspire to cause people to forsake private parlors and join with neighbors in public houses for entertainment. Vaudeville opens America to myriad traveling entertainers and an entertainment industry that is good for the national psyche as well as the national economy at the dawn of a new century. From sports (primarily baseball) to theaters (primarily along New York's Broadway), music is written for the ages. Billy

Murray records a popular version with the Haydon Quartet in 1903.

> *Katie Casey was baseball mad,*
> *Had the fever and had it bad.*
> *Just to root for the hometown crew*
> *Every soul Katie blew.*
> *On a Saturday her young beau*
> *Called to see if she'd like to go*
> *To see a show, but Miss Kate said "No,*
> *I'll tell you what you can do":*
>
> *Take me out to the ball game,*
> *Take me out with the crowd;*
> *Buy me some peanuts and Cracker Jack,*
> *I don't care if I never get back.*
> *Let me root, root, root for the home team,*
> *If they don't win it's a shame.*
> *For it's one, two, three strikes you're out,*
> *At the old ball game.*

Jack Norworth (words) and Albert Von Tilzer (music)
"Take Me Out to the Ball Game"
1908

This song is sung for another 100 years and more, between the 7th and 8th innings of baseball games too numerous to count, as Americans take the traditional "7th Inning Stretch." Norworth and Nora Bayes go on to compose another classic love song, "Shine On, Harvest Moon." Frank Stanley and Henry Burr make a popular Columbia recording in 1909 of that memorable fall song.

The night was mighty dark so you could hardly see,
For the moon refused to shine.
Couple sitting underneath a willow tree,
For love they did pine.
Little maid was kinda 'fraid of darkness
So she said, "I guess I'll go."
Boy began to sigh, looked up at the sky,
And told the moon his little tale of woe.

CHORUS
Oh, shine on, shine on, harvest moon
Up in the sky;
I ain't had no lovin'
Since January, February, June or July.
Snow time ain't no time to stay
Outdoors and spoon;
So shine on, shine on, harvest moon,
For me and my gal.

I can't see why a boy should sigh when by his side
Is the girl he loves so true,
All he has to say is: "Won't you be my bride,
For I love you,
I can't see why I'm telling you this secret,
When I know that you can guess."
Harvest moon will smile,
Shine on all the while,
If the little girl should answer "yes."
REPEAT CHORUS

Jack Norworth and Nora Bayes
"Shine On, Harvest Moon"
1908

The early 1900s are also a time of national growth as immigrants flock to American shores and with them, new and modern ideas flourish. Nearly 305,000 patents are registered at the U.S. Patent Office between the years 1900-1910 as new inventions are created that will have a lasting impact on life in the 20th century. A shocking new consciousness also grips the nation as President William McKinley is assassinated in 1901 by socialist fanatic/anarchist Leon Czolgosz while McKinley is standing in a receiving line in Buffalo, New York. Republican Vice President Theodore Roosevelt, who is forty-two, succeeds to the presidency in 1901. The 26th President of the United States, Roosevelt is the youngest president yet, a record that still stands today. Roosevelt is a former Navy Secretary and commander of the 1st U.S. Cavalry Regiment during the Spanish American War. His style and record mirror the regiment's nickname — the Rough Riders.

Roosevelt brings to the presidency an unconventional, progressive agenda. A frail child plagued with early health conditions, Roosevelt personifies later in life a daring, self-reliant and adventuresome persona. He promotes an environmental conservation movement to protect America's precious natural resources, a domestic policy position for which he will be revered decades later. He opposes big business and supports labor unions. He oversees construction of the Panama Canal, perhaps his most significant international achievement. An author, adventurer, populist and independent politician, Roosevelt will be known for championing the American foreign policy motto, "Walk softly, but carry a big stick, and you will go far," a statement he makes in 1901 in Minnesota. He serves as president until 1909, but runs in 1912 not as a Republican, but as a Progressive/Bull Moose Party nominee. Woodrow Wilson defeats him, and in the process Roosevelt is shot in the chest by fanatic John Schrank, a psychotic New York saloon keeper, before delivering a 90-minute campaign speech. But Roosevelt survives because the assassin's bullet struck the manuscript of Roosevelt's speech in his coat pocket, saving him from fatal injury — a testament to his toughness and "bull moose" constitution. When the Republican Party failed to nominate Roosevelt, it created a split that resulted in his third party candidacy that would divide the Republican Party for another twenty years and signal defeat for Republicans during and after the Great Depression years.

The 1900s are a time of immigration to America, a land of opportunity. As ragtime and vaudeville become part of the entertainment genre, songwriters and composers gain prominence. One such composer whose family emigrates from Belarus in 1893 will become one of the most prolific and memorable songwriters in American history. Irving Berlin, born of Jewish parents in 1888, is responsible for the welfare of his family after his father dies in 1896 in New York. Berlin finds work in the Tin Pan Alley/Broadway entertainment scene and discovers he has enormous talent for writing music and lyrics. A self taught pianist, Berlin composes a march, "Alexander's Ragtime Band," at age twenty-three. It continues the musical influence of Scott Joplin and is popularized on the New York stage. Edison Blue Amberol made a popular recording in 1913 that featured Billy Murray with orchestral accompaniment.

Oh, ma honey, oh, ma honey,
Better hurry and let's meander
Ain't you goin', ain't you goin',
To the leader man, raged meter man?
Oh, ma honey, oh, ma honey
Let me take you to Alexander's
Grand stand, brass band,
Ain't you comin' along?

Come on and hear,
Come on and hear,
Alexander's Ragtime Band,
Come on and hear,
Come on and hear,
It's the best band in the land,
They can play a bugle call
Like you never heard before,
So natural that you want to go to war.
That's just the bestest band that am,
Honey Lamb!

Irving Berlin
"Alexander's Ragtime Band"
1911

This song establishes Berlin as a success, and he writes more songs of the era that dominate the musical stage in New York. A patriot who loves the United States, Berlin joins the Army in 1917 to fight in World War I. He stages a musical revue for the troops in

1918 and includes a song that isn't released for another twenty years, but one that will be revered by generations of Americans. It is titled "God Bless America." Its World War I timing speaks not only of the threat of war, but also of the threat of harm to the United States. Berlin rewrites the song for Armistice Day (November 11) in 1938. Popular singer Kate Smith performs the new version on her radio show, and it becomes her signature song. Berlin gives the royalties of the song in perpetuity to the Boy Scouts of America (BSA) and the Girl Scouts of America (GSA).

'While the storm clouds gather far across the sea,
Let us swear allegiance to a land that's free,
Let us all be grateful for a land so fair,
As we raise our voices in a solemn prayer.

God bless America,
Land that I love.
Stand beside her, and guide her
Thru the night with a light from above.
From the mountains, to the prairies,
To the oceans, white with foam
God bless America, my home sweet home.

Irving Berlin
"God Bless America"
1938

In 1915, the United States under 28th President Woodrow Wilson is wary of entering World War I, a European war. Wilson is narrowly elected in 1916 for keeping America out of the war, but after Germany sinks five American ships in 1917, Wilson asks Congress for a declaration of war under Article I, Section 8 of the Constitution. Known as "The Great War," World War I engages more than seventy million military personnel and leads to the death of more than fifteen million. As countries and empires of Europe fall, the map of Central Europe is redrawn. On June 28, 1919, the Treaty of Versailles is signed, ending the war. Germany admits guilt for World War I and is prohibited from rearming. But it is a treaty that the U.S. Senate refuses to ratify. The post-war division of war-torn territory reshapes the world and sets the stage for World War II and the rearming of an aggressive Germany.

But the threat and reality of World War I would not be the only threat to fear. In 1918, the silent threat of disease causes more death across the globe than the Great War in which America finds itself. From March 1918 to June 1920, the world is gripped in fear of a deadly strain of influenza virus that kills twenty to forty million people, and by some later estimates, up to 100 million humans — as much as five percent of the world's population. Thought to have started in Spain, the "Spanish Flu" spreads worldwide, killing healthy men, women and children in tragic numbers. Although fewer than a million Americans lose their lives to the flu, its mortality rate exceeds that of American loss of life in World War I.

As the United States emerges weary from world war and world pandemic flu, American society is poised to embark on an era of social exploration and modernization. Women engaged in war and health relief efforts are anxious for a measure of affirmative social integration. The women's movement began in earnest in 1848 but stalls as the idea of equality matures and a coalition of additional supporters is recruited and developed over six decades. The massive March for Women in 1913 leads President Woodrow Wilson to support a Constitutional Amendment giving women the right to vote. The movement culminates on August 26, 1920, with the ratification of the 19th Amendment to the U.S. Constitution. Finally, women are given the universal, legal right to vote in American elections. The dreams and efforts of prominent suffragettes Elizabeth Cady Stanton and Susan B. Anthony are realized.

As the decade of the 1920s dawns, the United States has experienced 144 years of democracy, nineteen amendments to the U.S. Constitution, one world war, the development and maturity of a national military, numerous challenges to the Constitution, social equality for blacks and women (even though incomplete), threats and wars from outside American borders, numerous economic recessions, one attempted impeachment (Johnson, 1868), three assassinations of American presidents (Lincoln, 1865; Garfield, 1881, and McKinley, 1901), two assassination attempts (Jackson, 1835 and T. Roosevelt, 1912), a massive territorial expansion of United States land acquisition on the North American continent and technological developments that changed the social fabric of American society.

The United States census in 1790 shows 3,929,214 United States inhabitants. By 1930, the census documents 123,202,624 inhabitants. Yet with the passage of 144 years and growth by 120 million people, the American constitutional system and the Founders' vision of a free society survives and thrives, despite the challenges and painful growing pains of a representative democracy. The architecture of a capitalistic economy endures. The social obligations with basic individual freedoms evolve. The dignity and order of an equitable system of justice and the necessity of due process of law produce an elastic and dynamic society that endures attacks from within and without. Relations between the United

States and other nations of the world develop to produce a standard of living in the 1920s that never could have been envisioned by the Founders of the 1700s.

But despite the progress and advancements of technology that ease the lives of Americans, the threats to democracy and freedom pose challenges that the Founders also could never have imagined. A gift of representative, orderly government and individual freedom is given to several generations of Americans. That freedom, that form of government and that society will face national and worldwide circumstances that will test the endurance of the United States as never before. The 1930s and 1940s will be two pivotal decades of American history that will determine the fate and shape the destiny of the United States into the next century.

CHAPTER 5

REINVENTION
The Flag of Freedom's Nation

The new century marks the start of technological progress in the United States that fuels an emerging economy and sets a trend for American ingenuity that will last for more than 100 years. That ingenuity will help Americans struggle through two world wars and economic challenges and allow Americans to gradually raise their standards of living in a modern society. Progress at times will be uneven and discouraging to an American society developing rapidly and experiencing new and uncertain growing pains. But the United States receives a lively gift on Christmas Day, 1896 — one we still enjoy today. The gift, like the freedom we enjoy, is only perishable if we do not use it and keep it alive in our hearts and minds.

The gift is conceived in the mind of a young composer and bandleader while riding a ferry in Europe. The melody tumbles into his mind upon receiving news that his manager back home in the States has died. He writes down the musical score when he gets back home to America, including a full set of lyrics. While he will perform it with his band at every concert for the rest of his career, only one recording — made in 1909 — is known to survive today. It becomes his *magnum opus* and, by Act of Congress, the National March of the United States of America — "Stars and Stripes Forever."

FIRST VERSE AND CHORUS
Let martial note in triumph float
And liberty extend its mighty hand
A flag appears 'mid thunderous cheers,
The banner of the Western land.
The emblem of the brave and true
Its folds protect no tyrant crew;
The red and white and starry blue
Is freedom's shield and hope.

Other nations may deem their flags the best
And cheer them with fervid elation
But the flag of the North and South and West
Is the flag of flags, the flag of Freedom's nation.

John P. Sousa
"Stars and Stripes Forever"
1896

This song and many others brand John Philip Sousa as the "March King." Toward the end of his life, in his autobiography *Marching Along*, Sousa writes:

A march speaks to a fundamental rhythm in the human organization and is answered. A march stimulates every centre of vitality, wakens the imagination… But a march must be good. It must be as free from padding as a marble statue. Every line must be carved with unerring skill. Once padded it ceases to be a march. There is no form of musical composition wherein the harmonic structure must be more clear-cut. The whole process is an exacting one. There must be a melody which appeals to the musical and the unmusical alike. There must be no confusion in counterpoint.

Sousa called recorded music "canned music" and feared it would take away from America and musicians. He even testified in Congress against the recording industry and the dissemination of music "artificially," not live before an audience. Ironically, that industry was responsible for increasing the popularity of Sousa's music. Moreover, many people around the world have come to know about America and Americans through one of our most popular exports: music.

"Stars and Stripes Forever" becomes an anthem for a new century that will become known as the American Century. Just like the song, so many of the world's great inventions — conceived in the minds of Americans — will change the world.

We know what the Sousa band sounds like because we have phonograph recordings of it. The ability to write sound (phono = sound; graph = write) pre-dates the ability to read it. Edouard-Leon Scott creates the oldest known recording of the human voice in France in 1860 on a hand-cranked machine he calls a "phonautogram." Scott's invention records sounds on paper using a stylus blackened by smoke from an oil lamp. The device has a fatal flaw — it cannot reproduce sound. It isn't until computers are able to make sense of Scott's paper recording 150 years later that scientists at the Lawrence Berkeley National Laboratory are able to play it back.

The principle of acoustic analog recording is gloriously simple, yet each element must be invented separately: a diaphragm (microphone) detects changes in atmospheric pressure (sound waves) and records them with a stylus on some medium (phonograph). Acoustic analog reproduction employs these elements in reverse: a stylus responds to the grooves of a recording and activates a diaphragm (loudspeaker), which creates sound waves that are a facsimile of the original.

The French recording of the human voice (from the time of the American Civil War, which gives birth to speculation that an audio recording exists of President Lincoln) is a remarkable novelty, but practically useless until an American, Thomas Edison, invents the tinfoil cylinder phonograph that makes a very recognizable recording of the human voice in 1877. Upon hearing the human voice speak from a machine for the first time, Edison's employee, John Kruesi, exclaims: "Gott in Himmel!" (God in Heaven!) Edison himself says, "I was never so taken aback in my life." Edison's first cylinder recording no longer exists, but the recording of his 1927 re-enactment does:

> Here are the first words I spoke in the original phonograph. A little piece of practical poetry. Mary had a little lamb. Its fleece was white as snow. And everywhere that Mary went, the lamb was sure to go.

Edison's machine records the voice of Benjamin Harrison in 1889. It is the oldest known recorded voice of an American president.

> As president of the United States, I was present at the first Pan-American congress in Washington D.C. I believe that with God's help, our two countries shall continue to live side-by-side in peace and prosperity. Benjamin Harrison.

Edison's cylinder phonograph, patented in 1878, is wildly successful. An entire industry is born around the commercial recording, distribution and sale of sound recordings. Copies of popular titles sell in the many millions. Mass production techniques are developed which enable cylinder recordings to become a major new consumer item around the world. Edison moves on to inventing a practical incandescent lamp, large-scale generators and a nationwide system of electric distribution that revolutionize the way we work, live and play. Dubbed "the Wizard of Menlo Park," Edison is involved in the patenting of more than one thousand inventions in his lifetime — the most for any individual in American history. The phonograph, though, is his favorite. He calls it his "baby."

The oldest known recording of "My Country 'Tis of Thee" is performed by the Diamond Four in 1898. It is considered by many as the national anthem of the United States before the adoption of "The Star Spangled Banner."

(first verse only)
My country, 'tis of thee,
Sweet land of liberty,
Of thee I sing;
Land where my fathers died,
Land of the pilgrims' pride,
From every mountainside
Let freedom ring!

Lyrics by Samuel Francis Smith
"My Country 'Tis of Thee"/"America"
1831

As music is progressing at the close of the first full century of American evolution, so are changes in the United States Constitution. The Constitution of the United States is amended several times at the beginning of the 20th century. The 16th Amendment (1913) creates the income tax as we know it today; the 17th Amendment (1913) moves the election of Senators from state legislatures to the people and allows each state's governor to appoint a Senator between elections; and the 18th Amendment (1919) establishes Prohibition in the United States. Prohibition bans the manufacture, sale or transportation of "intoxicating liquors" for beverage purposes throughout the country. The amendment, promoted heavily by the Temperance Movement, does not ban the actual consumption of alcohol, but makes obtaining it legally very difficult after the law takes effect on January 29, 1920. It is the only constitutional amendment that takes away something that is previously a right, and that doesn't go down very well with Americans. The consumption of alcohol simply moves underground — figuratively speaking — where organized crime picks up the manufacture, sale and transportation of "bootleg hootch."

The Skillet Lickers sell more than 200,000 copies of their first record, released in the dark days of Prohibition. It is the golden age of mountain stills and old-time music when the band encourages its listeners to "never-mind" federal law, just "pass around the bottle and we'll all take a drink."

Pass around the bottle and we'll all take a drink (3x)
As we go marching on.

Glory, glory to old Georgia (3x)
As we go marching on
Hang Jim Davis on a sour apple tree (3x)
As we go marching on

(James "Methodist Jim" Davis was a fervent Temperance advocate)
The Skillet Lickers
"Pass Around the Bottle and We'll All Take a Drink"
(Sung to the tune of "John Brown's Body"
and "Battle Hymn of the Republic.")
1926

The 21st Amendment repeals the 18th Amendment in time for Christmas, 1933 — the only constitutional amendment to repeal another. The more than decade-long experiment with Prohibition will be a failure. Americans get to drown their sorrows with alcohol during the Great Depression.

The lead-in to international conflict early in the 20th century is the modern realization that the United States, despite all its internal progress on social, cultural and technological fronts, cannot avoid being a major defense force in the world. As technologies grow in the world and human nature's dark side leads men to try to dominate whole populations, the United States reluctantly answers the call to defend the freedoms of Americans and non-Americans across the globe. It is a role the United States will assume as the most powerful peace-loving country in the world and it will last for a period beyond the next century.

CHAPTER 6

WORLD WAR I

You're a Grand Old Flag

"She's a grand old rag" may be something you say to a person sitting next to you about our national flag but is probably not what you'd say if the whole world is listening. Bowing to formality, a "grand old rag" becomes a "grand old flag" and the first big hit song of the 20th century, selling over a million copies of sheet music — the first song ever to do so.

George M. Cohan is on stage as an infant. Born to Irish-Catholic vaudeville performers, he is "the man who owns Broadway" in the decade before the First World War. Cohan publishes more than 1,500 original songs, noted for their catchy melodies and clever lyrics. In 1906, he writes a song for the stage musical "George Washington Junior." Today, few remember the play, but most know the song.

There's a feeling comes a-stealing,
And it sets my brain a-reeling,
When I'm listening to the music of a military band.
Any tune like "Yankee Doodle"
Simply sets me off my noodle,

It's that patriotic something that no one can understand.
"Way down south, in the land of cotton,"
Melody untiring,
Ain't that inspiring?
Hurrah! Hurrah! We'll join the jubilee!
And that's going some, for the Yankees, by gum!
Red, white and blue, I am for you!
Honest, you're a grand old flag!

CHORUS
You're a grand old flag,
You're a high flying flag
And forever in peace may you wave.
You're the emblem of
The land I love.
The home of the free and the brave.
Ev'ry heart beats true
'neath the Red, White and Blue,
Where there's never a boast or brag.
But should auld acquaintance be forgot,
Keep your eye on the grand old flag.

George M. Cohan
1906

Cohan's parents are two of the more than twelve million people who enter the United States through Ellis Island, at the mouth of the Hudson River in New York harbor. Named for Samuel Ellis, a colonial New Yorker who once owned the island, it is the main point of entry for immigrants from January 1, 1892, to November 12, 1954. The first immigrant to pass through Ellis Island is a fifteen-year-old Irish girl, Annie Moore; the last is a Norwegian man, Arne Peterssen. The all-time daily high number of immigrants is recorded on April 17, 1907 when 11,747 people arrive to new lives in the United States. Those with health problems, discerned in a six-second medical examination, little more than a glance, are turned back and forever call this "the island of tears." The rest, who appear healthy, are asked 29 questions (Name? Occupation? How much money do you have?). They will forever call this "the land of opportunity." More than 100 million Americans can trace their ancestry to someone who arrives in America through Ellis Island.

Culture and tradition arrive with the immigrants across the Atlantic, including food and music. One of the first Italian foods to become popular here is pizza; one of the first Irish songs to become popular here is "Danny Boy." Elvis Presley will call it his favorite song. He records it in 1976. It is played at his funeral in 1977. In the century since it was written, such diverse talents as Johnny Cash, Willie Nelson, Judy Garland and Sarah Vaughn have recorded it.

The song tells the tale of an Irish lad who is called to war by the sound of distant bagpipes, and the sweetheart who promises to wait for him at home — her beloved Danny Boy.

Oh, Danny boy, the pipes, the pipes are calling
From glen to glen, and down the mountain side.
The summer's gone, and all the roses falling,
It's you, it's you must go and I must bide.
But come ye back when summer's in the meadow,
Or when the valley's hushed and white with snow,

It's I'll be here in sunshine or in shadow, —
Oh, Danny boy, O Danny boy, I love you so!

Lyrics: Frederick Weatherly
"Danny Boy"
1910

The melody for "Danny Boy" — "Londonderry Air" — emerges as a folk song from 17th century Ireland and, with different lyrics, becomes more than 100 different songs. Frederick Weatherly writes the most famous of these in 1910, though he originally sets them to a different tune. Weatherly is an attorney in England who writes songs on the side. When he pairs his new poem with the old melody in 1913, it becomes the timeless classic we know today.

Nineteen-ten is a difficult year for Weatherly because he loses both his father and his only son. While he publishes more than 1,500 songs in his lifetime, Weatherly gives life to his most famous song in the year of his greatest sorrow. The plaintive melody is, perhaps, never more touching than when it is played at the funeral for New York Fire Chief Peter Ganci, killed in the World Trade Center attack of September 11, 2001.

Thousands of songs are written every year, across time and around the world, yet few linger in our minds for very long. Those that do are often attached to times of hardship and trouble, like wars that separate families and too often result in heartache; difficult economic times that tightly squeeze family budgets and emotions; and national crises that foster public policy debates and citizen disagreement. But there is likely no greater impact on the human spirit than war; losing loved ones to it or surviving it, as a soldier or as a citizen.

"Danny Boy" gains worldwide popularity as thousands of young men go off to fight the Great War, the war to end all wars — which we, with hindsight, call World War I. One of the other signature tunes of this war invites troops to pack up their troubles in their old kit bags and smile, smile, smile.

Private Perks is a funny little codger
With a smile a funny smile.
Five feet none, he's an artful little dodger
With a smile a funny smile.
Flush or broke he'll have his little joke,
He can't be suppress'd.
All the other fellows have to grin
When he gets this off his chest, Hi!

CHORUS
Pack up your troubles in your old kit-bag,
And smile, smile, smile,
While you've a lucifer to light your fag,
Smile, boys, that's the style.
What's the use of worrying?
It never was worth while, so
Pack up your troubles in your old kit-bag,
And smile, smile, smile.

Words by George Asaf
Music by George Powell
"Smile, Smile, Smile"
1915

World War I is a global version of a brawl in which everyone's friends join the fight. The sides are chosen seventy-five years before the war begins — the *Central Powers*, which include the German Empire, Austro-Hungarian Empire, Ottoman Empire and the Kingdom of Bulgaria; and the *Entente Powers*, which include the British Empire (England, Australia, Canada, New Zealand, India and South Africa), Russian Empire, France, Italy, Romania, Belgium, Montenegro, Serbia and the Empire of Japan.

The largest war in history begins with a single gunshot on June 28, 1914. The shot is fired from the pistol of a Bosnian-Serb student and kills Archduke Franz Ferdinand of Austria, heir to the Austro-Hungarian throne. Within weeks, a series of alliances among almost all of the world's great powers is activated which mobilizes seventy million military personnel. At the start, the fighting is expected to be over by Christmas. At the end, the war lasts four years.

Austria-Hungary declares war on Serbia the day of the assassination, though the war doesn't really explode until a month later. On August 1, Germany declares war on Russia; August 3, Germany declares war on France; August 4, Britain declares war on Germany. U.S. President Woodrow Wilson declares the United States will remain neutral.

The major combatants throw all of their scientific and industrial capabilities at the war, which sees aircraft, tanks, machine guns, barbed wire, field telephones and poison gas (chlorine, mustard and phosgene) used in war for the first time. Exploding shells and fragmentation cause a large number of head wounds, leading to the invention of the modern steel helmet (1915). This is an especially brutal war, perhaps reflecting the puzzling propensity of mankind to do harm to itself in the age-old desire of one population to dominate another.

George M. Cohan writes another of his hit tunes in 1917, when — despite Wilson's pledge — the U.S. commits to the war, and able-bodied men on three continents are packing up their kit bags and heading "over there."

Johnnie, get your gun, get your gun, get your gun.
Take it on the run, on the run, on the run.
Hear them calling you and me,
Every son of liberty.
Hurry right away, no delay, no delay.
Make your daddy glad, to have had such a lad.
Tell your sweetheart not to pine, to be proud her boy's in line.

CHORUS
Over there, over there, send the word, send the word over there,
That the Yanks are coming, the Yanks are coming,
the drums rum-tumming ev'rywhere.
So prepare, say a prayer, send the word, send the word to beware.
We'll be over, we're coming over, and we won't come back
till it's over, over there.

George M. Cohan
"Over There"
1917

The entry-level rank for an enlisted man in the Army is a private; the highest, a sergeant. Army officers begin at the rank of lieutenant and go up to general. If an officer has eagles on his shoulders, he is a colonel. Would you rather be a colonel with an eagle on your shoulder or a private with a chicken on your knee?

FIRST VERSE

Once I heard a father ask his soldier son,
"Why can't you advance like the other boys have done?
You've been a private mighty long,
Won't you tell me what is wrong?"
And then the soldier lad
Said, "Listen to me, Dad":

FIRST CHORUS

"I'd rather be a private than a colonel in the Army,
A private has more fun,
When his day's work is done;
And when he goes on hikes,
In ev'ry town he strikes
Girls discover him
And just smother him
With things he likes.
But girlies act so shy
When colonel passes by,
He holds his head so high with dignity;
So would you rather be a colonel with an eagle on your shoulder
Or a private with a chicken on your knee?"

Lyrics by Sidney Mitchell
Music by Archie Gottler
"Would You Rather Be A Colonel With An Eagle On Your
Shoulder Or A Private With A Chicken On Your Knee?"
1918

The United States enters the war in April 1917 as an "Associated Power." By the summer of 1918, it is sending 10,000 fresh American soldiers to France every day. General John "Black Jack" Pershing commands the American Expeditionary Force. The "Harlem Hellfighters" are among the segregated regiments of African-American soldiers. The Espionage Act of 1917 makes free speech illegal in the United States. The Sedition Act of 1918 makes disloyal statements a federal crime. Postal censors (federal employees) remove from circulation all publications critical of the government. Eugene Debs — erstwhile candidate for president under the banner of the Social Democratic Party of America, later the Socialist Party, and one of the founding members of the International Workers Union and the International Workers of the World — is jailed for speaking out against the war.

There are few luxuries for American soldiers overseas. Among them are letters from home, familiar songs and cigarettes. "You ask me what we need to win this war," says General Pershing. "I answer tobacco as much as bullets. Tobacco is as indispensable as the daily ration; we must have thousands of tons without delay." In 1918, the War Department buys out the entire output of Bull Durham tobacco to provide cigarettes to the troops. An entire generation returns from the war addicted to cigarettes.

The First World War also brings the first recording of an anti-war song. It is written "for the ones who died in vain." Ed Morton's sensational anti-war song hit, "I Didn't Raise My Boy to be a Soldier," captures growing American skepticism about fighting what some see as "the European war."

Ten million soldiers to the war have gone
Who may never return again;

Ten million mothers' hearts must break
For the ones who died in vain.
Head bowed down in sorrow,
In her lonely years,
I heard a mother murmur through her tears:

CHORUS
I didn't raise my boy to be a soldier
I brought him up to be my pride and joy;
Who dares to place a musket on his shoulder
To shoot some other mother's darling boy?
Let nations arbitrate their future troubles,
It's time to lay the sword and gun away;
There'd be no war today,
If mothers all would say,
I didn't raise my boy to be a soldier.

Lyrics by Alfred Bryan
Music by Al Piantadosi
"I Didn't Raise My Boy To Be A Soldier"
1915

To say World War I is a bloodbath does not capture the complete truth of it. Advances in technology far outpace advances in military tactics; ability to attack outpaces ability to defend. Field officers command a massively efficient ability to kill. The British Army suffers 57,470 casualties (19,240 dead) in the first hour of the first day of the Battle of the Somme on July 1, 1916. It is the bloodiest day in British Army history. The entire Somme offensive costs the British Army nearly half a million men.

Many soldiers, on both sides, fight in trenches. For a defensive position, troops "dig in"; for an offensive position, troops go "over the top." In the diary of an unknown British soldier, we come to know the horror of a German gas attack across the trenches at Ypres, Belgium. The words are written on April 22, 1915:

> Utterly unprepared for what was to come, the (French) divisions gazed for a short while spellbound at the strange phenomenon they saw coming slowly toward them.
>
> Like some liquid the heavy-coloured vapour poured relentlessly into the trenches, filled them, and passed on.
>
> For a few seconds nothing happened; the sweet-smelling stuff merely tickled their nostrils; they failed to realize the danger. Then, with inconceivable rapidity, the gas worked, and blind panic spread.
>
> Hundreds, after a dreadful fight for air, became unconscious and died where they lay — a death of hideous torture, with the frothing bubbles gurgling in their throats and the foul liquid welling up in their lungs. With blackened faces and twisted limbs one by one they drowned — only that which drowned them came from inside and not from out.

More than fifteen million people are killed in World War I overall. Some participating countries lose 20 percent of their active male population. The last recorded casualty of the Great War is Canadian George Price, shot by a German sniper at 10:58 a.m. on the morning of November 11, 1918 (Armistice Day). World War I officially ends two minutes later, on the eleventh hour of the eleventh day of the eleventh month when German officers sign an armistice in a railroad car at Compiègne, France. Those who survive the war are called "veterans," the first use of the term to describe former military men (and later, women). Veterans of the Great War are said to belong to the "lost generation."

The "War to End All Wars" ends with a dramatically different map of Europe. Four empires are dissolved: German Empire, Russian Empire, Austro-Hungarian Empire and Ottoman Empire. Four dynasties, with ancillary aristocracies, fall: the Hohenzollerns, Habsburgs, Romanovs and Ottomans. Russia revolutionizes into the Soviet Union. The League of Nations is formed to prevent another European war. Germany's defeat and European nationalism, however, lead to a second world war in 1939, despite post-World War I efforts to "reconstruct" Germany through international gifts and loans from countries victorious in World War I. Through connivance, determination and misguided plans for racial domination, Adolf Hitler will rise as a fanatical German leader to resurrect the military capability of a Germany determined to rule the world.

On November 11, Remembrance Day (also known as Veterans Day and Armistice Day), British Commonwealth citizens wear red poppies (red as a symbol of bloodshed) in their left lapels (closest to the heart) to remember the Great War. The red poppies of Flanders are immortalized by the words of Canadian Expeditionary Force surgeon, Lieutenant Colonel John McCrae. McCrae witnesses a shell burst on May 2, 1915, in Flanders that kills his friend and former student, Lieutenant Alexis Helmer. Fellow soldiers gather Helmer's remains, place them in sandbags and lay them on an Army blanket. That night, McCrae presides over Helmer's funeral in the dark so as not to attract enemy snipers. The next morning, McCrae scribbles his thoughts in a notebook while watching a breeze comb the poppies across the field. His words survive as the most poignant poem of the war. It is often recited in remembrance every November 11.

In Flanders fields the poppies blow
Between the crosses, row on row,
That mark our place; and in the sky
The larks, still bravely singing, fly
Scarce heard amid the guns below.
We are the dead. Short days ago
We lived, felt dawn, saw sunset glow,
Loved, and were loved, and now we lie
In Flanders fields.
Take up our quarrel with the foe:
To you from failing hands we throw
The torch; be yours to hold it high.
If ye break faith with us who die
We shall not sleep, though poppies grow
In Flanders fields.

Lt. Col. John McCrae (1872-1918)
"In Flanders Fields"
1915

In the last moments of the Great War, a German lance corporal stumbles into the path of a British private. The private lifts his rifle, takes aim at the lance corporal, but decides he cannot shoot a wounded man and so lowers his rifle and lets him go. The German soldier nods in thanks and retreats with his fellow troops to Germany, where he languishes in the humiliation of defeat. History does not recall the name of the British soldier, twenty-seven-year-old Henry Tandy. History does not forget the name of the German soldier, twenty-nine-year-old Adolf Hitler.

CHAPTER 7

MUSICAL INTERLUDE:
SONGS OF THE U.S. MILITARY

Let These Colors Be 'Til All of Time Is Done

Whenever something has great value, it is common for people in uniform to guard it — sometimes even give their lives for it. The "something" we, as Americans, have, of greatest value is our freedom. The American flag is more than a symbol of a nation and a people: It is a mark of those who protect, and those who are remembered for protecting, our freedom. So it is that the American flag is sewn on every military and public service uniform in our country — so that we may rightfully regard those in uniform as freedom's champions.

There is nothing sweeter in American society than the aura of respect that surrounds a veteran of war, someone who suffers danger in combat or military exercise and survives to come home. Or young soldiers, fresh-faced and clean-cut, in military uniform, survivors of basic training and committed to a world of following orders and uniform dress, who make us smile when we see their eager enthusiasm for the life they have chosen. Or a military family that loses a loved one to war, gathered together to remember, which touches hearts and makes heads slowly shake at the loss of youth in service. We reverently attend late May's Memorial Day events, celebrate Veterans Day each November and cheer the loudest at parades for military bands and color guards. And why shouldn't we? We owe our freedom to enjoy life to those who fight for it on battlefields around the globe. The largest single discretionary federal budget item is national defense, and because of our love for veterans, Americans proudly budget a special government account for veterans' health and welfare benefits.

World history is full of stories and songs that chronicle man's struggle to survive and the seemingly inevitable conflict among nations. There is never a time when the world is free of conflict. There is rarely any nation that does not experience conflict with another. It seems to be part of the human condition that societies and populations fight. It is usually the young of one nation that fight against the young of another, and America is no exception.

United States military families are almost a sub-set of Americans because the military is known as more than just a service group committed to national values. It personifies a unique lifestyle that incorporates all that is good in American society: discipline, commitment, love of country, sacrifice, honor, duty, order. These are all words that describe and define the soldier, seaman, airman, Marine. People who serve in the military have a special stature because they commit themselves to the standards and legacy of military service, a legacy rich in tradition, born of the horrors of war and the rewards of freedom. It is not just the soldier who adopts military life — it is the commitment of the soldier's family and extended family that makes the military journey a family affair. Millions of anxious fathers and mothers, sisters, brothers, aunts, uncles and grandparents and children grieve over loss in war, nurture wounds to health, welcome the returning veteran home with love and understanding, and cry either tears of loss or tears of relief. Today's telecommunications resources, newspapers, magazines and special shows reveal war for those who remain home, secure in the freedoms won in prior wars, and safely enjoying the material fruits of a grateful society. Only the soldier and, to a greater extent than the public, the soldier's family have the true sense of what fighting for a country is really like.

Wars are usually fought and won by the young because they are the best fighting resource any nation could have. Fighting and winning a victory take the fitness and muscular development and energy of the young. These victories always come with great human loss. In 2008, the United States Department of Defense compiled statistics of war casualties from the Revolutionary War to the Iraq War. More than forty million Americans have served in war and conflict since 1775. Over one million deaths are officially recorded in such battles. Unofficial estimates are much higher. An estimated over one million deaths occur in the Civil War alone, making it the deadliest war in United States history.

The Founders know that defending the new nation is not only prudent, it is necessary for survival. Of the fifty-six men who sign the Declaration of Independence, one-third serve in the militia. They know the nation must be defended, and the War of 1812 is arguably the moment in history when the American military becomes a fixture, when 286,730 military personnel serve the United States. Later wars and conflicts find generations of Americans accepting the call to military service. World War II marks the most military personnel in war service — 16,112,566; the Mexican-American War the least — 78,718.

As the prosecution of war evolves, the military specializes into separate branches rooted in a common bond and tradition for service. Each service branch has its own slogans, mottos and songs — and we recognize them all.

The first American service branch is the Continental Army; it commences on June 14, 1775, and carries the United States successfully through the Revolutionary War. Nine years later to the day, Congress creates the United States Army. Its motto: "This We'll Defend." Its flag: red, white and blue with fringe of yellow, made of white silk and containing the War Office official seal and the blue numerals "1775." President Dwight D. Eisenhower, the 34th President of the United States and a five-star Army General, Supreme Commander of the Allied forces in Europe and graduate of the United States Military Academy at West Point, officially adopts the Army Flag on June 12, 1956. The flag is unfurled on June 14, 1956, at Independence Hall in Philadelphia, Pennsylvania by Army Secretary Wilber Brucker. Flag Day in the United States is thereafter celebrated on June 14 in honor of the establishment of the U.S. Army. On November 11, 1956, 150 days later, Brucker dedicates the "Caisson Song"[8] as the official song of the U.S. Army.

Over hill, over dale
We have hit the dusty trail,
And the Caissons go rolling along.
In and out, hear them shout,
Counter march and right about,
And the Caissons go rolling along.

REFRAIN
For it's hi! hi! hee!
In the field artillery,
Shout out your numbers loud and strong,
And where e'er you go,

You will always know
That the Caissons go rolling along.

In the storm, in the night,
Action left or action right
See those Caissons go rolling along
Limber front, limber rear,
Prepare to mount your cannoneer
And those Caissons go rolling along.

Was it high, was it low,
Where the hell did that one go?
As those Caissons go rolling along
Was it left, was it right,
Now we won't get home tonight
And those Caissons go rolling along.

Edmund L. Gruber with William Bryden and Robert Danford
"Caisson Song"
1908

Army General Edmund L. Gruber of Ohio composes this version. A West Point graduate, Gruber serves in the field artillery corps in the United States, the Philippines and the Panama Canal Zone. Along with two lieutenants, William Bryden and Robert Danford, Gruber composes the "Caisson Song" while stationed in the Philippines in 1908. Although the lyrics change slightly in 1956, the song is forever known as the Army song and is hummed by Army veterans for generations to come.

The United States Army has a hymn, too. The song is written for the centennial Fourth of July in 1876 by the rector of an

Episcopal church in Vermont. He borrows a phrase from the Bible for its original title, "God of Our Fathers." The song is a prayer for our country.

God of our fathers, whose almighty hand
Leads forth in beauty all the starry band
Of shining worlds in splendor through the skies
Our grateful songs before Thy throne arise.

Thy love divine hath led us in the past,
In this free land by Thee our lot is cast,
Be Thou our Ruler, Guardian, Guide and Stay,
Thy Word our law, Thy paths our chosen way.

From war's alarms, from deadly pestilence,
Be Thy strong arm our ever sure defense;
Thy true religion in our hearts increase,
Thy bounteous goodness nourish us in peace.

Refresh Thy people in their toilsome way,
Lead us from night to never ending day;
Fill all our lives with love and grace divine,
And glory, laud, and praise be ever Thine.

Lyrics by Daniel C. Roberts
Music by George C. Warren
"God of Our Fathers"/United States Army Hymn
1888

The oldest official song in the United States military is the Marines' Hymn, the official hymn of the United States Marine

Corps. Even though the Marine Corps copyrights the song on August 19, 1919, its original words are set to music in the mid-1800s:

FIRST VERSE

From the halls of Montezuma,
To the shores of Tripoli;
We will fight our country's battles
In the air, on land, and sea;
First to fight for right and freedom
And to keep our honor clean;
We are proud to claim the title
Of United States Marine.

BEFORE 1919

From the halls of Montezuma
To the shores of Tripoli,
We fight our country's battles,
On the land as on the sea.
Admiration for the nation,
We're the finest ever seen;
And we glory in the title
Of United States Marines.

"Marines' Hymn"
1800s

The United States Marine Corps is established in Philadelphia by adoption of the Second Continental Congress on November 10,

1775. The Marines are to serve as a weapon against the British Navy, and their forces are used to secure and board ships at sea. After Revolutionary War victory against the British, the Marine Corps lies dormant until 1798, when Congress creates the Navy and Marine Corps. Its motto, *Semper Fidelis*, from the Latin meaning "Always Faithful," is officially adopted in 1883. Its seal will date from 1800 and consist of an eagle, a globe and a foul anchor (the cable wrapped around the shank of the anchor, causing distress to the ship). That seal will become official in 1954, adopted by order of President Dwight D. Eisenhower. It will symbolize the continuous connection and affiliation between the Marines and the Navy, and their compatible functions of protection by land and sea.

The United States Navy's origin is a story in its own right. In Article I, Section 8 of the United States Constitution, Congress is specifically authorized to "Provide and maintain a Navy" and to "make Rules for the Government and Regulation of the land and naval Forces." Under Article II, Section 2, the "President shall be the Commander in Chief of the Army and Navy of the United States."

Like the Army, the Navy is a creature of the Continental Congress, formed to fight the Revolutionary War in 1775. Its original adversary, the British Royal Navy, is established over 700 years earlier and is the most powerful navy on earth, able to compete against any nation anywhere. With its veteran navy, England boasts of massive fleets and victories over the Dutch, the Spanish and the French spanning centuries. It engages the French again before century's end in the Napoleonic War. In 1794, the United States Congress adopts the Naval Act of 1794 and commissions six frigates — square-rigged warships with three masts — to establish American sea power. Even though the Continental Congress vigorously debates the necessity of a naval force, it ultimately decides to perfect a navy to protect American vessels at sea and defend American coastlines. If America is to stand against the British, its military must include a sea force.

George Washington supports a viable navy after successfully taking steps to interdict the supply lines of British cargo ships. October 13, 1775, is an important date: It marks the birth of the United States Navy, the date when Washington commands armed vessels engaging the enemy with success. Even though the United States suffers numerous losses at sea, border protection ensures the continuation of a naval buildup starting in Delaware that assures future victories in war. The Navy Department is created as a separate military division on April 30, 1798; its first Secretary is Benjamin Stoddert.

Even though the Navy and Marines remain functionally connected, the Navy's identity is distinct. Though the Navy has no official motto, the Latin words, *Non sibi sed patriae* (Not self, but country) are accepted as the Navy Motto. Its colors — navy blue, white and gold — mark the Navy Flag. The Navy Jack, adopted in the Revolutionary War, consists of thirteen white and red stripes as a backdrop for a coiled Timber rattlesnake with thirteen coils, representing the original colonies and symbolically prepared to strike when provoked. The phrase "Don't Tread on Me" is adopted as a statement of American intent, a message of self-assurance and confidence.

Sixty years later, a clergyman from the Church of England, Rev. William Whiting — a survivor of storms at sea — writes the words that will become the Navy Hymn. Titled "Eternal Father, Strong to Save," it is set to the music of Rev. John B. Dykes in 1861:

FIRST OF FOUR VERSES
Eternal father, Strong to save,
Whose arm hath bound the restless wave.
Who bid'st the mighty Ocean deep
Its own appointed limits keep;
O Hear us when we cry to thee,
For those in peril on the sea.

Rev. William Whitney/Rev. John B. Dykes
"Eternal Father, Strong to Save"/The Navy Hymn
1861

The melody of the hymn, Melita, is particularly powerful and inspiring. It is a plaintive melody that is alternately sweet and compelling. Even though the words change slightly over the years, it is a tune attached to Navy service and reminds us of those who die on duty at sea. It is played at the funeral of President Franklin D. Roosevelt, formerly Secretary of the Navy, and in commemoration of the death of President John F. Kennedy, a Navy veteran of World War II. The tradition of concluding Sunday church services at the United States Naval Academy with the hymn's first verse commences in 1879 and continues to this day.

In 1906, Lieutenant Charles Zimmerman and Navy Midshipmen Alfred Miles compose a tune that is adopted as the Navy March. It is performed as a tribute to the Naval Academy Class of 1907 and becomes the unofficial song of the Navy, played at thousands of public events in recognition of Navy service.

Stand Navy, out to sea, Fight our Battle Cry;
We'll never change our course, So vicious foe steer shy-y-y-y.
Roll out the TNT, Anchors Aweigh. Sail on to Victory
And sink their bones to Davy Jones, Hooray!

Anchors Aweigh, my boys, Anchors Aweigh.
Farewell to foreign shores, We sail at break of day-ay-ay-ay
Through our last night on shore, Drink to the foam.
Until we meet once more,
Here's wishing you a happy voyage home.

Blue of the Mighty Deep, Gold of God's Sun
Let these colors be till all of time is done-done-done,
On seven seas we learn Navy's stern call:
Faith, Courage, Service true, with Honor, Over Honor, Over All.

Charles Zimmerman and Alfred Miles
"Anchors Aweigh"
1906

Two World Wars later, the United States Air Force is established as a separate service branch. The United States Army Air Corps fights the air wars necessary in the first half of the 20th century, but the functional and specialized nature of a modern air corps only becomes more essential with the increasing sophistication of battle plans and warplanes.

The United States Air Force is formed under the National Security Act of 1947 (September 18, 1947). Aerial warfare becomes an indispensable, state-of-the-art asset in time of war. The official

Air Force song is composed in 1939, while the service is under the jurisdiction of the Army Air Corps, even before the official commissioning of the Air Force as a separate branch. Captain Robert MacArthur Crawford graduates from Princeton University in 1925. In 1937, General Hap Arnold, a five-star General in the Army and later the Air Force, believes the men of the Air Corps of the United States need a song unique to their aviation service, so he proposes a contest to select a song with a prize to the winner. *Liberty Magazine* takes up the cause, offering $1,000 to the winner. In 1939 the magazine receives 757 entries, and a song by Captain Crawford is selected. Its unofficial name: "Off We Go into the Wild Blue Yonder."

FIRST OF FOUR VERSES
Off we go into the wild blue yonder,
Climbing high into the sun;
Here they come zooming to meet our thunder,
At 'em boys, give 'er the gun!
Down we dive, spouting our flame from under,
Off with one hell of a roar!
We live in fame or go down in flame.
Nothing can stop the US Air Force!

Robert MacArthur Crawford
"Off We Go Into the Wild Blue Yonder"/US Air Force Song
1939

The United States Air Force hymn traces its ancestry to the early days of aviation in World War I. It begins its life as a poem, later set to music composed by Mozart. It offers a prayer-like plea for protection of those who fly.

FIRST OF FOUR VERSES
Lord, guard and guide the men who fly
Through the great spaces of the sky;
Be with them traversing the air
In darkening storms or sunshine fair
Amen

Words by Mary C.D. Hamilton
"Lord, Guard and Guide the Men Who Fly"
1915

President Woodrow Wilson recognizes the United States Coast Guard as a separate military branch on January 28, 1915 — relatively late given its early, rich history 125 years before. In 1790, Alexander Hamilton is the first Secretary of the Treasury under the presidency of George Washington. Much of the revenue to the struggling new government comes from tariffs on imported goods. Smuggling is rampant along the unpatrolled United States coastline. Hamilton, as Treasury Secretary responsible for the nation's revenues, commissions a maritime fleet to guard against smuggling and enforce United States tariff laws. On August 4, 1790, Congress authorizes the Revenue-Marine (later Revenue Cutter Service) in order to assist Hamilton in enforcing the maritime laws. The Service expands its mission in order to assist mariners and vessels in need during the winter months when sea travel is especially treacherous. As the Cutter Service evolves, it fights alongside, and later under, the United States Navy, meeting the nation's maritime challenges in wartime and providing additional national security offshore.

The Coast Guard Motto is *Semper Paratus*, Latin for "Always Ready" or "Always Prepared." Its colors: white, orange and blue. Its core values: honor, respect, devotion to duty. Its song bears the same name as its motto. The words are originally composed by USCG Captain Francis Saltus Van Boskerck in 1922 in the cabin of the Cutter Yamacaw in Savannah, Georgia, and the music in Unalaska, Alaska five years later.

From North and South and East and West
The Coast Guard's in the fight.
Destroying subs and landing troops,
The Axis feels our might.
For we're the first invaders
On every fighting field
Afloat, ashore, on men and Spars
You'll find the Coast Guard shield.

We're always ready for the call
We place our trust in Thee.
Through howling gale and shot and shell,
To win our victory.
"Semper Paratus" is our guide
Our pledge, our motto too.
We're "Always Ready" do or die!
Aye! Coast Guard, we fight for you.

Francis Saltus Van Boskerck
"Semper Paratus"/US Coast Guard Song
1922

Hundreds of thousands of men and women wear the uniform of the U.S. military for over two centuries. From such service, their lives change. They make and lose friends in service. They see parts of the world they never expected to see. They experience death and destruction on a scale never imagined. They bear the scars of war silently and usually without complaint. They live the mottos of their service branches. From them, the United States chooses its finest leaders, serving publicly and privately, and the military is responsible for some of the greatest technological developments the world sees, technologies that end wars, and technologies that cause death but ultimately save lives as war fighting secures the peace. The American military is an outstanding example of American democracy — achievement on merit, common standards of conduct and lines of authority that are certain and orderly for a universal objective.

There is a common thread that weaves through American military service, and it is worth remembering as modern history unfolds. This thread is evident in the songs that military veterans sing, the phrases they adopt, the mottos they chant, the flags they salute. Each military branch, and each serviceman or woman is bound by the same five standards which comprise that common thread: devotion to duty, commitment to honor, love of country, prepared for battle, service before self.

The Pentagon — the five-sided polygon in Arlington, Virginia, that houses 23,000 personnel devoted to U.S. national security in a building on less than 30 acres — is constructed in 1941 as a consolidation of all the military might of the United States. It is a figure of five equal sides that represent the five equal standards to which all service personnel and service members subscribe. The Pentagon is a place of national and international significance. It is there that men and women devoted to the defense of the United

States make a commitment to keep safe the country they love. The history of the United States military is a testament to heroism, sacrifice and the protection of national ideals and American life, as well as the lives of millions around the world, and the protection of liberty and the cause of freedom — that each of us may live in freedom from oppression and tyranny to pursue happiness, the happiness that comes in knowing that we can go to sleep each night assured that the United States military will fight to protect the freedoms we enjoy.

The Commander in Chief of the armed forces of the United States is the President of the United States (POTUS). At President James Polk's inauguration (March 4, 1845) a song — written for the play, "Lady of the Lake," by a British violinist — is played to announce his arrival. The song (without lyrics) has been played for presidents ever since: "Hail to the Chief."

Lyrics by Sir Walter Scott/Adam Gamse
Music by James Sanderson
"Hail to the Chief"
1821

The lyrics written by Gamse are set to James Sanderson's music but are rarely sung.

Hail to the Chief we have chosen for the nation,
Hail to the Chief! We salute him, one and all.
Hail to the Chief, as we pledge cooperation
In proud fulfillment of a great, noble call.
Yours is the aim to make this grand country grander,
This you will do, that's our strong, firm belief.
Hail to the one we selected as commander,
Hail to the President! Hail to the Chief!

The original lyrics, written by Scott, read:

Hail to the chief, who in triumph advances,
Honored and bless'd be the evergreen pine!
Long may the tree in his banner that glances,
Flourish, the shelter and grace of our line.
Heav'n send it happy dew,
Earth lend it sap anew,
Gaily to bourgeon and broadly to grow;
While ev'ry highland glen,
Sends our shout back again,
"Roderigh Vich Alpine dhu, ho! i-e-roe!"

Our country can only pray that the military that keeps us free and strong as a nation will continue to keep us free and strong as a people. It is more than a prayer of thanksgiving; it is a prayer for salvation.

To everyone who wears a uniform, those of us who enjoy freedom say "thank you."

Emotive songs continue to be written about our armed services. One of these is written in 2002 for the motion picture, "We Were Soldiers," starring Mel Gibson. The song touches so many people that it becomes the unofficial funeral song of the United States Army and is performed at the National Cathedral in Washington, D.C. in 2004 as the concluding music for the funeral of our 40th president, Ronald Reagan. President Reagan's burial site, at the Ronald Reagan Presidential Museum in Simi Valley, California, is engraved with these words:

I know in my heart that man is good, that what is right will eventually triumph, and that there is purpose and worth to each and every life.

To fallen soldiers let us sing
Where no rockets fly nor bullets wing
Our broken brothers let us bring
To the Mansions of the Lord.

No more bleeding, no more fight
No prayers pleading through the night
Just divine embrace, eternal light
In the Mansions of the Lord.

Where no mothers cry and no children weep
We will stand and guard though the angels sleep
All through the ages safely keep
The Mansions of the Lord.

Words by Randall Wallace
Music by Nick Glennie-Smith
"The Mansions of the Lord"
2002

CHAPTER 8

ECONOMICS AFTER 1900

Brother, Can You Spare a Dime?

Amerca searches for macroeconomic balance in the early 1900s. Americans have, at this time, lived with the ups and downs of capitalism for more than 100 years. The Founders' concept of a free enterprise system is largely implemented and mostly successful. The moral foundations of the nation are best illustrated and complemented by the economic system that society and government adopt. In America's case, freedoms for the individual, guaranteed by the Constitution, extend to economic freedom. The rights to live freely, to pursue happiness without undue restriction and with due respect for the freedoms and individual rights of others and society as a whole, and to make of ourselves what we will are important guarantees, secured by the moral and legal imperatives of the government.

The Constitutional assurance of the individual's pursuit of happiness in the early days of the Republic has to be tempered by the greater understanding that there is a proper place for government. The challenge for the Founders is to define that balance successfully. As we read the Constitution's Article I, Section 8,[9] it is obvious that the General Welfare Clause purports to do just that. It does more than authorize Congress to tax and spend for the general welfare. It permits spending for the nation's general welfare only and for the enumerated ends listed — to restrain state power and allow Congress to regulate commerce so that states have some limitations, and to ensure the free flow of goods and services among the states. Those restraints on government are further refined by the division of the national government into three equal branches (Executive, Legislative and Judicial) so no one branch will be dominant and the states will have maximum opportunity for the free exercise of their separate powers.

World War I takes an economic toll on the nation. The Great War triggered great economic growth, as national preparations for war often do. Economies adjust to manufacture goods and services that will be used in war fighting. The end of war results in the collapse of the manufacturing sector as demand for goods lessens and the post-war return of troops creates the influx into the economy of an abundance of labor. For economies that rely on foreign trade, the end of war usually reduces trade because the vanquished nations have weak economies and low productivity, limiting a country's ability to purchase from victorious nations.

In post-World War I America, troops come home, and the wartime economy adjusts to peacetime needs. The 1920s are a time of progress in product development and manufacturing. As modern goods are produced, women who worked in the wartime economy make way in the work force for men returning home. Post-war recession is relatively short-lived as economic activity increases.

America opens a window and fresh breezes blow through new curtains after the Great War. Markets, hemlines and optimism are up. Henry Ford is making a car almost everyone can afford; radio is bringing popular music into parlors across the country; Lady Liberty is learning a new dance step called "The Charleston." (The song has lyrics, but is most often performed as an instrumental.)

The song is recorded by Paul Whiteman and his Orchestra on May 7, 1925.

FIRST OF THREE VERSES
Charleston, charleston
Made in Carolina
Some dance, some prance
I'll say better than finer
Than the charleston, charleston
Boy, how you can shuffle
Every step you do
Leads to something new
Man, I'm telling you
It's a lollapazoo

Music by James P. Johnson
Words by Cecil Johnson
"The Charleston"
1923

As James P. Johnson composes "The Charleston," it is paired with a dance of the same name for the Broadway show, "Runnin' Wild," in 1923. Many see the country as running wild through the 1920s with every "new" thing becoming increasingly provocative and immoral. The "Roaring Twenties" encourage many to ask, "Why keep the brakes on? Let's misbehave!"

You could have a great career,
And you should;
Yes you should.
Only one thing stops you dear:
You're too good;
Way too good!

If you want a future, darlin',
Why don't you get a past?
'Cause that fateful moment's comin' at last...

We're all alone, no chaperone
Can get our number
The world's in slumber — let's misbehave!

Cole Porter
"Let's Misbehave"
1927

The period 1920-1929 is a time when the United States prospers economically and socially. This is a carefree time when jazz music is born, bathtub gin is consumed, "flapper girls" define fashion, bootleg liquor predominates in an era of prohibition, gangsters drive big cars and women get their first vote. The skies are sunny, the dress is formal and fancy, money flows, morals decline and consumption is the order of the day. Spending, dancing "The Charleston" and the "Fox Trot" and living high characterize the culture — remembering a time of war, but now enjoying a time of high-living and fun.

Americans gain confidence through the 1920s as technology helps us assert our place in the world. American soil, watered by capitalism, becomes the most fertile in the world, bearing inventions from the zipper (1891) to the airplane (1903). In 1927, the world's first international celebrity is an American — Charles Lindbergh, who is the first person to fly solo across the Atlantic Ocean. He receives a tickertape parade in New York where millions of people there and across the nation revel in his, and America's, triumph. From Australia to Zanzibar, almost every person on earth knows the story of "Lucky Lindy," performed by Nat Shilkret and the Victor Orchestra and Chorus in a May 26, 1927 recording.

From coast to coast, we all can boast
and sing a toast
to one who's made a name
By being game.
He was born with wings as great as any bird that flies
A lucky star
Led him afar!

CHORUS
Lucky Lindy! Up in the sky
Fair or windy, he's flying high.
Peerless, fearless — knows every cloud
The kind of a son makes a mother feel proud!
Lucky Lindy! Flies all alone
In a little plane all his own,
Lucky Lindy shows them the way
And he's the hero of the day.

Just like a child, he simply smiled
while we went wild
with fear
That Yankee lad!
The world went mad!
Everywhere we prayed for him to safely cross the sea
And he arrived
In gay Par-ee!

L. Wolf Gilbert/Albert Baer
"Lucky Lindy"
1927

Musician Ray Henderson and lyricist Mort Dixon team up in 1926 to compose a song that says goodbye to the pressures of life and hello to fun and laughter.

Pack up all my care and woe,
Here I go,
Singing low,
Bye bye blackbird,
Where somebody waits for me,
Sugar's sweet, so is she,
Bye bye
Blackbird!

No one here can love or understand me,
Oh, what hard luck stories they all hand me,
Make my bed and light the light,

I'll be home late tonight,
Blackbird bye bye.

Ray Henderson/Mort Dixon
"Bye Bye Blackbird"
1926

The following year, Harry Woods teams with Mort Dixon for another hit that speaks of the good times that grace the 1920s.

I'm looking over a four-leaf clover
That I overlooked before
One leaf is sunshine, the second is rain,
Third is the roses that grow in the lane.
No need explaining, the one remaining
Is somebody I adore.
I'm looking over a four-leaf clover
That I overlooked before.

Harry Woods/Mort Dixon
"I'm Looking Over a Four-Leaf Clover"
1927

These songs, and scores of others like them, are sung and whistled as the nation enjoys a period of prosperity, wealth, technological development and sheer excess, but only for some. As the stock market soars in the 1920s under 30th and 31st Presidents Calvin Coolidge and Herbert Hoover, the industrialized society prospers through the likes of Henry Ford's production of the gasoline automobile and many other booming industries, such as the radio industry. But there are millions of Americans who don't share in the prosperity. For the poor, the side of the street they walk is not sunny, the blackbirds they shoo away don't leave and the clovers they find only have three leaves. They are the agriculture workers in an economic world that is changing to a modern world of industry. Even though the nation's Gross Domestic Product in 1929 is almost $90 billion, the top one percent of the population earns more than the bottom forty-two percent. In short, the rich get richer and the poor get poorer.

The government policies of the 1920s greatly favor the wealthy — income taxes drop and the United States Supreme Court even finds the minimum wage unconstitutional. Because the rich have plenty and the poor have little, a new age of credit and borrowing hits the 1920s. Installment credit soars from 1925-1929, even as corporate wealth accelerates so that some 200 American corporations control half the corporate wealth. Investments in common stock increase as the Dow Jones Industrial Average rises to 381 in the late part of the decade, at that time a huge increase. Americans with money to invest try to catch a rising stock market as 1928 dawns, expecting massive profits and riding the wave upward, even though corporate balance sheets tell a different story.

As the technology industries prosper, the agriculture industry flounders. Farm prices drop precipitously as huge commodity surpluses pile up in farm country. The farm worker, a significant part of the American labor force, makes less that $300 per year. The disparity in income among industry sectors is gaping.

Believing that the way to continue the prosperity of the nation is to favor business and modern industry, President Calvin Coolidge and later President Herbert Hoover believe the 1920s should continue as a period of low taxes, corporate growth, cheap credit and favoritism for the corporate business sector over the agriculture sector. In the aftermath of World War I and interaction with European nations, in order to protect American business, the government imposes high tariffs on foreign imports, and Europeans cannot bring their goods cheaply into the United States. There is no money, and trade relations falter and economic consequences result.

September 1929 turns out to be the beginning of the end for all sectors of the American economy. Even though stock prices soften some, speculators optimistically flock to get in to the market just before they flock to get out of the market barely weeks later. October becomes a deadly financial month. October 25 finds the stock market crashing. The blackbird who is told to fly away decides to stay put. The nation crashes on October 29, 1929 — "Black Tuesday" — the day the Great Depression begins. Financial markets in the United States collapse; many economies around the world quickly follow. The stock market continues a trend downward that will last through the end of 1929. With the combination of high tariffs, massive disparity between rich and poor, a tightening of credit under uncertain market circumstances, lost jobs, overstocked inventories and little purchase and sale of goods, the United States enters the Great Depression. As the decade of the 1930s unfolds, the stock market loses ninety percent of its value; unemployment among non-farm workers reaches thirty-seven percent; homebuilding drops by eighty percent; the average family income drops by forty percent; 11,000 banks fail. Faced with no money, no jobs, no food, no credit and no economy, some Americans commit suicide. Material goods all but disappear. Families fall apart.

One quip coined during the Great Depression has found relevance in subsequent generations: "A recession is when your neighbor loses his job; a depression is when you lose yours!" In the late 1920s and early 1930s, the poor are especially hard hit —

particularly, the ethnic poor. Renowned composer and musician Quincy Jones says years later, "We were in the heart of the ghetto in Chicago during the Depression, and every block — it was probably the biggest ghetto in America — every block is the spawning ground for every gangster, black and white, in America too."

In the black community, the Depression (the "Panic") is deeply and spiritually felt. Steel mills shut down, unions are non-existent, factories close and millions of black Americans relate to a song sung by Hezekiah Jenkins in 1931.

What this country is coming to
I sure would like to know
If they don't do something by and bye, the rich
will live and the poor will die
Doggone, I mean the panic is on

Can't get no work, can't draw no pay
Unemployment getting worser every day
Nothing to eat no place to sleep
All night long folks walking the street
Doggone, I mean the panic is on

Hezekiah Jenkins
"The Panic Is On"
1931

The 1932 musical, "New Americana," features a new song that becomes an anthem for the shattered dreams of the era: "Brother,

Can You Spare a Dime?" On October 5, 1932, the song is recorded by the Leo Reisman Orchestra with vocals by Milton Douglas.

TWO OF FIVE VERSES

They used to tell me I was building a dream,
and so I followed the mob,
When there was earth to plow, or guns to bear,
I was always there right on the job.
They used to tell me I was building a dream,
with peace and glory ahead,
Why should I be standing in line,
just waiting for bread?

Once I built a railroad, I made it run,
made it race against time.
Once I built a railroad; now it's done.
Brother, can you spare a dime?

Lyrics by E.Y. "Yip" Harburg
Music by Jay Gorney
"Brother, Can You Spare a Dime?"
1931

The nation is struggling for leadership, and salvation. During the most challenging times in American history, qualified individuals with attractive personalities usually emerge to respond to the call to leadership. But the Great Depression calls for a special type of leader. In the elections of 1932, a leader for the times emerges who offers national hope and self-confidence to a population hungry for a solution. That leader is the 32nd President of the United States, Franklin Delano Roosevelt. He is elected as president to an unprecedented four terms, serving from March 4, 1933 to April 12, 1945. He brings America a "New Deal" in 1933, a series of programs designed to end the Depression and boost a nation's spirits through tough times. His campaign song is "Happy Days Are Here Again." It is a song copyrighted in 1929 by pianist Milton Ager with lyrics by Poland-born Jack Yellen. It is a song of hope, recorded by Lou Levin with Leo Reisman and his Orchestra on January 20, 1929.

So long sad times
Go 'long bad times
We are rid of you at last

Howdy gay times
Cloudy gray times
You are now a thing of the past

Happy days are here again
The skies above are clear again
So let's sing a song of cheer again
Happy days are here again

Altogether shout it now
There's no one
Who can doubt it now
So let's tell the world about it now
Happy days are here again

Your cares and troubles are gone
There'll be no more from now on
From now on...

Happy days are here again
The skies above are clear again
So, let's sing a song of cheer again

Happy times
Happy nights
Happy days
Are here again!

Milton Ager/Jack Yellen
"Happy Days Are Here Again"
1929

The optimism of the lyrics and the buoyancy of the music are just right for the time. The song is being played and enjoyed in parlors across the country, and the movie "Chasing Rainbows" features it in 1930. It is played at the 1932 Democratic Convention and becomes Democrat challenger Franklin Roosevelt's signature song, propelling him to victory. He soundly defeats Republican President Herbert Hoover with fifty-seven percent of the popular vote. Today, the song continues as the unofficial theme song of the Democratic Party.

Roosevelt is raised in a very wealthy New York family. He becomes Governor of New York, a state senator and Assistant Secretary of the Navy. In the 1920 presidential election, Roosevelt runs for Vice President on the unsuccessful ticket with Ohio

Governor James Cox. That election is won by President Calvin Coolidge. Twelve years later, Roosevelt promises a new era of government activism that will leave its mark on the policies of the United States for successive generations. In speaking to the unemployed and to the need for economic recovery and reform of economic and banking policies, Roosevelt, with a compliant Congress, creates an alphabet soup of new government initiatives: the Works Project Administration (WPA), the National Recovery Administration (NRA), the Agriculture Adjustment Administration (AAA), the Federal Deposit Insurance Corporation (FDIC), the Tennessee Valley Authority (TVA), the Securities and Exchange Commission (SEC), the Social Security Administration (SSA) and the National Labor Relations Board (NLRB), among others.

With Roosevelt in the White House, bringing change to the country, a new song captures the mood of the day. The song is featured in the 1933 film, "Gold Diggers." While few at the time can say it, anyone can sing it: "We're in the money." Popularly performed on May 2, 1933, by Fred Astaire with Leo Reisman and his Orchestra, it is a song of hope and expectation in uncertain times.

We're in the money, we're in the money;
We've got a lot of what it takes to get along!
We're in the money, that sky is sunny,
Old Man Depression you are through, you done us wrong.

We never see a headline about breadlines today.
And when we see the landlord
we can look that guy right in the eye

We're in the money, come on, my honey,
Let's lend it, spend it, send it rolling along!

Oh, yes we're in the money, you bet we're in the money,
We've got a lot of what it takes to get along!
Let's go we're in the money, Look up the skies are sunny,
Old Man Depression you are through,
you done us wrong.

We never see a headline about breadlines today.
And when we see the landlord
we can look that guy right in the eye
We're in the money, come on, my honey,
Let's lend it, spend it, send it rolling along!

Words by Al Dubin
Music by Harry Warren
"We're in the Money"
1933

Further optimism is reflected in songs such as "There's a New Day Comin,'" recorded by Sam Ross Silver Town Orchestra in December 1932. It speaks to a national yearning for getting back to work and getting back to a normal life.

New day's comin',
As sure as you're born!
There's a new day comin',
Start tootin' your horn,
While the cobbler's shoeing,

The baker will bake,
When the brewer's brewin',
We'll all get a break!

Now, a new day's comin',
For Levee and Burke,
New day's comin',
For boss and for clerk,
No more bummin',
We'll all get to work,
There's a new day coming soon!

A new day is coming, but the Depression is not to be over for a decade. It is a slow recovery. Real gross domestic product (GDP), which is all the goods and services produced by all of the people and companies in the United States, falls some thirty percent between the years 1929-1933. Real GDP is the same in 1939 as in 1933, evidence that the Depression lasts a long time, a more sustained downturn for the economy than for the spirits of the American people. Government jobs largely supplant jobs in the private sector during these years. They put people to work, even if artificially, and they result in the development of a national infrastructure. Dams on rivers that harness the energy of hydropower and national energy production are a byproduct of the Depression. These projects create jobs fueled by the federal investment. In the decade of the 1930s, President Roosevelt triples government spending. Critics charge he is turning America into a socialist state. The federal programs help, though future generations will realize that once government programs are put in place they are not easily displaced. Ultimately, it will take the massive spending of World War II to bring the national economy back to life.

The Great Depression, for the first time in American history, puts the nation's longstanding free enterprise system in question. The economic system in which America is born and grows up is capitalism. It centers on the private ownership and trading of goods, land, labor and capital. Private individuals or business enterprises control business decisions in a market-based economy that prices goods and services depending on their abundance. The market concept of supply and demand sets prices and therefore sets profits. If there are more goods available and wider choices for purchasers, the price of goods will be lower. If there are fewer goods and fewer choices for purchasers, the price of such goods will be higher. Free enterprise allows the entrepreneur to take a business risk by investing capital in a business idea, structure the idea so that a good or service is produced to make a profit, and then prosper, or not, by the strength of the idea, good, service and business judgment employed. The entrepreneur competes with other entrepreneurs for the consumer's attention and trade.

Capitalism is an evolving economic system, in the world since the Middle Ages, but develops further between the 13th and 16th centuries and provides a primary method of industrialization of the modern world. Socialism is an economic theory by which the state or public owns and administers the means of production and distribution of goods and services to the people of a nation. Socialists complain that capitalism concentrates power and wealth in a limited segment of society and creates a wealth disparity between rich and poor. Capitalists argue that socialism reduces the productivity and ingenuity of a market-based economy and is a disincentive for citizens to work and realize the fruits of their own labor for private consumption. Socialists want the government to assure a fair distribution of capital and wealth rather than leaving an economy subject to the uses and abuses of a free market system.

Capitalists want low taxes and maximum freedom for private business to achieve success based on merit, ingenuity and competition, and they oppose bigger government and more rules, regulations and the attendant costs on the private sector, because such restrictions tend to suppress entrepreneurial spirit.

The Roosevelt election results in the implementation of the economic model of economist John Maynard Keynes as a means to assure the fair distribution of the nation's income and assets. Rather than leave the effects of the Depression to market remedies and realities, Roosevelt uses the economic power of the federal government to increase employment at a time when the private sector cannot do so. He creates federal agencies that will employ the unemployed and act as a distributor of wealth through regulation of the economy. Productivity and worker output drop in 1929 and gradually increase over the following ten years. Critics of the Roosevelt plan argue that the Depression lasts longer than it should because of so much government control, and resulting inefficiencies, over the national economy. Supporters say that without the Roosevelt plan, the economy might never have recovered and that market forces would not correct the income disparities that existed before the crash. They contend the plan provided a lifeline to a public desperate for human survival.

Besides economic policy changes, other aspects of the national government change as well. As President Roosevelt takes office, his first year, 1933, turns out to be full of challenges and opportunities. The United States Constitution is amended twice on Roosevelt's watch.[10]

One of the great pillars of our national system of government is underlined by our relative unawareness of it — a peaceful transition of power between administrations. Some housekeeping is done to this process in the 20th Amendment to our Constitution.

Before Amendment XX, new Presidents, Vice Presidents and Members of Congress must wait four months following their election to take office — an amount of time deemed necessary in the 18th century when communication and travel are time-consuming. Two administrations demonstrate, however, that a transition needs to happen sooner: President Lincoln, to deal with the Civil War; and President Roosevelt, to deal with the Great Depression. After Amendment XX, the terms of new Senators and Representatives begin at noon on the third day of January; the terms of new Presidents and Vice Presidents begin at noon on the 20th day of January. Previously, they began on March 4.

The 21st Amendment to our Constitution is the only Amendment, to date, that is passed to repeal another. Amendment XXI — ratified on December 5, 1933 — repeals Amendment XVIII, thereby making it legal to consume liquor in the United States.[11] It is also the only Amendment, to date, ratified by state conventions rather than state legislatures (both methods are provided by Amendment V) — state legislators are believed to be beholden to, or fearful of, the temperance lobby of the times.

President Herbert Hoover calls Prohibition a "great economic and social experiment — noble in motive and far-reaching in purpose." But bootleg liquor sales boomed as organized crime and human nature responded to true market forces. Americans wanted to consume alcohol. Black-market sales and bootlegging became a multi-million dollar business under Prohibition. Speakeasies became the market vehicle for consumer consumption that illustrated the futility of further efforts to prohibit liquor sales in the marketplace. Recognizing the widespread consumption of alcohol, prohibition was repealed. Gangster Al Capone, who became wealthy in the 1930s from liquor sales and other illegal activity, uttered a capitalistic truism: "All I ever did was supply a demand that was pretty popular."

The gloom of depression begins to lift as Americans prepare to date their checks in a new decade — the 1940s. Not all storm clouds are past, though it seems most people are now walking on the sunny side of the street.

Grab your coat and get your hat
Leave your worries on the doorstep
Life can be so sweet
On the sunny side of the street

Can't you hear the pitter-pat
And that happy tune is your step
Life can be complete
On the sunny side of the street

I used to walk in the shade with my blues on parade
But I'm not afraid...this rover's crossed over

If I never had a cent
I'd be rich as Rockefeller
Gold dust at my feet
On the sunny side of the street

Jimmy McHugh/Dorothy Fields
"On the Sunny Side of the Street"
1930

Parlor games and board games become a popular pastime through the 1930s. The quintessential example of these is introduced by Parker Brothers in 1935 — Monopoly. It sells 20,000 copies in one week. Horse racing and baseball also become national phenomena, each with its own celebrities: War Admiral and Sea Biscuit at the track, Lou Gehrig and Joe DiMaggio on the field.

While the newspaper reminds people about what they don't have, popular singers tap into a vein of patriotism to celebrate what we do have. Kate Smith records her signature song in the spring of 1939.

God bless America, land that I love.
Stand beside her and guide her,
through the night with the light from above.
From the mountains to the prairies,
to the oceans white with foam,
God bless America, my home sweet home.

Irving Berlin
"God Bless America"
1918/1938

As the Great Depression recedes in 1939, another crisis looms — the threat of a resurrection of Germany from the ashes of World War I, which imperils Europe and the rest of the free world. It will be a second great crisis for President Roosevelt to confront and overcome. It will result in the restructuring of the world geographically, socially and politically, establishing the United States as the world's dominant national power for the rest of the 20th century. That great crisis is World War II.

CHAPTER 9

WORLD WAR II
AND NATIONAL RECOVERY

God Gave Me the Right to be a Free American

I f all the generations known to Americans living today are ranked for their valor and commitment to the preservation of American ideals, the generation which comes of age in the 1930s and 1940s will rank at the top — at the top for the plethora of challenges history presents to its members and their heroic response to it all, which still greatly affects us today. When the members of that generation are born (1901-1924), they come of age near the time of the Great Depression (1929-1933) and near the time that World War II is fought (1941-1945). It is called the "Greatest Generation" because of the hardships it endures and the courage it displays in saving the world from the tyranny of Nazi Germany, Fascist Italy and Imperialist Japan. This generation is also instrumental in lifting the United States from the greatest economic collapse it endures before World War II and setting the United States on a course of prosperity after the war.

But it is also a generation revered for its courage, ethics, self-sacrifice and leadership qualities, producing leaders such as Dwight D. Eisenhower, John F. Kennedy, Joe DiMaggio and Billy Graham, who leave legacies of excellence and honor, both on and off the battlefield. Like the people of the Greatest Generation, the songs of the World War II generation leave a descriptive legacy that defines the times.

Paul Roberts and Shelby Darnell (aka Bob Miller) compose a wartime song in 1942 that sells more than three million copies under the name "There's a Star-Spangled Banner Waving Somewhere."

FIRST OF THREE VERSES

There's a Star Spangled Banner waving somewhere
In a distant land so many miles away.
Only Uncle Sam's great heroes get to go there
Where I wish that I could also live some day.
I'd see Lincoln, Custer, Washington and Perry,
And Nathan Hale and Colin Kelly, too.
There's a Star Spangled Banner waving somewhere,
Waving o'er the land of heroes brave and true.

Paul Roberts/Shelby Darnell aka Bob Miller
"There's a Star Spangled Banner Waving Somewhere"
1942

The song captures the attitude of Americans: They want to be part of the global fighting which threatens free civilizations and democracies. It is a time of willing self-sacrifice for a greater cause — freedom — that is embraced by Americans of all ages, but particularly young men anxious to fight for their country. Future presidents — including George H.W. Bush, John F. Kennedy, Ronald Reagan and Jimmy Carter — heed the call to enlist and serve their country in World War II. The human values they bring to their future presidencies will help define their legacies as prominent Americans.

Emotions emerge as parents, sadly but proudly, send young boys off to war, sweethearts kiss young soldiers and sailors good-bye, perhaps for the last time, and the whole of America invests itself in winning a war against a ruthless foreign enemy. Letter exchanges take weeks, phone communications are not available and the fate of a loved one is always uncertain. Instant messaging, cell phones and e-mails are decades away, but music and tender songs are ways for families and lovers to sweetly think of and miss each other.

A favorite of the times is a song titled "I'll Be Seeing You," popularly performed by Jo Stafford with Paul Weston's Orchestra.

I'll be seeing you in all the old familiar places
That this heart of mine embraces all day through
In that small café, the park across the way
The children's carousel, the chestnut trees, the wishing well

I'll be seeing you in every lovely summer's day
In everything that's light and gay
I'll always think of you that way
I'll find you in the morning sun
And when the day is new
I'll be looking at the moon
But I'll be seeing you

Irving Kahal and Sammy Fain
"I'll Be Seeing You"
1938

As Americans today speak of global economies and global markets, the globe of the 1940s becomes infected by global military conflict without boundaries, led by countries and leaders whose names would represent the best and the worst of humanity. Enemies of freedom are aggressively emerging in 1939, when Hitler's Nazi Germany invades Poland, its neighbor to the east. The Axis countries (Germany, Italy and Japan) are dictatorships led by right-wing extremists — fascists, really, who combine radicalism with authoritarian nationalism . The names of the leaders of the Axis countries personify evil and destruction in world history. Adolf Hitler creates a Nazi Germany dedicated to a cruel disrespect for people of Jewish faith and heritage and engages in a systematic elimination of their existence. Benito Mussolini leads a fascist Italy into World War II on June 10, 1940, when it becomes a second Axis power by declaring war against Great Britain and France. Mussolini believes in strong nationalistic sentiments, opposes democracy, supports militarism, creates a warrior youth movement and develops an increasingly strong hand of military might. Japan's Emperor Hirohito, a continent away, becomes increasingly influenced by aggressive military leaders — particularly Hideki Tojo, Japan's prime minister in 1941 who ordered the attack on Pearl Harbor — and becomes a member of the Axis Powers as a third imperialist government opposed to democracy and freedom.

A common characteristic of the Axis countries under dictatorial leadership is their national policy of developing youth organizations, using subjugation of the mind and indoctrination through propaganda to build a military and civilian force that puts the state above the individual by means of force and coercion. Hitler, Mussolini and Hirohito have grand visions of oppression and control of the world in the 1930s and 1940s. Had they succeeded, one can only wonder and fear the world condition that would have resulted and the consequences for humanity.

On the side of freedom are the Allied countries of Great Britain, the United States and the Union of Soviet Socialist Republics. These three countries, which have developed militaries, also have strong civilian leaders: Great Britain's Winston Churchill, the Soviets' Joseph Stalin (ironically killing more people under his leadership than Hitler did) and the United States' Franklin Delano Roosevelt. The United States will be a reluctant entrant into World War II, perhaps deterred by President George Washington's counsel that the United States should avoid war with other nations.

The sounds of war, however, cause great anxiety across the country, brought home by the microphone of a young reporter who becomes the father of broadcast journalism. Edward R. Murrow receives his undergraduate degree in speech at Washington State College in Pullman, Washington. In 1935, Murrow becomes Director of Talks at the fledgling Columbia Broadcasting System (CBS); in 1937, the director of its European operations. Murrow speaks words of war into his CBS microphone while air raid sirens blare across London, on the evening of August 24, 1940, and millions across the globe listen intently to the drama of war.

Murrow returns to the United States in 1941, a national celebrity. CBS hosts a dinner in his honor at the Waldorf-Astoria Hotel in New York on December 2. Eleven hundred guests crowd the room to hear a now-familiar voice; millions more listen in on the radio. President Roosevelt sends a "welcome home" telegram, which is read at the dinner. The Librarian of Congress, Archibald

MacLeish, rises to speak poignantly about the power of Murrow's wartime dispatches:

> You burned the city of London in our houses and we felt the flames. You laid the dead of London at our doors and we knew that the dead were our dead ... were mankind's dead without rhetoric, without dramatics, without more emotion than needed be. You have destroyed the superstition that what is done beyond 3,000 miles of water is not really done at all.

The United States enters the war less than a week later.

A surprise attack by Japan against the United States at Pearl Harbor, Hawaii, on Sunday, December 7, 1941, makes it impossible for Roosevelt to keep the United States out of the war. The President addresses a Joint Session of Congress on Monday, December 8. Millions of Americans huddle around their radios to hear their president speak. The recording is iconic for the 20th century:

> Yesterday, December 7th, 1941 — a date which will live in infamy — the United States of America was suddenly and deliberately attacked by naval and air forces of the Empire of Japan.

Less well-known is what President Roosevelt says to the American people the next day, in a broadcast from the Oval Room of the White House. The President summarizes the state of world affairs that compels the United States to action:

> The sudden criminal attacks perpetrated by the Japanese in the Pacific provide the climax of a decade of international immorality. Powerful and resourceful gangsters have banded

together to make a war upon the whole human race. Their challenge has now been flung at the United States of America. The Japanese have treacherously violated the longstanding peace between us. Many American soldiers and sailors have been killed by enemy action. American ships have been sunk; American airplanes have been destroyed. The Congress and the people of the United States have accepted that challenge. Together with other free peoples, we are now fighting to maintain our right to live among our world neighbors in freedom, in common decency, without fear of assault.

Roosevelt sets a tone of nationalism for a beneficial and unifying purpose in his address to Americans:

There is no such thing as security for any nation — or any individual — in a world ruled by the principles of gangsterism. The true goal we seek is far above and beyond the ugly field of battle. When we resort to force, as now we must, we are determined that this force shall be directed toward ultimate good as well as against immediate evil. We Americans are not destroyers — we are builders. We are now in the midst of a war, not for conquest, not for vengeance, but for a world in which this nation, and all that this nation represents, will be safe for our children. We expect to eliminate the danger from Japan, but it would serve us ill if we accomplished that and found that Hitler and Mussolini dominated the rest of the world. So we are going to win the war and we are going to win the peace that follows. And in the difficult hours of this day — through dark days that may be yet to come — we will know that the vast majority of the members of the human race are on our side. Many of them are fighting with us. All of them are praying for us. But, in representing our cause, we represent theirs as well — our hope and their hope for liberty under God.

What follows is a national effort to prepare for war. Mobilization of the vast resources of the United States creates a boost to the national economy as American factory workers build cars, trucks, airplanes, guns, bullets, bombs and other implements of war. At the same time, heeding the Roosevelt call to arms and action, thousands of young men and women enlist in the war effort, committed to Roosevelt's vision of American liberty under God. Besides preparing a country for war, the economy at last receives a Depression-ending boost that will last into the second half of the 20th century.

The Allies' dogged determination to win the war against fascism is no better illustrated than by the windswept, chalky cliffs of Dover, England, which stand resolute against the pounding waves of the Atlantic Ocean — and survive. In 1941, these cliffs inspire Nat Burton and Walker Kent to collaborate on a song that is remembered by veterans of World War II as a song of hope for peace and freedom from the war of nations and safe return home for fighting men. It is popularly performed by Jimmy Dorsey and his Orchestra.

There'll be bluebirds over
The white cliffs of Dover,
Tomorrow
Just you wait and see.

There'll be joy and laughter
And peace ever after,
Tomorrow
When the world is free,

The shepherd will count his sheep
The valleys will bloom again,
And Jimmy will go to sleep
In his own little room again,

There'll be bluebirds over
The white cliffs of Dover,
Tomorrow
Just you wait and see.

Nat Burton/Walker Kent
("There'll Be Bluebirds Over") "The White Cliffs of Dover"
1941

Burton also goes on to compose another American classic, "I'll Be Home for Christmas."

The Almanac Singers perform a wartime song titled "Round and Round Hitler's Grave" that summarizes American sentiments about the Axis leaders in 1942. Folk singers Pete Seeger and Woody Guthrie are members of the group, and they compose lyrics to the tune of Old Joe Clark to emphasize their feelings about Hitler and Mussolini.

Now I wished I had a bushel
Wished I had a peck
Wished I had old Hitler
With a rope around his neck.

Mussolini (Hermann Göring) won't last long
Tell you the reason why

We're a-gonna salt his beef
And hang him up to dry.

Pete Seeger/Woody Guthrie
"Round and Round Hitler's Grave"
1942

Popular song becomes a serious weapon in the war — some of it silly, some of it sinister. On the silly side, Walt Disney Studios releases an animated short called "Der Fuehrer's Face," in which Axis leaders Hirohito, Herman Göring, Goebbels and Mussolini appear as members of an "oompah band" singing the virtues of Nazi doctrine while marching through a German town in which everything — including the clouds and trees — is decorated with swastikas. Spike Jones parodies the cartoon's signature song and captures the collective attitude of Americans when his band of City Slickers says we'll "Heil! Heil! Right in Der Fuehrer's Face."[12]

On the sinister side, Germany's minister of propaganda, Joseph Goebbels — who outlaws "degenerate jazz" at home — comes up with the swing era's most improbable jazz band: Charlie and his Orchestra. Bandleader Karl "Charlie" Schwedler performs cover versions of the latest swing sensations on German shortwave broadcasts in 1941 beamed to London every Wednesday and Saturday nights at 9 p.m., local time, when Goebbels knows British citizens will be at home with the blinds closed. Every tune sounds so familiar to Allied soldiers listening in on the radio, but these songs deliver a sarcastic sting.

Let's go slumming, take me slumming,
Let's go slumming on Park Avenue.

Let us hide behind a pair of fancy glasses
and make faces when a member of the classes passes.
Let's go smelling where they're dwelling,
sniffing everything the way they do.
Let us go to it, let's do it
why can't we do it too.
Let's go slumming, nose-thumbing on Park Avenue.
Here is the latest song of the British airmen:
Let's go bombing, oh, let's go bombing,
just like good old British airmen do.
Let us bomb the Frenchmen who were
once our allies!
England fights for liberty, we make them realize,
from the skies.
Let's go shelling where they're dwelling,
shelling Nanette, Fifi and Lulu.
Let us go to it, let's do it, let's sink
their food-ships too.
Let's go bombing, it's becoming quite the thing to do.

Charlie and his Orchestra make almost 100 recordings between March 1941 and February 1943. The *Propagandaministerium* writes the lyrics for each one while band members are free to come up with their own musical arrangements. British Prime Minister Winston Churchill will reveal after the war that he enjoys the broadcasts and finds the lyrics hilarious.

The National Defense Savings Program commissions Irving Berlin to write its war campaign theme song in 1941, to encourage every American to be part of the war effort by buying defense bonds and savings stamps. Over the course of the war, eighty-five million Americans purchase bonds totaling about $186 billion.

FIRST OF THREE VERSES
The tall man with the high hat and the whiskers on his chin
Will soon be knocking at your door and you ought to be in
The tall man with the high hat will be coming down your way
Get your savings out when you hear him shout "Any bonds today?"

Any bonds today?
Bonds of freedom
That's what I'm selling
Any bonds today?
Scrape up the most you can
Here comes the freedom man
Asking you to buy a share of freedom today

Irving Berlin
"Any Bonds Today?"
1941

As the United States flexes its national muscle and the giant within it awakens, lives are put on hold to face the battle for national survival. On May 22, 1942, baseball superstar Ted Williams takes a leave of absence from the Boston Red Sox, after hitting an astonishing .406 batting average in 1941, to join the Navy. He later receives his wings as an outstanding Marine pilot and will ultimately go on to serve America in the Korean War. Actor Jimmy Stewart is not only a superstar film actor: he voluntarily enlists in the Army in March 1941, the first major movie star to serve in World War II. The actor becomes a decorated Army Air Corps officer and flight instructor, interrupting a successful movie career to serve his country but credited with helping liberate France. After the war, he achieves the rank of Air Force Brigadier General in 1959.

Two future United States Presidents demonstrate their valor during World War II. Twenty-four-year-old John F. Kennedy tries to enlist in the Army in the spring of 1941 but is rejected because of a bad back. Born into a wealthy family, Kennedy uses family influence to join the Navy and achieves the rank of Lieutenant. He becomes commander of a patrol torpedo boat (PT-109) that is rammed by a Japanese vessel. Kennedy's courage and bravery are tested as he survives the incident and later receives military decoration for his injuries and performance under fire. Another future president, George H.W. Bush, graduates from boarding school at age eighteen and in 1942 joins the Navy, becoming the youngest naval aviator in the military at that time. Assigned to the Pacific theater in 1944, Lieutenant Bush pilots a bomber during an attack on a Japanese installation. Coming under heavy anti-aircraft fire, Bush's plane is hit, and he parachutes into the Philippine Sea in the Northern Pacific Ocean. Four hours later, the life raft he clings to is found, and a Navy submarine rescues him. Throughout the war, Bush will fly fifty-eight missions and is later decorated with three Air Medals, the Distinguished Flying Cross and a Presidential Unit Citation.

Not only the famous devote themselves to the cause of freedom called for by President Roosevelt. A sense of patriotism inspires millions of men and women across the United States to devote themselves to some part of the war effort. The Civil Defense Corps encourages restricted use of tires, fuel, steel and other resources so they can be used for defense manufacturing. As Americans prepare at home for possible air raids, they sense an unspoken obligation to provide meaningful contributions to national mobilization. Those who cannot serve in the active military can serve domestically, as cooks, auxiliary fire and police patrol, nurses, canteen corps members, Red Cross contributors, debris cleaners and rescue squads. Buying United States Savings Bonds to fund the war treasury is an act of patriotism. While food is plentiful, America suffers from a shortage of metals.

President Roosevelt does not identify serving the national defense as a sacrifice; he calls defending the cause of freedom a "privilege." An estimated eighteen million women take wartime jobs across America, building ships, airplanes and other products in factories, steel mills and on farms. Many serve as nurses and aides in the military. Millions of women volunteer for the Red Cross and the United Service Organization (USO). "Rosie the Riveter," appearing in a pose showing her well-developed bicep, becomes the face of American women in service to country. Posters show women with sleeves rolled up, hands in gloves and hair in a bandana, a soldier in the background, beside the slogan, "The Girl he left behind is still behind him — she's a WOW." Roosevelt will later commend the women of America for their efforts to support the soldiers and the war. And these women also support their families with a newfound paycheck and as a support service for families recovering from the Great Depression.

Gracie Fields sings for the many factory workers who may not know the purpose of the "thing-ummy-bob" that they're so busy making in the factory, but they know it's "going to win the war."

FIRST OF FIVE VERSES
I can't pretend to be a great celebrity
But still, I'm quite important in me way,

The job I have to do may not sound much to you
But all the same, I'm very proud to say.....

I'm the girl that makes the thing that drills the hole
that holds the ring that drives the rod that turns the knob
that works the thing-ummy-bob
I'm the girl that makes the thing that holds the oil
that oils the ring that takes the shank that moves the crank
that works the thing-ummy-bob.

Gordon Thompson/David Heneker
"The Thing-Ummy-Bob (That's Going to Win the War)"
1942

The war also produces heroes and leaders who display courage and bravery on the battlefield. It reveals the talents and promise of an array of leaders, some of whom earn five stars as Generals in the military: Army General Dwight D. Eisenhower, the Supreme Commander of the Allied Forces in Europe; Army General Omar N. Bradley, who commands the Allied forces in North Africa and Europe; Army General George C. Marshall, who becomes Chief of Staff of the Army and directs the war effort under President Roosevelt; the colorful General George S. Patton, a military genius who courts controversy on the battlefield and shows an intolerance for disagreement with his superiors, both military and civilian; and Army General Douglas MacArthur, who fights in three wars during his career and becomes General of the Army, but he is ultimately relieved of his command by President Harry S. Truman in a disagreement over Korean War policy.

War's product is heroic men in battle, young men who sacrifice life and limb to the cause of freedom and victory in war for the

United States and its World War II allies. A unique generation of survivors returns home as the Allied forces of the war prevail in the liberation of Europe and Africa, obtaining surrender in Asia by the Japanese and cessation of hostilities around the world.[13] The war defines that generation: It possesses elements of strengthened character, both heroic and sacrificial, personifying the longstanding American attitude about conflict and reconstruction and non-aggressive postwar policy. Contrasted with the war-ending violence of the atomic bombs dropped by the United States on Japan, which bring World War II to a close in June 1945, the policy of tolerance and mercy exhibited by American and Allied leaders is true to the 169 years of American existence. In fact, the war does not expand the geography of the United States by one square inch (except by territories such as Guam and other Pacific Islands which seek affiliation with the United States). Americans crave peace, not expansion or control over other nations or peoples of the world in order to establish a world empire.

The No. 1 song of 1943 is performed by trumpeter/bandleader Vaughn Monroe. Titled "When the Lights Go on Again All Over the World," it represents the American attitude toward war.

When the lights go on again all over the world
And the boys are home again all over the world

And rain or snow is all that may fall from the skies above
A kiss won't mean "goodbye" but "Hello to love."

When the lights go on again all over the world
And the ships will sail again all over the world

Then we'll have time for things like wedding rings
and free hearts will sing
When the lights go on again all over the world
When the lights go on again all over the world

Eddie Seller/Sol Marcus/Bennie Benjamin
"When the Lights Go On Again (All Over the World)"
1943

The overall death toll of World War II has been estimated in the tens of millions of lives lost. American military casualties totaled over 290,000. An estimated six million Jews die at the hands of Nazi Germany. President Roosevelt also becomes a casualty of war by implication. Having returned from an emotional and exhausting trip to the Middle East and a meeting in Yalta with Stalin and Churchill to discuss postwar settlement and relations, Roosevelt is ill. He suffers from the mental stress of foreign relations and a reelection in 1944, and he also has a host of physical maladies, including high blood pressure and heart disease. Roosevelt collapses and dies on the afternoon of April 12, 1945, only eighty-two days after commencing his historic fourth presidential term. Vice President Harry S. Truman succeeds him as president.

Roosevelt's death counters the jubilation of victory for a war-weary nation celebrating the survival of freedom and the return home of military men and women. As the nation grieves, Harry S. Truman becomes the nation's 33rd President. A Missouri native, the unsophisticated, plain-speaking Truman differs in style and substance from his patrician predecessor, and his postwar management of domestic and foreign affairs is not without controversy or challenge. It is Truman's decision to try to end World War II by the first-ever use of nuclear weapons — the development of which is kept secret from him as Vice President — that signals the beginning of a nuclear weapons race that will change the foreign relations of the world's major powers and mark the start of the Cold War. More than 240,000 people die in Hiroshima and Nagasaki when the atomic bombs are dropped by the United States on Japan in August 1945, resulting in Japan's immediate surrender and the end of World War II. Truman holds clear in his mind that the bomb will shorten the war and save thousands of lives. He never looks back on his decision.

> The world will note that the first atomic bomb was dropped on Hiroshima, a military base. We won the race of discovery against the Germans. We have used it in order to shorten the agony of war, in order to save the lives of thousands and thousands of young Americans. We shall continue to use it until we completely destroy Japan's power to make war.

In 1945 Truman oversees the contentious conversion of the American economy to peacetime, which brings out issues that had lain dormant during the war. Labor strikes and the first-ever railway strike in 1946 lead Truman to unprecedented nationalizing of the railroads. He makes famous the slogans, "The buck stops here" and "If you can't stand the heat, get out of the kitchen." They reflect the challenges he faces in his presidency and his resolve to make bold public policy moves and accept the potential fallout. Truman's decisions while in office from 1945-1953 have lasting implications: he supports the United Nations; he establishes the Truman Doctrine to support free peoples against oppressive governments in order to contain the emboldened Soviet Union; he recognizes in 1949 the nation state of Israel in Palestinian territory; he secures the treaty establishing the North Atlantic Treaty Organization (NATO) (see Appendix H); he oversees the separation of Taiwan from Mainland China; he recognizes the newly created state of Pakistan as a nation in 1947; he calls for a blockade of North Korea in 1950 after North Korea invades South Korea, and oversees American commitment to war there. The Korean War is often called the "Forgotten War" because it ended in a stalemate between North and South Korea, divided ever since by a heavily armed bookended demilitarized zone. Nevertheless, it was a story of heroic American military service.

Domestically, Truman faces coal miners' strikes, the rapid focus on communism and the possibility that the American government is infested with communist spies under the control of the Soviet Union. It is an accusatory period in the United States as Americans struggle with the fear of internal communism, balanced by their desire to remain true to the American sense of justice and respect for individual rights. The early 1950s are marked by the political ascension of a future president, Richard M. Nixon, and the notoriety of controversial Joseph McCarthy, both United States Senators focused on combating communism in a post-war period of political change. Both of these men incorporate the destructive element of citizen suspicion with the offsetting fear of Soviet threats to liberty and international peace.

Postwar, post-Depression Americans celebrate their new birth of freedom in very personal ways — we buy more, go out more and make more babies. Deprived of so much for so long, we gather close the people and the things we love most. Many youngsters of the postwar baby boom are weaned on comic books, dime store candy and cowboy heroes. Gene Autry — the singing cowboy — is among the first "stars" of broadcasting. He has his own national radio show from 1940-1956 and transitions to television. Thousands of young cowboys and cowgirls consider him a hero and endeavor to keep his

Cowboy Commandments — considered by some as powerful as scripture and still valuable today:

A Cowboy

1. must never shoot first, hit a smaller man, or take unfair advantage.
2. must never go back on his word, or a trust confided in him.
3. must always tell the truth.
4. must be gentle with children, the elderly and animals.
5. must not advocate or possess racially or religiously intolerant ideas.
6. must help people in distress.
7. must be a good worker.
8. must keep himself clean in thought, speech, action and personal habits.
9. must respect women, parents and his nation's laws.
10. is a patriot.

As families reunite and plan postwar futures, the 1950s usher in opportunity, political anxiety, material affluence and social development and international challenge. Author David Halberstam in his book, *The Fifties*, describes this decade as one filled with technological and social changes, challenges to old order, and growth of an American "middle class" that sees the essential goodness of American society. Trust exists between citizen and national leader, especially with the 1952 election of Dwight D. Eisenhower, perhaps the most reliable and trustworthy leader to emerge from Allied victory in World War II.

The Fifties are marked by dramatic changes in music and technology. The decade sees the public's devotion to conventional music and ballads that can be sung and understood, contrasted with the music of Elvis Presley and other rock and roll artists. Modern music is not political music, but it has political consequences and pits the generation of children born in the early to mid 1940s against their parents — Frank Sinatra v. Elvis, Hello Young Lovers v. Hound Dog performers, standing still v. young musicians gyrating. The political consequences amount to an early and modest rebellion by young people against the predictable behavior patterns of their parents of the 1930s and 1940s. The rebellion is not anarchy; it is a challenge to accepted authority and conventional standards. Teenage enjoyment of the hip-swinging performances of Elvis singing "All Shook Up," the pounding piano of Jerry Lee Lewis' "Great Balls of Fire" and the guitar boogie of Chuck Berry's "Johnny Be Good" are a way for teenagers to be daring, but not too daring.

The technology of television, introduced commercially in the 1940s, becomes widespread in the 1950s, changing entertainment and the transmission of news and social trends. It is a new medium that generates a profound impact on society that will shrink, and change, the world. The reality of seeing an actual event or news item is far superior to merely hearing or visualizing it through the medium of radio or newsprint. TV will spawn a new era of political activism that will affect society for the rest of the 20th century. Television not only communicates — it mobilizes, tantalizes and enfranchises a generation of Americans who see a post-war world differently than their parents.

As America's generational divide is changing the nation, so is the international world changing. President Eisenhower presides over a nation engaged in a Cold War (no shots fired, but no communication, either, between countries that support either communism or democracy and have the capacity to wage serious war against each other — peace without peace) with the reclusive and aggressive Union of Soviet Socialist Republics (USSR) and its brand of communism designed to oppress, not liberate. The nation's information highway experiences connectivity with the widespread enjoyment of the television, invented in the 1920s, but popularized in the 1950s. Likewise, transportation connectivity emerges in 1956 when President Eisenhower develops the Interstate Highway System, a program of modernizing the nation's transportation networks.

In foreign affairs, Eisenhower crafts the "Eisenhower Doctrine" that affirms America's resolve to oppose the imposition of communism on unwilling nations. He also opposes unconstitutional racial policies at home, supporting the landmark decision in the 1954 case of *Brown v. Board of Education of Topeka*, and pushes through two separate civil rights laws that precede comprehensive civil rights legislation of 1965. The *Brown* case, decided by the United States Supreme Court, does away with the "separate but equal" doctrine of segregation in public schools and is a major step forward to achieving racial equality in America. Eisenhower's relatively successful and peaceful presidency comes to an end in the election of 1960, since the 22nd Amendment to the Constitution limits a president to two terms. The 1960s mark the start of a new era of American political and social activism.

Symbolic of the decade to follow, Eisenhower is President on May 1, 1960, when American pilot Francis Gary Powers is shot down in a U-2 spy plane over Soviet Union territory. The Cold War tension between countries — the United States and the USSR — and their forms of government — democracy and communism — will last well beyond the 1960s and will test the resolve of six future presidents and millions of Americans anxious about the potential for nuclear war and the mutually assured destruction of the world's superpowers, and perhaps humanity. It is a time when the world seems twisted in a political knot that will determine policy and progress for the last half of the century.

The fifth most popular song of the 1960s is "The Twist" by Chubby Checker.

CHAPTER 10

TIMES OF CHANGE: 1960S AND 1970S

And I Grew Strong and Learned How to Get Along

The rebellious rock and roll culture of the 1950s gives way to a second American Revolution, this one smaller, but more assertive and internal than the original American Revolution of 1776. It is a generational revolution that focuses less on the existence of the country and more on the nature of that existence. It pits the students of the 1960s against their parents and against particular government policies and leaders and the conventionality of the past against the unconventionality of the present.

Elvis Presley, the hip-swinging "King of Rock and Roll," and former teen-idol crooner Frank Sinatra, still have hit songs, despite their differing musical styles. Rock and roll still dominates the music charts. A dashing, young new leader, John F. Kennedy, is elected president in 1960, ushering in a new excitement and style as younger voters help elect the first Catholic president in America's history. Kennedy describes himself as a president who happens to be Catholic rather than a Catholic president — no small distinction in 1960. Frank Sinatra changes the lyrics of his 1959 hit single, "High Hopes," and expresses the optimism of a new decade and a new political generation in the Kennedy campaign song.

FIRST OF TWO VERSES
Everyone is voting for Jack
'Cause he's got what all the rest lack
Everyone wants to back Jack
Jack is on the right track
'Cause he's got high hopes, he's got high hopes
1960's the year for his high hopes
So come on and vote for Kennedy, vote for Kennedy
And we'll come out on top
Whoops there goes the opposition ker-
Whoops there goes the opposition ker-
Whoops there goes the opposition ker-plop.

Jimmy Van Heusen/Sammy Cahn
"High Hopes" (original version)
1959

Kennedy represents a new order in American politics, breaking an unspoken barrier where religion and politics blend. Kennedy and the election of 1960 represent a rebellion from the past orderly and predictable practices of choosing American presidents. The Kennedy-Nixon debates are the first presidential debates on television, exposing millions of voters to the images presented on an electronic screen to be viewed, and talked about, in the privacy of voters' homes. During this decade television will become Americans' window on the world and the United States, allowing instant viewing of cultural, political and international changes that will affect public opinion. Television will bring a distant war (Vietnam) to American living rooms, news of the assassination of three public figures (John F. Kennedy, 1963, Robert F. Kennedy and Martin Luther King, Jr., both 1968) and mankind's first steps on another world (moon landing, 1969) before the decade ends.

Sinatra releases an album titled "All the Way." Elvis releases one called "Something for Everybody." These albums define the decade that questions and challenges all previously accepted ways of life in America. War, social unrest and turmoil will be commonplace, representing a period of generational conflict and testing the tolerance of Americans for change. All aspects of society will be affected: music, dress, manners, social norms, role of government, authority, national education, international relations and American identity.

This is also a period of testing social limits. The miniskirt is born. The Twist is the popular fad dance of the period, thought by some to be a physical release from the anxieties of the Cold War. The psychedelic drug era begins, and drug use becomes a form of "dropping out" of society. As the United States in 1960 gets involved in fighting communism in Vietnam, a war-torn area of Southeast Asia, Americans aged eighteen to thirty find an anti-government cause that matches well with the counter-cultural practices of the times and embraces a new sensitivity and engagement in the public policy practices of the United States government.

A black Baptist minister and civil rights leader, The Rev. Martin Luther King, Jr., leads a "March on Washington for Jobs and Freedom" on August 28, 1963. His stirring remarks, which he delivers from the steps of the Lincoln Memorial to more than a quarter-million civil rights supporters gathered along the National Mall, are considered to be one of the greatest speeches in history. It is originally titled "Normalcy, Never Again." Halfway through, Gospel songstress Mahalia Jackson shouts from the crowd, "Tell them about the dream, Martin." King departs from his script and repeats the phrase by which the speech will forever be known.

> I have a dream that one day this nation will rise up and live out the true meaning of its creed: "We hold these truths to be self evident, that all men are created equal." I have a dream that one day on the red hills of Georgia, the sons of former slaves and the sons of former slave owners will be able to sit down together at the table of brotherhood. I have a dream that one day even the state of Mississippi, a state sweltering with the heat of injustice, sweltering with the heat of oppression, will be transformed into an oasis of freedom and justice. I have a dream that my four little children will one day live in a nation where they will not be judged by the color of their skin but by the content of their character. I have a dream today!

Shortly after the march, King is named Man of the Year by TIME magazine for 1963; in 1964, he is the youngest person ever to be awarded the Nobel Peace Prize.

A culture-changing English rock group is introduced to America in 1964. The Beatles bring an unconventional style of appearance, dress and music that captures the excitement of young people around the world, feeding the era of protest and social unrest, and fueling the importation of other English rock groups including The Rolling Stones, The Who, The Kinks and The Animals. At the same time, black and white Americans embrace a form of racial healing through the popularity of a cultural phenomenon known as the "Motown Sound." Called "The Sound of Young America," artists such as Stevie Wonder, The Supremes, Smokey Robinson, Gladys Knight and the Pops, Marvin Gaye, The Four Tops, The Temptations, the Velvettes and the Marvelettes bring worldwide attention to the "Motown Sound."

As more Americans are sent to fight the Vietnam War, another genre of music is born — the protest song. In the mid-1960s, P. F. Sloan writes a protest song that captures an American mood. It is called "The Eve of Destruction," and Barry McGuire records the song. It reaches No. 1 on the charts in September 1965.

FIRST VERSE AND CHORUS

The eastern world, it is explodin'
Violence flarin', bullets loadin'
You're old enough to kill, but not for votin'
You don't believe in war, but what's that gun you're totin'
And even the Jordan River has bodies floatin'

But you tell me
Over and over and over again, my friend
Ah, you don't believe
We're on the eve
Of destruction

P. F. Sloan
"The Eve of Destruction"
1965

The song refers to the Kennedy assassination, the Vietnam War, the existence of racial prejudice, the American space flight, hate in America and distrust of politicians. Along with Marvin Gaye's "What's Going On," "The Eve of Destruction" becomes a theme song for the protest era and the list of complaints of students and activists. The song becomes a movement typified by a counterculture figure collectively known as the Hippie, a member of a subculture group that advocates separation from conventional society, embracing drug use and sexual freedom and an anything-goes lifestyle. Its impact will last through the end of the century in music, dress and food influence.

The 1960s is a decade of assassination in America. As the nation is still reeling from the November 22, 1963, Kennedy assassination, President Kennedy's killer, Lee Harvey Oswald, is himself killed two days later by a Dallas nightclub owner, Jack Ruby. Ruby is convicted and sentenced to death, but his conviction is overturned. Before he can get a new trial, Ruby dies in 1967. A federal Kennedy assassination review commission, headed by U.S. Supreme Court Justice Earl Warren, concludes that Oswald acted alone. It finds no conspiracy to overthrow the government.

Two years later, after Lyndon B. Johnson, President Kennedy's Vice President, has succeeded to the presidency on November 22, 1963, civil rights issues become prominent in the American conscience. President Johnson, the 36th President, chooses Minnesota Senator Hubert H. Humphrey as his Vice President. Johnson is responsible for passing the Civil Rights Act of 1965, which had been introduced by President Kennedy in 1963. This legislation to outlaw racial segregation in schools, public places and employment, creates the Equal Employment Opportunity Commission (EEOC) and has been viewed as the most far-reaching equality legislation in history. It is passed under the Commerce Clause of the Constitution (Article I, Section 8) in order to protect the law from challenges to congressional limitations on legislative enforcement. Standing with President Johnson at the White House signing ceremony of this historic civil rights legislation is The Rev. Martin Luther King, Jr. It is through King's "civil disobedience" practices (active refusal to obey laws) in the southern United States that civil rights laws are changed.

Then, tragically, King is assassinated by James Earl Ray, a fugitive from a Missouri prison, on April 4, 1968, outside of Room 306 of the Lorraine Motel in Memphis, Tennessee — now the home of the National Civil Rights Museum. The assassination creates outrage in the black community and throughout America. More than sixty major American cities suffer damage from riots over the assassination, primarily from the frustration of black Americans at the killing of their greatest leader. A plaque marks the step of the Lincoln memorial on which King delivered his "I Have a Dream" speech. A national holiday is later named in his honor.

The King assassination occurs four days after President Johnson suddenly withdraws his pending presidential candidacy on March 31, 1968. His decision is largely influenced by the growing anti-war sentiments in the Democratic Party over the course of the Vietnam War and the introduction of ground troops he had ordered there. Two prominent Democratic Party candidates run against Johnson because of the war: Senator Eugene McCarthy of Minnesota and New York Senator Robert F. Kennedy. Kennedy had served as his brother John's Attorney General from January 1961 to November 20, 1963, and stayed on as Johnson's Attorney General until September 1964, when he resigned to run for the United States Senate in New York. Victorious in the 1964 election, along with President Johnson's election, Sen. Kennedy had broken with President Johnson on the Vietnam War by opposing American ground troops there. Fifteen days before President Johnson withdraws his candidacy, Kennedy declares for president on March 16, 1968, and becomes the national anti-war favorite. By late April 1968, Johnson's Vice President, Hubert Humphrey, joins the Democratic field as a presidential candidate.

Robert Kennedy wins the California primary on June 4, 1968, and gives a victory speech at the Ambassador Hotel in Los Angeles early on June 5. As he exits the hotel's ballroom via a kitchen, he is suddenly struck by an assassin's bullet and dies instantly, creating heartbreak among his millions of supporters, including many younger generation activists, and chaos in the 1968 presidential election.

In late 1968, Richard Holler writes a tribute to four of history's assassinated leaders: Abraham Lincoln, John F. Kennedy, Martin Luther King, Jr. and Robert F. Kennedy, commemorating their commitment to racial equality. The gentle song becomes a hit sung by Dion in the United States and Canada.

Has anybody seen my old friend Abraham? (John, Martin)
Can you tell me where he's gone?
He freed a lot of people
But it seems the good they die young
You know, I just looked around and he's gone.

Didn't you love the things they stood for?
Didn't they try to find some good for you and me?
And we'll be free
Some day soon, and it's a-gonna be one day…

Anybody here seen my good friend Bobby?
Can you tell me where he's gone?
I thought I saw him walk up over the hill
With Abraham, Martin and John.

Richard Holler
"Abraham, Martin and John"
1968

Political parties have selected presidential nominees of the two major parties since 1831. Since 1940, most political conventions are nationally televised. In 1968, televised coverage of the Democratic National Convention in Chicago gives national voters the chance to see political activism explode in the aftermath of three politically significant assassinations. The combination of aggressive social and cultural changes, an emerging national opposition to the Vietnam War, a near-anarchical segment of the protest population interested in the Democratic Convention, and a commitment to retain order at the Convention makes for a domestic political conflict never before seen on television at a national convention.

The scene is startling to traditional Democrats in attendance and to television observers, but it reflects a changing society and illustrates the power of public sentiment over an issue as divisive as American attitudes toward war. By 1963, President Kennedy has deployed 16,000 American troops to Vietnam. By 1964, the troop level has increased to 184,000. In 1968, the troop numbers total 537,000. In 1967, American casualties reach 770 per month — in 1968 they total 1,200 per month. A sizable anti-war segment of the American public is fed up with the war, and many come to Chicago to force the political party in control of the American government to change policy and end the war. Violence and anarchy prevail in Chicago as worldwide television viewers watch the police make forceful arrests as the protesters fight back. The city of Chicago fights the violence of the protesters with violence of its own. It is an embarrassing spectacle and an unsettling phenomenon for law-abiding Americans to observe. In the aftermath of the convention, the Walker Commission concluded that the Chicago police overreacted and were primarily responsible for the riot.

The 1968 presidential election is between Republican nominee Richard M. Nixon and Democratic nominee Vice President Hubert H. Humphrey. Nixon is viewed as the leader of the nation's "Silent Majority" (dutiful citizens, not activists) in the aftermath of the violence of the Democratic National Convention. Experienced in foreign policy and promising a law-and-order domestic platform, Nixon urges a policy of "Peace with Honor" in Vietnam. With strict-conservative, anti-integration, states-rights candidate George Wallace of Alabama competing as an independent candidate, Nixon defeats Humphrey by more than 500,000 votes to become the 37th President of the United States on November 5, 1968. He secures victory with former Maryland Governor Spiro Agnew as Vice President. The team offers and delivers on a promise of troop withdrawal from Vietnam and the establishment of the Nixon Doctrine — that armed forces of countries seeking democracy will defend themselves so that Americans can avoid long-term military commitments far from home.

But the Vietnam War continues until 1975. As the war continues, so does the threat to established order in America. The counterculture of political activism, the sexual revolution and drug use fostered in the 1960s and the generation devoted to peace, love and "doing their own thing" meet for three days in mid-August 1969 on a 600-acre field in Woodstock, New York, for a festival in the Age of Aquarius (an era that occurs every 2,500 years or so that ushers in a time of true fellowship of humankind). Officially known as "An Aquarian Exposition," it becomes a venue for folk music, songs of peace and love, and music created by artists partaking in the products of a drug culture. Shocking in its unabashed consumption of drugs, uninhibited sexual freedom and promiscuity and abandonment of conventional behavior, Woodstock becomes a metaphor for anti-establishment activities and a rejection of authority. Three days worth of nonstop music performances vault musical artists like Joan Baez, Richie Havens, Jimi Hendrix, Ravi Shankar, Arlo Guthrie, John Sebastian, Santana, Janis Joplin, Credence Clearwater Revival, Grateful Dead, The Who, Joe Cocker, Jefferson Airplane, Crosby, Stills, Nash & Young and Sly and the Family Stone into commercial prominence and barely exhaust the 500,000 attendees.

As the 1960s draw to a close, an age of technology emerges with the creation of the first automated teller machine for fast-cash dispensing. Texas Instruments develops a handheld calculator. Computer chips and computer technology get their start. When Neil Armstrong and Buzz Aldrin walk on the moon in the summer of 1969, the world marvels as human beings set foot on Earth's nearest celestial neighbor. A contact light signals the first words spoken from the moon (notice how close they come to an empty fuel tank).

Mission Control: Sixty seconds (of fuel remaining).

Aldrin: Lights on…Down 2½. Forward. Forward. Good. 40 feet, down 2½ Kicking up some dust. 30 feet. 2½ down. Faint shadow. 4 forward. 4 forward. Drifting to the right a little. Okay. Down a half.

Mission Control: 30 seconds (of fuel remaining)

Armstrong: Forward drift?

Aldrin: Yes. Okay. Contact light. OK, engine stop.

Armstrong: Houston, Tranquility Base here. The Eagle has landed.

Mission Control: Roger, Tranquility. We copy you on the ground. You got a bunch of guys about to turn blue. We're breathing again. Thanks a lot.

While Aldrin speaks the first words from the moon, the words Armstrong says while stepping onto the lunar surface become one of the world's most famous sentences: "That's one small step for a man, one giant leap for mankind." It is estimated that more than a billion people — one-fourth of the world's population — see and/or hear these words live from the lunar surface via radio and television.

Two pieces of the massive Saturn V rocket that is Apollo 11 exist today: the Command Module returns to earth and is on display at the Smithsonian Air and Space Museum in Washington, D.C. The Descent Stage of the Lunar Module remains on the surface of the moon. Mounted on its ladder is a plaque which reads: "Here men from the planet Earth first set foot on the Moon July 1969 AD. We came in peace for all mankind." A chalice used by Neil Armstrong to celebrate the first communion on a planet other than Earth is preserved at Webster Presbyterian Church in Webster, Texas.

President Kennedy's challenge to America to reach the moon in this decade is met, and the success of the American space program will spawn another decade of progress for humanity, creating technologies related to space travel and opening the world to scientific research only heretofore imagined. The 1970s, though, will be as heartening and as heartbreaking as the predecessor decade, full of political, social and cultural challenge as America's world expands and new leaders fulfill America's promise to offer opportunity, foster international understanding, bolster America's economy, protect the nation and manage its resources, and explore new frontiers created by new-found inventions.

THE 1970S

While the decade of the 1960s is often referred to as a time of rebellion and revolt, the 1970s is less rebellious and more targeted on reform and American evolution. The rock and roll dancing of the 1960s yields to the Disco dancing of the 1970s. In the aftermath of Woodstock, the nation calms down. Folk singer soprano and activist Joan Baez leads the massive anti-war movement in a country divided by war, and more pressure is placed on President Nixon to quickly end the Vietnam War and bring American troops home. The Paris Peace Accords are adopted in 1973, signaling an end to hostilities and an orderly withdrawal of American troops. The nuclear threat of Mutual Assured Destruction (MAD) and the expectation of war between the two major superpowers of the world, the USSR and the United States, lead Americans in the peace movement to demonstrate against the nuclear age and for an end to war. Environmental protection takes national center stage, with the recognition of Earth Day in 1970, and President Nixon's creation of the Environmental Protection Agency in 1973. It represents intolerance for environmental waste and support for a national effort to clean up the planet. In 1974, Spokane, Washington, hosts the World's Fair, Expo 74, with a theme of "Celebrating America's Fresh, Clean Environment." President Nixon opens the Fair. It is the first international event focused on global environmental health. Spokane remains the smallest city ever to host a World's Fair.

The peace movement shows all generations that peaceful protest can yield policy results. The American population is now more than 200 million, and the Vietnam War continues to force changes in government. The release of the "Pentagon Papers," military documents that reveal top-secret strategies of the Vietnam War, undercuts confidence in government authority and feeds the anti-establishment attitude of a growing number of younger Americans. Satirical comedy is a growing branch on the tree of individual rights and the breakdown of traditional societal norms.

The sexual revolution continues amid a growing women's rights movement. More women enter the workforce and assert their social rights as the United States Supreme Court makes a landmark ruling in 1973 that creates a woman's right to privacy and makes abortion legal in the United States. That decision, *Roe v. Wade*, will divide Americans on the subject of abortion rights, human rights, states' rights, women's rights, religious rights and legal rights into the new century. It helps define the decade as one variously called the Me Decade, Decade of Retreat, Decade Under the Influence, Anything Goes Decade, Decade of Greed, Identity Decade and the Decade of Firsts. It is all of these and more, and music continues to define it further. The most popular song of the 1970s is "Hotel California," performed by the Eagles. Eagles lead singer Don Henley comments in a later *London Daily Mail* interview, "Some of the wilder interpretations of that song have been amazing. It was really about the excesses of American culture and certain girls we knew. But it was also about the uneasy balance between art and commerce."

The separation between policymakers and the constitutionally important free press widens further in the 1970s as President Nixon remains in office after the turn of the decade. An intensely private leader steeped in the traditions of the dignities accorded presidents, Nixon finds himself disrespected by the national press, and the disrespect is mutual. Aware that President Kennedy was beloved by the press and likely bitter from his 1960 presidential election loss to Kennedy, Nixon famously declared at a press conference in 1962 after losing the California Governor's race, "You won't have Nixon to kick around anymore because, gentlemen, this is my last press conference."

The press corps treatment of Nixon also signals a breakdown in the courtesy historically accorded presidents: The press demands accountability from the president regarding the Vietnam War. Presidential press conferences become more combative as White House correspondents shout for recognition and are more confrontational in their questions. As Nixon responds in-kind, the nation observes television coverage of the drama of Nixon's service in tumultuous times and the demand for government accountability by press representatives.

It is an angry time in America, but less so than the 1960s. Public weariness with war creates aggressiveness in citizens, policymakers and editorialists toward office-holders responsible for national policies. But the music of the decade is less so. Talented musicians and bands respond to the anger of the 1960s with happier songs of the 1970s by popularizing such pop groups as the upbeat Beach Boys and the Bee Gees, with their happy and danceable disco sound. Elton John, Chicago, James Taylor, the Eagles, Michael Jackson, Marvin Gaye, Stevie Wonder and John Lennon continue to produce happier melodies of love and relationships, not angry message music. Even musical variety shows like the "Sonny and Cher Comedy Hour" become popular between 1971 and 1975 (Sonny Bono is elected to the U.S. House of Representatives in 1994). The modern clothing fads of bell-bottom pants and long hair are new and different, but harmless, and they sweep the nation.

The boundaries of political aggressiveness, though, are elastic, stretching further with every discovery of governmental missteps.

The greatest public misstep of the post World War II era with the most prominent legacy is the series of events occurring in the early 1970s collectively known as Watergate. In 1973, members of the Nixon Administration staff are aware of and variously involved with a June 1972 late-night break-in at the Washington, D.C. offices of the Democratic National Committee in a hotel/office/apartment complex near the Potomac River called the Watergate Hotel. Even though government officials are not part of the break-in, they are part of its cover-up, eventually implicating President Nixon through his knowledge of White House personnel involvement. Fed by press corps' dislike of Nixon, the issue becomes a constitutional crisis when top Nixon aides testify before Congress that evidence of Nixon's dishonesty is discoverable through secret White House Oval Office recordings. Faced with a Supreme Court ruling that denies presidential protection of the tapes and pending Impeachment Articles in the House of Representatives, Nixon announces his resignation from the Oval Office on August 8, 1974, and leaves the presidency and the White House the next day. As President Nixon leaves office, his approval rating is a mere twenty-three percent. It is a dark day for the Nixon presidency, but a bright day for the integrity of the constitutional system in America.

Vice President Gerald R. Ford, formerly a Michigan Congressman, becomes the 38th President of the United States at noon, August 9, 1974, declaring,

> My Fellow Americans, our long national nightmare is over …
> Our Constitution works; our great Republic is a government of laws, and not of men. Here the people rule. But there is a higher Power, by whatever name we honor Him, who ordains not only righteousness but love, not only justice but mercy…

On September 8, 1974, President Ford issues a broad preemptive presidential pardon of Richard Nixon under Article I, Section 2 of the Constitution as a means of putting aside past recriminations against Nixon and preventing a continuation of the discord that marked the final years of the Nixon presidency.

The Watergate years also mark the emboldening of the national press. The *Washington Post* employs two reporters, Bob Woodward and Carl Bernstein, who are instrumental in discovering the details of Nixon's involvement with the Watergate fiasco. They receive a Pulitzer Prize for their Watergate book of 1974, *All the President's Men*.

As technology becomes a tool of journalism, news outlets employ the speed at which news is discovered and reported to increase and use investigative journalism as a weapon in public policy accountability. One of the most pressing stories of the early part of the decade is the economic crisis that grips the United States. The 1973 Arab oil embargo raises gasoline prices to more than $1.50 per gallon, forcing motorists to sit in long lines at gas stations. By 1979, mortgage interest rates skyrocket to sixteen percent and rates of inflation exceed thirteen percent. President Ford vows to "Whip Inflation Now," signified by the public distribution of "WIN" buttons. A measure is defined to help consumers calculate how miserable they have it in the economy. Adding the unemployment rate to the inflation rate produces a "Misery Index" that can be used to gauge the economic climate and serve as a weapon against incumbents holding office.

Americans become familiar with Middle Eastern energy policies promulgated by the Organization of Petroleum Exporting Countries through the use of an acronym, OPEC. American consumers, who suffer rationing of United States oil and gas imports in the 1970s, receive a harsh lesson in the economic concept of supply and demand — they will revile it. Because the American appetite for gasoline that runs automobiles creates demand, the suppliers (OPEC) can raise gas prices by curtailing supply, resulting in a public outcry for conservation and energy responsibility.

The Nixon Administration disgrace, high oil and gas prices, high interest rates and a stagnant economy open the door for a "new" kind of politician: one not from the seasoned Washington, D.C. political class. In 1976, a one-term Georgia Governor named Jimmy Carter bursts onto the national political scene by claiming to be an "outsider" and not responsible for any problems suffered by the national government. Perceived to be a fresh face with down-to-earth innocence and strong religious faith, Carter rockets ahead of his rivals by enjoying favorable news coverage and receives the 1976 Democratic Party nomination for president. The Republicans nominate a politically wounded President Ford, but Carter uses anti-Washington rhetoric against Ford and barely wins the election to become the 39th President of the United States, the first Southerner to be elected in 130 years.

An even higher Misery Index marks the Carter presidency, and Carter is viewed as an inexperienced leader not up to the expectations Americans have of the presidency. In his four-year term, he faces a continuing domestic energy crisis and high inflation at home. Foreign affairs conflicts, particularly in the Middle East, occupy Carter Administration energy and time. Carter is roundly criticized for accusing Americans of being stricken with a "malaise," a calculated political move meant to inspire Americans, but which does the opposite. As Iranian student-militants seize fifty-two American diplomats on November 4, 1978, and occupy the American Embassy in Tehran, Carter is helpless to secure their release after 444 days. An American military team tries to free the hostages, but they fail because of military equipment problems, and Carter is held responsible. The public is disgusted that American hostages are mistreated for so long in a foreign land and blames President Carter for their plight.

That responsibility carries into the 1980 presidential election, when another governor challenges President Carter. Notwithstanding the Carter record of creating the United States Department of Energy and focusing on energy diversity, working to achieve peace in the Middle East, devoting a stronger emphasis to human rights around the world and establishing a United States Department of Education, the failures of his presidency mark his legacy. Returning the Panama Canal Zone to Panamanian control, canceling American participation in the 1980 Olympic Games in the Soviet Union because the Soviets invaded Afghanistan, placing an American embargo on Soviet trade, which hurt American exports, failing to improve the American economy and secure the Iranian hostage release are unpopular enough in America that Massachusetts United States Senator Ted Kennedy mounts an unsuccessful challenge to Carter for the 1980 Democratic presidential nomination. With President Carter as the Democratic nominee, the 1970s conclude for Carter and America much as they started: American frustration with inefficiencies and incompetence in the Nation's Capital; Americans are hungry for a competent leader and a competent government.

Beyond the political intrigue of the late 1970s, another significant development affecting mankind ends the decade. Mozart, Beethoven, Washington and Lincoln all survive a disease that disappears in the 1970s — smallpox. Originally discovered around 10,000 BC, the virus is responsible for killing millions of people throughout history. In 1796, Dr. Edward Jenner, a physician in rural England, discovers that immunity to smallpox can be produced by inoculating a person with material from a cowpox lesion, a non-lethal poxvirus in the same family. Jenner names his technique using a *vacca* (the Latin word for cow) "vaccination." For nearly two hundred years after his discovery, children around the world are routinely vaccinated for smallpox. In December 1979, the World Health Organization certifies the eradication of the smallpox virus. Smallpox is the first and, to date, only human disease driven to extinction.

It is hardly a cure, though, for what ails the national economy and the failures attributed to the Carter presidency. The medicine for the national illness will be delivered by American voters at the start of the new decade.

CHAPTER 11

OPTIMISM: 1980S AND 1990S
It'll be Here, Better than Before

The pendulum of American politics and popular culture swings back to conservatism and traditional values in the decade of the 1980s. Americans have their fill of music and style that are "far out," and politics and policy that "sock it to me." We yearn for someone who reminds us of America's greatness and affirms our national principles. We find a leader who literally steps off the movie screen and declares, "It's dawn in America." His name is Ronald Wilson Reagan.

Ronald Reagan is the perfect personality for a national makeover. His movie star good looks, genial nature, positive personality and political history make him the ideal communicator for a nation deeply anxious for inspiration. Reagan is a familiar face to Americans. As host of the series, "General Electric Theater," from 1954-1962, Reagan, with his soothing voice and kindly smile, visits the living rooms of millions of Americans through the powerful new medium of television. He hosts and stars in "Death Valley Days," a popular Western television series, from 1964-1965. Reagan takes his Hollywood charm to the political arena, where he is elected Governor of California, the nation's largest and most diverse state. He makes unsuccessful runs for President in 1968 and 1976. By 1980, however, Republicans flock to his principled issue-positions and sunny optimism. As a reformed Democrat, comfortable with his conservative political philosophy and sense of self, Reagan is well liked by Southern Democrats who embrace a commonsense conservatism that rejects the wasteful policies of President Carter and the idealism of the left. Reagan embodies a political force that is about to erupt.

Eruptions are occurring around the world in 1980: the Iran-Iraq War commences, there is an upheaval in Turkey, and at home, John Lennon, perhaps the most famous Beatle, is senselessly assassinated outside his luxury apartment in New York City. In Washington State, the eruption of Mt. St. Helens, an active 9,677-foot volcano and the fifth highest mountain in the Pacific Northwest's Cascade Mountain Range, kills fifty-seven people. It symbolizes the letting off of national steam when it erupts in May 1980, creating two serious earthquakes and sending an ash plume 60,000 feet high. Because Jimmy Carter's presidency is uncertain after four years, the Democratic Party is poised to change leaders and direction for the 1980 presidential election. Turmoil around the world and disillusionment in the faltering national economy cause Americans to search for a new direction. The year's best-selling book is *Crisis Investing* by Douglas Casey, a reflection of existing economic uncertainty. The United States hockey team wins a gold medal at the 1980 Winter Olympics in Lake Placid, New York (the XIII Winter Olympic Games), scoring a miraculous victory over the Russian team and stirring the emotions and national pride of Americans everywhere. It is a burst of optimism in a pessimistic political year, and it signals a coming rejuvenation and the potential for national improvement. The mood of the nation favors positive change, for a change.

Age and maturity, experience and success swirl around Ronald Reagan, forming an aura of personal strength that translates directly to political strength. The lure, and allure, of Hollywood glamour add to his attraction. Americans respect success, good looks, transparent ideas and self-assurance without arrogance. Reagan has all those qualities and a simple message that offers a positive alternative to the dismal record of the Carter presidency.[14] Reagan also brings to the 1980 presidential campaign a new approach to national economics. Urging a return to simple values of hard work, low taxes and smaller government, Reagan strikes a chord with American voters fed up with a growing and failing federal government under President Carter and an economy with high interest rates and high taxes. Reagan's personality and acting skill in delivering clever one-liners endear him to voters at the beginning of his campaign. On Labor Day 1980 in New York Harbor, with the Statue of Liberty behind him, Reagan matter-of-factly with a smile declares in his kickoff speech: "Recession is when your neighbor loses his job, depression is when you lose your job, and recovery is when Jimmy Carter loses his." Voters embrace Reagan's version of America. He crushes President Carter by carrying forty-four states and amassing 489 electoral votes to Carter's 49.

At noon, January 20, 1980, as Reagan takes the oath of office as America's 40th president and promises a stronger and more forceful United States in world affairs, the captors of the fifty-two American hostages in Iran set them free. It is symbolic of the international respect for Reagan and a slap at outgoing President Carter. The release of the hostages is also due in part to America's release of a freeze on Iranian assets worth billions.

Singer/songwriter Neil Diamond captures the mood of the day and releases in April 1981 a song titled "America." The song, written for a patriotic movie titled "The Jazz Singer," pays tribute to the United States as a welcome place for immigrants and celebrates their contributions to American culture and society. It is a modern patriotic song.

Far
We've been traveling far
Without a home
But not without a star

Free
Only want to be free
We huddle close
Hang on to a dream

On the boats and on the planes
They're coming to America
Never looking back again
They're coming to America

Neil Diamond
"America"
1981

Reagan brings to his presidency a return to a previous faith in America, a remembrance of a bygone era when times are simple, humor simpler and problems solvable. At age seventy when he takes office in 1981, Reagan presents a grandfatherly image, accompanied by calm and wisdom. So effective is Reagan at selling his message that he is nicknamed "the Great Communicator," a moniker that no succeeding president possesses in the same fashion. He is able to successfully communicate his unwavering love of country, belief in America's promise and time-tested theories of public policy to the national political scene. His larger-than-life persona is enhanced through adversity: an assassination attempt is made on his life on March 30, 1981. He survives a bullet wound to the chest, nearly killing him, and cleverly quips to the hospital surgical team, "I hope you're all Republicans!"

In 1984, Reagan wins every state's electoral votes except those of Minnesota, the home state of his Democratic opponent, Walter Mondale, President Carter's former Vice President. Reagan's national campaign manager is Edward J. Rollins, who will be part of another important campaign in 1994. During his eight years as President, Reagan maintains a simple and clear philosophy: End the Cold War and defeat the Soviet Union by rebuilding America's defenses; jump-start and grow the American economy with massive tax cuts and control on government spending; and restore pride in American enterprise and the cause of freedom around the world. Reagan essentially will stay true to this formula, despite a major increase in federal spending caused in part by American military build-up. His landslide reelection in 1984 affirms the public support for Reagan the President and Reagan the man. Reagan's campaign slogan "Morning in America" is a call to recognize the promise of greatness for the United States. Reagan has an abiding faith in the exceptional nature of the United States, pledging that anything is possible. After all, he declares with conviction, "We are Americans." The inimitable Ray Charles version of "America the Beautiful" is performed to widespread acclaim at Reagan's Second Inaugural in 1985.

FIRST OF 8 VERSES
O beautiful for spacious skies,
For amber waves of grain,
For purple mountain majesties
Above the fruited plain!
America! America!
God shed his grace on thee
And crown thy good with brotherhood
From sea to shining sea!

Words by Katharine Lee Bates
Melody by Samuel Ward
"America the Beautiful"
1895/1910

By 1985, the Cold War is forty years old. It is symbolized by a period of tension, suspicion and conflict between the United States and the Soviet Union, the two reigning superpowers that embrace opposite systems of government: democracy v. communism. President Reagan intends to dismantle the Soviet system by pressure from the inside and by his words and actions of challenge from the outside. He proposes to outspend a failing Soviet economy by accelerating American defenses, knowing that the Soviets cannot compete and that their system will break under such pressure. Berlin, Germany, is the perfect setting for Reagan's influential weapon of dramatic rhetoric. The Berlin Wall has divided West Germany from East Germany since the end of World War II as the Cold War began. People are brutally shot and killed trying to escape from East to West Berlin. Secret tunnels are dug and quiet plots are hatched as the quest for freedom continues for those suffering under the oppression of communism. The Wall is a metaphor for the division between the light of freedom in the West and the darkness of communism and oppression in the East. When Reagan issues a dramatic challenge to Soviet leader Mikhail Gorbachev, saying, "Mr. Gorbachev, tear down this wall," it is a challenge to the Soviets to end the oppression of communism and expose the people of East Berlin, and the communist system, to the liberating nature of freedom. But Reagan's bold declaration is also designed to give additional hope to millions laboring under communism in Europe and around the world that they can, in fact, achieve the blessing and hope of freedom.

Reagan delivers a lesson to the international community: that through timing, coalition-building and the power of personality, world affairs can change. Reagan's freedom partnership with Great Britain's Prime Minister Margaret Thatcher, his outreach to Soviet Communist Party Secretary General Mikhail Gorbachev and his driving belief in international human freedom cause the world to change. The people of the United States and the people of the Soviet Union both clearly benefit from the end of the Cold War. Yet the ramifications extend to all of humanity. The end of the Cold War reduces the threat of state-to-state nuclear war and the buildup of more dangerous nuclear weapons with mass destructive capability.

As the 1970s disco music is replaced by synthesizers and electronic keyboards, so does the music industry look outward with a worldwide vision for underserved continents. "We Are the World" is a song written and performed by pop stars Lionel Richie and Michael Jackson in January 1985 in a collaborative effort with twenty-two solo musical stars and seventeen supporting artists. It is a song written to counteract famine in Ethiopia and Africa. Its producer and conductor is Quincy Jones, a five-decade veteran of the music entertainment industry and one of the most decorated black musical artists in Grammy Award history. Jones is credited with successfully bringing the performers of this song together by the simple admonition, "Check your ego at the door." The Live Aid concerts held in cities throughout the world also raise money and draw attention to the plight of those suffering from famine in Ethiopia.

There comes a time when we heed a certain call
When the world must come together as one
There are people dying
Oh, and it's time to lend a hand to life
The greatest gift of all

CHORUS
We are the world, we are the children
We are the ones who make a brighter day
So let's start giving
There's a choice we're making
We're saving our own lives
It's true we'll make a better day
Just you and me

Lionel Richie and Michael Jackson
"We Are the World"
1985

"We Are the World" marks a turning point in America's attitude toward national charity, fueled both by the prosperity of the

1980s and the cheerleading by the entertainment industry to embrace international support for the plight of the world's less fortunate. It is a time of heightened social consciousness as advances in communications technology shrink the world and highlight problems heretofore unreported on the nightly news. The AIDS (Acquired Immune Deficiency Syndrome) phenomenon starts in the early 1980s in San Francisco and will become a worldwide pandemic affecting homosexuals and unsanitary drug users, but will also spread to the greater population. The plight of African AIDS incidence will become a recognized tragedy, particularly for African children, and will garner broad support efforts for medical research, and federal expenditures by the United States and other countries over the next two decades.

In the United States, First Lady Nancy Reagan mounts a "Just Say No" campaign in a War on Drugs against the growing use of illegal drugs among young people. Fueled by strong economic conditions, cocaine becomes the drug of choice, even as widespread marijuana use continues. Cocaine is an expensive drug, with Latin American countries (particularly Mexico) serving as the primary cross-border suppliers to a burgeoning American demand. With heightened drug use comes heightened popularity for hard rock, punk rock, hip hop, new wave and heavy metal bands. These are publicized in many instances by a new television format titled "Music Television," or MTV. Music videos are a different genre of music, a new source of revenue for musicians and a new art form that makes musicians actors in their own productions. They also reflect the culture of the younger generation's penchant for unconventional music style — less message and lyrics and more noise, choreography and pounding beat. It signals a changing society, a self-directed modernism separated from the predictability of convention, characterized by lyrics supporting abuse. The black community adopts the hip hop and rap genre that will last through the turn of the century and will reflect a style of dress, actions and separateness that becomes its own sign of self-dignity, selfishness and racial pride.

The decade of the 1980s also ends the two-term presidency of Ronald Reagan. By the campaign of 1988, the Reagan Revolution is well underway with the hallmarks of "Reaganomics" in place — tax cuts, private sector development and free enterprise as cornerstones. The popular appointment of the first-ever female Supreme Court Justice, Sandra Day O'Connor, is historic as she is confirmed by the United States Senate by a vote of 99-0, and begins service on the Court on September 25, 1981. But Reagan's legacy is tarnished by the 1986 Iran-Contra affair. High officials in the Reagan Administration were caught selling armaments to Iran (prohibited by law) to fund the freedom fighters (Contras) in Nicaragua, even though Congressional hearings revealed later that Reagan never knew of or authorized such illegal sales. Eleven administration officials are convicted of crimes relating to charges of selling arms, which also led to the release of the American hostages held at the Embassy in Tehran.

Reagan's Vice President, George H.W. Bush, strives to carry on the legacy of his former boss, becoming the Republican candidate for the 41st President of the United States against Michael Dukakis, the Democratic Governor of Massachusetts. With government spending higher than expected due to a strong military buildup, the nation faces the challenge of whether to raise taxes or cut spending. Bush receives the Republican nomination with the rousing pledge to "Read My Lips, No New Taxes." It is a pledge that will ultimately haunt his presidency.

Not convinced that a liberal from Massachusetts is the proper Reagan successor, American voters elect George Herbert Walker

Bush as the 41st President of the United States, even though Bush was born in Massachusetts in 1924 and is the product of a privileged upbringing. Bush's victory over Dukakis is resounding as he wins 53.4% of the popular vote and carries forty states.

THE 1990S

Bush enters the presidency with a long and successful history of accomplishments, both in and out of government. The son of a United States Senator and a graduate of exclusive New England schools, Bush serves his nation as a Congressman from Houston, United States Ambassador to China, Ambassador to the United Nations, Central Intelligence Director and Vice President. As President, he presides over the fall of the Berlin Wall, signaling the end of communist division in Germany and symbolizing the literal end of the Cold War and communist rule in Europe with the dissolution of the Soviet Union in 1991.

A decorated Navy veteran of World War II, President Bush launches and presides over the Persian Gulf War, a major military conflict in the Middle East. Saddam Hussein, the ruthless dictator of Iraq, invades neighboring oil-rich Kuwait, a sovereign country, on August 1, 1990. In response, Bush assembles a coalition of multinational forces, led by the United States and endorsed by the United Nations, to force Iraqis out of Kuwait and back to Iraq. In doing so, Bush sets forth the concept of a "New World Order," a phrase that embodies a new set of standards of conduct among nations.

A new era — freer from the threat of terror, stronger in the pursuit of justice, and more secure in the quest for peace. An era in which nations of the world, East and West, North and

South, can prosper and live in harmony....A world where the rule of law supplants the rule of the jungle; a world in which nations recognize the shared responsibility for freedom and justice; a world where the strong respect the rights of the weak.

In January 1991, coalition forces successfully repel the reckless Iraqi attack against Kuwait in only 100 hours, pushing Iraqi forces out of Kuwait and winning the Gulf War. Yet questions are raised about President Bush's decision not to use force to remove Saddam Hussein as Iraq's leader and eliminate the threat of future aggressive activity by Iraq. It is a decision that will have profound consequences for the future presidency of Bush's son, George W. Bush.

The invasion of Iraq to rescue and liberate Kuwait is not the only significant foreign policy activity undertaken by the Bush Administration. Panama's shady President Manuel Noriega, acting as a drug smuggler and confidant of other Latin American dictators, is an irritant to President Reagan's Administration during the 1980s. After Noriega undermines elections there and a United States soldier is killed, Bush orders American troops into Panama to capture Noriega. Named "Operation Just Cause," the successful invasion results in the capture of Noriega and stabilizes the Panamanian government.

The Bush presidency is marked by another major international accomplishment related to trade relations with Canada and Mexico, two of America's largest trading partners. Under Bush's leadership, steps are taken to create a tariff-free zone for the three major nations of the North American continent. The Bush Administration pursues the North America Free Trade Agreement (NAFTA) as an example of trade creativity and trade relations among neighbors. Although its adoption must await the next president, President

Bush is credited with creating an agreement satisfactory to all three countries.

While Bush achieves success in foreign affairs, his attention to domestic policies falters, creating for him a major challenge in the 1992 presidential election. The start of the 1990s brings an economic recession to the United States and the rest of the world, starting with the stock market crash of October 1987 and the failures of various savings banks. In an effort to reduce a federal deficit of some $220 billion in 1990, Bush signs a deficit reduction measure, which Congress passes, that raises taxes — a violation of his "No New Taxes" pledge in 1988.

Facing a recession in 1992 and an angry Republican Party because of his capitulation on tax increases, Bush is confronted by a charismatic Arkansas Governor as his Democratic opponent in the 1992 presidential campaign. Out-talked by Governor Bill Clinton and seemingly out of touch with domestic issues, President Bush faces a challenging campaign and more than one political opponent. The 1992 presidential race is actually a three-candidate campaign. A third-party candidate, billionaire businessman H. Ross Perot, enters the race in February 1992, running on a strong economic platform with a libertarian philosophy: balancing the federal budget, trade protectionism and domestic support for jobs retention. He is identified with and strongly supported by a third-party organization, United We Stand America, composed of voters disgruntled by the two major political parties. The straight-talking Perot with his simplistic campaign message is polling ahead of President Bush and Governor Clinton in 1992.

But in mid-summer 1992, Perot abruptly drops out of the race, citing anticipated dirty tricks by the Bush team. Perot — to the surprise and dismay of President Bush and Governor Clinton — then reverses course and just as abruptly re-enters the presidential race in October. He aggressively participates in presidential debates, spends $65 million of his own money and ends up with nineteen percent of the popular vote, the best showing of any third-party candidate in history, but a losing candidacy nevertheless. William Jefferson Clinton becomes the 42nd President of the United States, winning forty-three percent of the popular vote and achieving a solid victory over Bush in electoral votes: 370-168.

On election night, Bill Clinton and his Vice President Al Gore become the new generation of America's elected leaders, dancing to a song by British rock group Fleetwood Mac that symbolizes the forward-looking intentions of the new American leadership.

If you wake up and don't want to smile,
If it takes just a little while,
Open your eyes and look at the day,
You'll see things in a different way.

Don't stop, thinking about tomorrow,
Don't stop, it'll soon be here,
It'll be here, better than before,
Yesterday's gone, yesterday's gone.

Why not think about times to come,
And not about the things that you've done,
If your life's been bad to you,
Just think what tomorrow will do.

Christine McVie
"Don't Stop"
1977

It is a song that marks a fresh start for the decade of the 1990s. Technology and economic growth bring astonishing expansion of the world economy. In the United States, the Dow Jones Industrial Average surges to more than 10,000, the Internet becomes a new and fast method of commerce and communications, and 1992 is designated the "Year of the Woman" as the role of women in society grows in equality of pay, corporate responsibility and election to office. Social changes advance at lightning speed as the world comes under a new post-Cold War management structure bringing greater national independence and capital expansion. There are no longer only limited dominant superpowers (heretofore the USSR and the United States), but numerous nations accumulating political and economic power (China, Middle East nations, European and Asian nations).

A new enemy of freedom develops as a force against the Middle East policies of the Western world and the undisciplined social practices of modern society. It is an enemy with an unconventional disruptive potential that threatens the nation-state in the late stages of the 20th century. The enemy is collectively known as terrorism — the intentional violent infliction of fear upon innocent populations for political purposes. Reflecting the growth of the Islamic religion worldwide, it is led by factions of Middle Eastern radicals who detest undisciplined Western lifestyles and what they consider to be the permissive and immoral nature of free societies. In 1996, according to United Nations statistics, twenty-six percent of the world's population (about 1.6 billion) is Muslim, reflecting more than six percent annual growth, compared to Christian population growth of less than two percent. With the concentration of Muslim populations in the Middle East and Africa, representing oil-rich centers of the world, oil-consuming modern nations like the United States become a target for Islamic radicals opposed to Western values and the international interventionist nature of the United States. The radicals are well funded and violently aggressive.

The early incidents of terrorism experienced by the United States occur in the early 1990s. With the designation of Osama bin Laden as an Islamic Extremist Financier involved in the Afghan resistance to the Soviet Union in the 1980s, from which he built a terrorist network identified as Al Qaida and the Taliban in Afghanistan, the seeds of terrorism take root, sprout and grow. On February 26, 1993, the World Trade Center in New York is bombed, killing six people. It is the first terrorist attack on American soil by Middle Eastern extremists.

The June 25, 1996, bombing of the Khobar Towers housing complex in Saudi Arabia kills nineteen American soldiers and wounds more than 500 others, including more than 200 Americans. Together with the 1998 bombings of American embassies in Africa, the attacks signal a warning about the depth and breadth of terrorist activity aimed at the leading nation of the free world — America. In this decade of prosperity, terrorism poses an ominous threat to world standards of sovereignty and safety. It threatens to reorder relationships among nations and portends the realignment of traditional alliances and resources. It will have profound social and economic consequences and unpredictable political results. It will also require extraordinary political leadership. Terrorism violence even occurs at home as the Alfred P. Murrah Federal Building in downtown Oklahoma City, Oklahoma, is bombed by militia movement sympathizers, Timothy McVeigh and Terry Nichols, killing 168 innocent people.

American political moods are usually unpredictable. The impossible is always somehow possible, especially in elections, but also in political trends. Americans historically reserve the right to change political directions when moved to do so, and the American system of government is elastic enough to withstand voter mood changes. Such a change occurs in the elections of 1992 and 1994.

President Clinton enters office in 1992 with sizable Democratic Party majorities in the U.S. House of Representatives and in the Senate. The Democrats' margin in the House is 255-173; in the Senate, it is 56-44. One-party control means one-party praise when things go well and one-party blame when things do not. President Clinton is perceived to be highly intelligent and firmly on the left side of the political center, but not on the far left. A political pragmatist at heart who adores public approval (what politician doesn't?), Clinton announces early in his Administration a plan to reform the American health care system, putting his wife, Hillary Rodham Clinton, in charge of a health care task force. President Clinton also announces a new policy affecting the open service of gays and lesbians in the military, "Don't ask, don't tell." Both policy pronouncements draw heavy attention and criticism. Clinton passes through Congress two legislative measures in 1993 that cause controversy — the Earned Income Tax Credit for the poor and tax increases on wealthy Americans — and a gun control law called the Brady Bill. Named for Jim Brady, President Reagan's press secretary, who was seriously wounded in the Reagan assassination attempt in 1981, it imposes a five-day waiting period for the purchase of a weapon. A personnel controversy, labeled "Travelgate," involves the summary firing of long-time, non-partisan White House travel office personnel in favor of Clinton associates; it is perceived that the Clintons use dishonest favoritism in government contracting. While an independent investigation reveals no Clinton wrongdoing, positive public perceptions about the Clintons diminish.

Disillusioned by the threats of a bureaucratic national health care system from President Clinton and the Democrats, frustrated by high taxes and high numbers of federal welfare recipients and federal budget deficits, and irritated by the potential for a larger, unwieldy federal government, American voters are susceptible to a political alternative in the elections of 1994.

For forty years, since 1954, Republicans serve as a minority party in the U.S. House of Representatives. Through the leadership of a handful of young House Republicans, led by a brash, intellectual Congressman from Georgia, Newt Gingrich, a blueprint for a Republican resurrection in the House is proposed — it is the "Contract with America." It sets forth ten policy provisions affecting national security, economic prosperity, personal responsibility and job creation. It promises action within 100 days of Republicans becoming a majority in the House; it is a contract for action and an assurance of results between public officials and the public. It is a unique assurance of accountability by elected officials, and it is widely popular.

In the elections of 1994, the excitement of the new generation of leadership represented by the Clinton-Gore team from 1992 diminishes. The Democratic majority is dramatically replaced by seventy-three new House Members riding on the wave of voter dissatisfaction with incumbent Democrats in office and the hope and promise of the Contract with America (see Chapter 12). It is the first time in forty years that Republicans have the opportunity to simultaneously lead the Senate and the House. True to the Contract, the first 100 days of Republican control lead to the consideration of all ten Contract measures. Though not all Contract measures pass into law, the commitment of the first 100 days is met.

Domestic policies take priority in the 104th Congress of 1995-96. Welfare reform, putting welfare recipients to work, is a

Republican priority. Tax relief benefiting small businesses and entrepreneurs is adopted as the national economy flourishes. For four straight years (1996-1999), the federal budget is balanced, with more revenue than expenditure, and more than $500 billion of national debt is "paid down." The "split government" of a Clinton White House and a Republican Congress results in dynamic tension but effective results for which both parties can take credit. But although Clinton is easily reelected President in 1996, he will later be beset by a personal challenge that will affect his presidency and strain the Constitution.

The Impeachment process is set forth in Article 2, Section 4 of the Constitution. A two-step process, it calls for the United States House of Representatives to issue Articles of Impeachment, amounting to an indictment, against a federal official, to be followed by a trial on the Articles in the United States Senate. Federal officials may be removed upon conviction for committing "Treason, Bribery or other High Crimes and Misdemeanors." It is an extraordinary process set forth by the Constitution to permit "the people" to take action against federal officials for specific misconduct in office. Intentionally burdensome, the impeachment process is rarely used but is available to assure public service accountability. Only seventeen federal officials have been impeached in American history: thirteen federal judges, two presidents, one U.S. Senator and one cabinet secretary.

After Clinton lies under oath in a lawsuit brought by a young woman charging him with sexual misconduct, and after the revelation of Clinton's affair with a White House intern, the Republican-led House of Representatives passes two Articles of Impeachment against Clinton on December 19, 1998, involving charges of perjury and obstruction of justice. On February 12, 1999, after more than a thirty-day trial in the Senate constitutionally presided over by Supreme Court Chief Justice William Rehnquist, Clinton is not convicted of any charges of impeachment and remains in office until his second term expires on January 20, 2001.

It is the second time in United States history that a president has been "acquitted." President Clinton joins President Andrew Johnson (1868) in the exclusive club of presidents who are impeached, but acquitted, and allowed to remain in office. While it is a cloudy day for Clinton in 1999, it is a bright day for the United States and its system of presidential accountability under the Constitution. Clinton's political survival assured, all Americans must be relieved that a crisis of government stability has been avoided. Even though the Constitution is rarely tested outside the federal courts, impeachments of federal officials are exclusively within Congressional jurisdiction. Serving as a means of assuring proper conduct in the sacred trust of public office, impeachment offers a means of straining the Constitution, but not breaking it, balancing political disagreement with objective findings of wrongdoing. It also assumes that those who sit in judgment in any impeachment proceeding are protective of the American system of government and able to set aside political preferences for institutional integrity and achieving a just result.

Survival of the federal government and avoidance of a leadership interruption become secondary at the end of 1999, as the world faces the start of a new millennium on January 1, 2000, also referred to as Y-2K (year 2000). Fearful of calamitous consequences of computers unprepared for the turn of the new century, and with recognition that the world runs on computer technology, attention turns to millennium preparedness and potential emergencies caused by computer breakdowns. Despite warnings to the contrary on this significant New Year's Eve, time marches on and a collective sigh of relief accompanies the passage from 11:59:59 p.m. on

December 31, 1999, to midnight. Like the thousands of millennia before it, the darkness yields once again to the dawn of a new day, a new century and a new millennium.

Even though President Clinton later loses his law license in response to the impeachment proceedings, he leaves office with high approval ratings and a record of working with Republicans to enhance the economic prosperity of the United States during his eight years as president. The Clinton scandals of Whitewater,[15] independent criminal and civil investigations (Bill Clinton's Arkansas law license was suspended by agreement in 2001), marriage infidelity, controversial legislative policies, and claims of his aversion to difficult leadership challenges, especially as to the growing threat of terrorism, dominate much of his presidency. However, he is rightly credited with forceful leadership in Bosnia, strong attempts to forge peace in the Middle East, welfare reform, economic prosperity and crime control.

The end of Clinton's presidency will set the stage for a successor who enters the White House under election controversy in 2001 with a pledge to "restore honor and dignity to the White House." That restoration of honor and dignity, however, will not protect America from suffering the first foreign attack on American soil since World War II. It will be an attack that will transform the free world and fully define a new enemy to freedom.

CHAPTER 12

INTERLUDE:
ANATOMY OF A MODERN
POLITICAL CAMPAIGN
There's a Time for Everyone

The United States of America is a representative republic. Each of us, therefore, has a hand in running our country, whether indirectly by voting for our elected representatives or directly as an elected representative. In the Congress of the United States, we have 100 Senators (two from every state) and 435 Representatives (elected by population). The supreme authority in the U.S. Senate is the Senate President, who also serves as Vice President of the United States. In the House of Representatives, the Speaker of the House is chosen by its Members. This dialogue clip, from the 1939 film, "Mr. Smith Goes to Washington," accurately captures how a new member is sworn in.

> *Senate President:* The Gentleman will raise his right hand: Do you solemnly swear to support and defend the Constitution of the United States, against all enemies, foreign and domestic; and that you will bear true faith and allegiance to the same; that you take this obligation freely without mental reservation or purpose of evasion; and that you will well and faithfully

discharge the duties of the Office upon which you are about to enter, so help you God?

Smith: I do.

Senate President: Senator, you can talk all you want to, now.

What effect can one person have on American politics? "Mr. Smith Goes to Washington" receives eleven Academy Award nominations and wins the Oscar for Best Screenplay as it explores that question. In the film, an idealistic young man from a Western state, played by Jimmy Stewart, replaces a man by the name of Foley in Washington, D.C., and stands up to entrenched leadership. Stewart's character — Senator Jefferson Smith — embodies the difference that one individual can make in our country. In the big filibuster scene near the end of the picture, Stewart's character speaks to the heart of our representative republic:

It's a funny thing about men, you know. They all start life being boys. I wouldn't be a bit surprised if some of these Senators were boys once. And that's why it seemed like a pretty good idea to me to get boys out of crowded cities and stuffy basements for a couple of months out of the year and build their bodies and minds for a man-sized job, because those boys are gonna be behind these desks some of these days.

And it seemed like a pretty good idea, getting boys from all over the country, boys of all nationalities and ways of living — getting them together. Let them find out what makes different people tick the way they do. Because I wouldn't give you two cents for all your fancy rules if, behind them, they didn't have a little bit of plain, ordinary, everyday kindness and a little lookin' out for the other fella, too.

The Library of Congress places "Mr. Smith Goes to Washington" on its National Film Registry in 1989 for being culturally, historically and aesthetically significant.

Fast-forward a few decades and this fictional story becomes reality in Spokane, Washington.

The year is 1994. "From the Beginning" is a Top 10 song by Pink Floyd. The song "Landslide" by Smashing Pumpkins is a top hit. Kurt Cobain commits suicide. OJ Simpson is arrested for the murder of his ex-wife. A young lawyer and his wife, Mary Beth, travel to Washington, D.C., in January 1994 to explore the possibility that someone who has never run for public office could successfully run against the third-most-powerful official in the United States. In this case it is the Speaker of the United States House of Representatives, who, according to the Presidential Succession Act of 1947, would succeed to the presidency if the President and Vice President could not serve.

The author of the book you are now reading is that young lawyer. The Speaker of the United States House of Representatives is Thomas S. Foley, the Congressman who represents Washington's 5th Congressional District.

Thomas Foley is a thirty-year veteran of the House. He is elected in 1964 and reelected fourteen more times without defeat or interruption. Foley is a legend: distinguished, intelligent, experienced, and respected. George Nethercutt is a virtual unknown in Eastern Washington, even though he was born and raised in Spokane, the population center of Eastern Washington.

A poll is conducted in early 1994. The findings: Foley is known by ninety-nine percent of the people of the 5th Congressional District of Washington, the District he has represented for three decades. Nethercutt is known by three percent of the people, but there is a four percent margin of error! The good news for

Nethercutt: three-fourths of the three percent who know him, like him. The bad news for Foley: He's liked by barely half of all who know him.

In Washington, D.C. in late January 1994, Nethercutt meets with Congressman Newt Gingrich, an outspoken, bright rising-star from Georgia. He meets with Congressman David Drier, an experienced, well-spoken Member from California. Gingrich suggests that Nethercutt use a 1964 automobile as a campaign car, symbolizing how long Foley has been in office. Drier reveals that Foley is highly respected but is not a Speaker in the rough and tumble style of Tip O'Neill, a more ruthless leader who served as Congressman from Massachusetts for thirty-four years and Speaker from 1977-1987. Nethercutt meets with the Republican National Committee. The young staff members muffle their amusement at the prospect of defeating Speaker Foley. They pat Nethercutt on the back and say, "Call us when you've won your primary election in ten months." Nethercutt meets with Congresswoman Jennifer Dunn of Washington State, the only Republican House Member of nine from the State — the other eight are all Democrats. She is warm and welcoming, gracious and encouraging. A former State Republican Chairman, she says, "Run."

Returning home, Nethercutt contemplates a race: the cost, the time, the expected abuse inherent in modern campaigns, and the money to raise. He has never before run for public office. Where in the world does he start? His first telephone call is to an old friend, Edward J. Rollins. Rollins was the campaign manager for President Ronald Reagan in 1984, the year Reagan carried forty-nine of fifty states, winning the Electoral College vote 525-13. Reagan racked up more than fifty-four million votes to Walter Mondale's thirty-seven million votes. The winning Reagan percentage was 58.8% to 40.6%. By any calculation, it was a landslide, and it was engineered by Ed

Rollins — perhaps the premier American political strategist. (Rollins also helped manage the 1992 Ross Perot candidacy for president.)

In March 1994, Rollins accepts Nethercutt's invitation to come to Spokane for a meeting. He and Nethercutt have a twenty-year friendship dating back to Washington, D.C. when they are both young staffers working in government in the 1970s. They play football together on the Senator Ted Stevens Capitol Hill League football team for three years. They are boxing sparring partners off and on, with Rollins the coach. Over a lunchtime sandwich, Rollins asks, "What is the biggest criticism of Foley?" Nethercutt says, "People say he doesn't listen." Rollins says, "Hmmm, a Speaker who won't listen. This District doesn't need a Speaker, it needs a Listener. And that Listener is you!"

Suddenly — a campaign is born!

Nethercutt rounds up twenty of his best friends to have lunch. He announces that he wants to run for Congress — against Speaker Tom Foley. After the laughter dies down, they listen to Nethercutt's rationale and agree to help with a "Breakfast of Champions" as the first campaign kickoff event. For $25, attendees will get a box of Wheaties, a banana and a cup of coffee. Everyone agrees to bring ten people, hoping to produce a respectable crowd of 200. The kickoff date is set for April 21, 1994. Nethercutt's campaign is very late getting started. It has no money and no real organization. As of February, he has not yet announced his candidacy, but when the local newspaper announces that he is considering running, Nethercutt receives seventy encouraging phone calls in one day. He telephones local advertiser John Robideaux, who agrees to design a campaign logo and take photos for a campaign brochure.

At the 1994 Academy Awards, "Forrest Gump" receives an Oscar for Best Picture. The top box office draw is the animated

"Lion King." One of the top songs of the year is "Can You Feel the Love Tonight," the Academy Award, Golden Globe Award and Grammy Award-winning song.

There's a calm surrender to the rush of day
When the heat of the rolling world can be turned away
An enchanted moment and it sees me through
It's enough for this restless warrior just to be with you

And can you feel the love tonight
It is where we are
It's enough for this wide-eyed wanderer
That we got this far
And can you feel the love tonight
How it's laid to rest
It's enough to make kings and vagabonds
Believe the very best

There's a time for everyone if they only learn
That the twisting kaleidoscope moves us all in turn
There's a rhyme and reason to the wild outdoors
When the heart of this star-crossed voyager
beats in time with yours

Elton John
"Can You Feel the Love Tonight"
1994

"Forrest Gump," a story of the improbable achieving the outstanding, and the "time for everyone" lyric set to Elton John's melody seem oddly prophetic and symbolic of the campaign about to unfold.

In 1994, the United States Congress is an institution fraught with problems. Many members of the House have abused a special bank set up for themselves, and some are caught up in their own personal scandals. The Clinton Administration health care proposal has offered a complicated plan that is opposed by doctors, nurses, senior citizens, patients and particularly Republicans. It is viewed as an unwieldy, bureaucratic takeover of the fee-for-service health care system that has made America preeminent in the delivery of health care services. The Democrats have now been in control of the House Majority for forty years. They have not balanced the federal budget since 1969 — a quarter century in the red. The approval rating of Congress is low, about eighteen percent. Taxes are high and so is the national debt, about $18,000 for every man, woman and child in America. There are fourteen million people in the United States on welfare in 1994, about six percent of all Americans. Abuse of social programs at the federal level is rampant, and reports of federal agency mismanagement are too numerous for the public's comfort.

CLARITY OF VISION FOR CAMPAIGN STRATEGY

Singer Jimmy Cliff records a Johnny Nash song called "I Can See Clearly Now," which becomes a hit of 1994, and provides the Nethercutt campaign with language outlining a goal for the dramatic political battle which looms ahead, and the hope for a history-making miracle.

I can see clearly now, the rain is gone,
I can see all obstacles in my way
Gone are the dark clouds that had me blind
It's gonna be a bright, bright Sun-Shiny day.

I think I can make it now, the pain is gone
All of the bad feelings have disappeared
Here is the rainbow I've been prayin' for
It's gonna be a bright, bright Sun-Shiny day.

Look all around, there's nuthin' but blue skies
Look straight ahead, nuthin' but blue skies

I can see clearly now, the rain is gone,
I can see all obstacles in my way
Gone are the dark clouds that had me blind
It's gonna be a bright, bright Sun-Shiny day.

Johnny Nash
"I Can See Clearly Now"
1972

While Nethercutt's political path ahead is not always clear, on April 21, 1994, the cavernous Spokane Convention Center is filled with a standing-room-only breakfast crowd. The event is truly a Breakfast of Champions, and Nethercutt can clearly see in this startling response to a simple breakfast invitation more than 1,000 people in the room who believe that they can now clearly see a chance to make national election history.

He delivers a message that speaks directly and personally to the citizens of the 5th Congressional District. It is an announcement speech that favors the young family burdened by high taxes, the small business owner struggling against a growing federal bureaucracy and a generation of young professionals who had heretofore never engaged in a political campaign. This is the symbol of a new generation of leaders, one that would listen. "The people of the 5th District don't need a Speaker — they need a Listener!" As the crowd roars approval, the campaign is rocket-launched into orbit for this first-time candidate. It will be a time of excitement, anxiety, challenge, fear and immeasurable personal growth. Its outcome will be historic.

The biggest obstacle for any challenger's campaign is to convince the electorate that a change in leaders should be made. Voters who have repeatedly voted one candidate into office need a solid reason to change their vote. Changing a voter's mind is a tall order. It takes the right message, the right candidate, sometimes the right political party affiliation, but particularly the right personal connection between challenger and voter. In the case of the House Speaker, simply quadruple the difficulty scale. Upsetting a sitting Speaker had only occurred once previously in American history.

Incumbents have a ninety-five percent chance of being reelected because they usually have massive campaign funds on hand, they know the District or state, and they are supported by various constituent groups and leaders. They know the issues before Congress better than any challenger because the incumbent lives those issues every day, at work. They are insiders. The Speaker is the insider's insider. He runs the Congressional show. His voice is powerful, and he is omnipresent.

In Foley's case, he is larger than life. Tall in stature, white-haired, well-spoken, immaculately tailored and groomed, a champion debater, he is the picture of a prominent politician, straight out of central casting. Born and raised in Spokane, and the son of a highly respected former Superior Court Judge, Foley ran for Congress in 1964 at age thirty-five after serving on the staff of beloved United States Senator Henry "Scoop" Jackson of Washington. In his 1964 campaign against twenty-two-year incumbent Republican Walt Horan, Foley exclaimed, "No one should serve so long in Congress. Twenty-two years is enough." Foley won in 1964, never expecting that those words would come back to haunt him thirty years later.

A lawyer, Foley worked his way up through the ranks of the Democratic Congress through the decades of the 1970s and 1980s. His election in 1986 as Majority Leader paved the way for his election in 1989 as Speaker, the first-ever from Washington State. Even though Foley lived a scandal-free Congressional life, he led an institution in 1994 that the public believed was broken. As Speaker, he was President Clinton's point person in the House. House Speakers carry the legislative water for the President if they are of the same political party. Whether he wants to be or not, Speaker Foley and President Clinton are locked at the political hip in 1994.

Nethercutt's challenge between his April 21 announcement and Washington State's primary election on September 20 is to raise his three percent name identification and convince enough voters who have supported Foley for fifteen consecutive elections to change their minds — a tall order. Campaigns require candidates to meet two important obligations: raise campaign money and meet voters. In House elections, votes are earned one at a time, through personal contact. Candidates must go door-to-door, parade-to-parade, community-to-community, and face the grueling but usually enjoyable task of meeting and greeting voters: "Hello, I'm George

Nethercutt, and I'm running for Congress." Every day, every weekend, at every venue, that is the message.

The Nethercutts lend their campaign $25,000 as seed money to pay for initial signs, brochures, pictures, travel, and a venue for a campaign kickoff. Foley has more than $1 million in the bank in early 1994. He spends most of his time in Washington, D.C., likely unafraid of someone with little name identification and even less campaign cash on-hand. He is, after all, the Speaker of the House, with reelection history on his side.

The Washington State Republican Party offers two young staffers for hire, Mike Gruber and Ken Lisaius. The Nethercutt campaign hires them as its first employees. They are dedicated, smart, and barely experienced, but eager to pursue a campaign that could set the standard for political underdogs. They want to help David defeat Goliath. They want to help their man become the Giant Slayer.

Now age forty-nine, Nethercutt campaigns with energy and commitment after April 21. He attends virtually every Republican event in all twelve counties covering some 20,000 square miles of the 5th District. Talks to Chambers of Commerce, meetings with Rotary Clubs and Lions Clubs, meetings with local elected officials and discussions with farm groups, doctors, small businesses, teachers, seniors and countless others fill every weekday and every weekend. A Spokane native, Washington State University graduate and Gonzaga Law School alumnus, Nethercutt has practiced law for eighteen years in Washington State. The focus of his law practice is estates and probates, adoptions and occasional trial work. He handles the legal work for some 2,000 adoptions during this period, helping bring joy and security to adoptive children and families. In the 1980s, he and a group of caring citizens led by founder Bill Bialkowsky start a respite-care facility for children, the Vanessa

Behan Crisis Nursery, to help protect children from the horrors of child abuse. He is a Lion, a Mason and president of the Spokane Chapter of the Juvenile Diabetes Foundation, a cause to which he has devoted his heart in honor of his fourteen-year-old daughter, who contracted diabetes in 1986 at age six. As an active part of the Spokane community, George Nethercutt and the priorities in his life qualify him as a legitimate candidate for public service. But he is not the only qualified candidate in the race.

Two Republican candidates have previously challenged Foley and lost. Dr. John Sonneland, a reputable and wealthy surgeon, has tried four times and failed to topple Tom Foley. Duane Alton, a successful tire dealer, has tried and lost twice. They are joined by another Republican, Edward Larish, who decides to throw his hat into the political ring by the July filing date. There are now four candidates. The Republican National Committee will neither endorse nor put its network of party support behind any candidate until after the primary election, if then. Each candidate is on his own.

Another obligation of any challenger is to assemble a staff to help with fund-raising, scheduling, transportation, issue development and education, and the preparation of a workable campaign plan that is supported by a budget that can pay for the plan. With Ed Rollins' advice, a presidential-level team is put together. The day-to-day manager is James Moore, former operative of the successful Christine Todd Whitman race for Governor of New Jersey. He knows campaigns inside and out. Smart and serious, Moore works with Lisaius and Gruber to design and create a campaign that can have a chance for victory. Nethercutt's trusted friends, James F. O'Connell and Rick Melanson, take the lead on local fund-raising. Rollins, now running a California United States Senate campaign for Congressman

Michael Huffington, visits Spokane regularly to check on his friends, the Nethercutts. He is the campaign overseer and the candidate's confidant.

The campaign takes shape. Nethercutt Campaign County Chairmen are set up in all twelve counties. Volunteers are assembled and enthusiastic to join in this effort. The campaign becomes a movement, and Spokane's own "Mr. Smith" going to Washington becomes a possibility.

From May through August, Nethercutt immerses himself in parades, door-belling, fund-raising, meetings, candidate forums and volunteer organizing. Nethercutt has engaged the assistance of ordinary citizens of every profession and avocation. A trusted lawyer and friend, Richard W. Kuhling, is the campaign's general chairman. A trial lawyer, Kuhling is a taskmaster, a wordsmith, a strategist and an intellect. Single-minded and loyal, he wants his friend to beat Speaker Foley. Dr. Eric S. Johnson, a highly respected anesthesiologist and civic leader, is Nethercutt's personal adviser. With unequaled loyalty, with family ties in Walla Walla, Washington, an important part of the 5th District, Johnson will provide trustworthy advice and personal commitment that will be an indispensable element of the campaign.

Nethercutt's visits to rural counties are usually in the company of another loyal adviser, Karl Zacher. Formerly a burly small-school athlete, Zacher drives Nethercutt town-to-town in his white Chevy pickup, never hesitating to offer free political advice, but always with sincerity and commitment to the Nethercutt cause. Tom Foley largely stays in Washington, D.C., in the run-up period to the September 20 primary election.

Just after Labor Day, September 5, 1994, ten-thousand blue "Nethercutt for Congress" yard signs spring up throughout the 5th District. The level of visual support is stunning. Between Labor Day and Primary Day, Nethercutt airs limited television commercials produced by Larry McCarthy, a veteran of television ad work for various statewide and national elections. Thoughtful and highly intelligent, he is part of the Nethercutt Campaign A-Team. He deals masterfully in words and messages.

Under Washington campaign laws, all candidates seeking a Congressional seat appear on the same primary ballot, even if unopposed, by political party affiliation. Foley has no Democratic Party opponent. Nethercutt and the three Republican challengers must run against each other to earn the "opportunity" to face Foley in the general election only forty-nine days later. Any voter is allowed to vote for any candidate on the Congressional ballot, regardless of party affiliation.

By now, Nethercutt has visited every 5th District county more than once. He has ridden in countless parades, run in numerous local fun-runs, eaten more than his share of pancakes and hot dogs, ridden in buses full of volunteers to county fair celebrations, given news interviews and speeches to anyone who would listen and shaken thousands of hands in every corner of the District. Winning the primary is entirely possible.

On September 20, 1994, 128,350 people vote in the Congressional primary election. The four Republicans collect 65% of the total votes cast; Foley gets 35% and racks up 44,829 votes; Nethercutt gets 37,844 votes, nearly thirty percent of the total vote, second to Foley's total. Despite dire predictions about his odds of winning the primary, Nethercutt is announced as the victor early in the evening. The die is cast: Foley v. Nethercutt on November 8.

Will the Speaker or the Listener be victorious?

An unofficial KHQ News poll taken soon after the primary has Nethercutt leading Foley by nineteen points. The attention of the 5th District voters, the Republican National Committee and the news media is suddenly focused on this race. They sense a historic moment may be at hand. Nethercutt receives a phone call from famous columnist George Will. "How does it feel to be at the center of the universe?" Will asks.

The sentiments "Could the Speaker be in trouble?" and "Who is Nethercutt?" are usually raised simultaneously in both Washingtons on both coasts of America. Both candidates' teams spring into action. The Washington, D.C., money machine of lobbyists and trade associations starts directing massive campaign contributions to Foley. Less money pours into Nethercutt's campaign, but the Nethercutt budget for the month of October and up to Election Day can be met. Challenger candidates do not have to match an incumbent dollar-for-dollar, but in 1994, the challenger must have enough to meet the budget and air the all-critical last round of television and radio ads. Small donors are Nethercutt's salvation, and so are his volunteers. A check of activity level at the two campaigns shows a high energy level for the challenger and a subdued atmosphere in the incumbent's headquarters.

Two more important campaign experts join the Nethercutt team: Joe Justin from California and Erik Skaggs from Spokane. They will be on-site in Spokane, the region's most populous city and county, managing operations. The post-primary press inquiries and scheduling requests require a professional and experienced press secretary. Campaign veteran Terry Holt flies in from Florida to handle national press. The Tarrance Group, led by Ed Goeas, perhaps tops in the nation, is drawn to the race and joins as the polling team.

Foley has a top-level Democratic campaign veteran, Bob Shrum, leading his team, and has the support of every Democratic, and some Republican, big business and major company executives in both Washington State and across the nation. They not only support his reelection, they use all corporate personnel and resources available to campaign for him. The Nethercutt side has people devoted to smaller business enterprises, including waitresses, non-executive workers and those generally unassociated with the power center in Washington, D.C. They are from every walk of life, and their desires are simple: They just want to elect someone who will go to Washington, D.C., to represent their interests. The contrast between the candidates is evident on paper:

FOLEY	NETHERCUTT
Age 65	Age 49
30-year incumbent	newcomer
No children	two children
Democrat	Republican
Lawyer (non-practicing)	Lawyer (practicing)
Spokane apartment tenant	Spokane homeowner
Moderate to liberal philosophy	Conservative to moderate philosophy
Washington, D.C. resident	Spokane resident

Most candidates who run against incumbents participate in no more than two debates, unless the incumbent is behind in the polls, as Foley is. The reason: Why should an incumbent give any challenger publicity or the chance at legitimacy, for the voters to see? The safer course of action is to stiff-arm a challenger and give him no opportunity to gain recognition and traction.

Of the nine Foley-Nethercutt debates conducted during the month of October, most nationally televised, the first one is held in Walla Walla, Washington, a lovely community deep in rich farmland and the home of Whitman College. On October 6, 1994, at 11:30 a.m., Nethercutt enters the Walla Walla Elks Club to meet Speaker Foley to debate the issues of the day. Nethercutt is alone.

The first thing he sees is a bank of television cameras aimed at the head table and a podium. His heart sinks as he realizes he will soon confront the political equivalent of heavyweight boxer Mike Tyson, the champion. Nethercutt fears that he will be injured.

As Foley enters the room, the crowd surges to and around the Speaker, the champ. To Nethercutt, Foley does not seem to be his normal 6-foot-3, but rather ten feet tall, calm, courteous, obviously at ease in this contest. Nethercutt's normal 6-foot-height shrinks to 5-foot-9 as he sits down to prepare mentally for what will unfold.

Campaign debates are normally not very helpful to voters or viewers. With a format of sixty-to-ninety-second answers, debaters cannot fully explore a subject area or offer a sensible solution to the questions posed or subjects raised — there just isn't time. So they take on the task of answering questions by laying out concepts or themes that give a listener the chance to gauge the depth of a candidate's knowledge or to outline a philosophy. Skilled debaters have a reservoir of information and succinct points to reveal when given the chance to verbally strike an opponent. The best debaters try to sound knowledgeable and avoid making misstatements in the process. The Walla Walla debate is a draw, no knockouts or knockdowns, but Nethercutt and his supporters consider it a victory simply because he is still standing when the final bell rings.

Traditionally, the Speaker of the House does not vote in Congress like other Members, nor does he serve on any House committees. Nethercutt's message to blunt the Speaker's natural position advantage: "I want to cast a vote for the people of the 5th District, and I want to fight for their interests on a committee, just like other Congressmen. Mr. Foley does neither." That message will recur throughout the campaign.

There is nothing healthier in American politics than two strong candidates who sincerely support competing policy positions and have the ability to discuss and debate their differences effectively, for ultimate voter consumption and decision. The voters and the integrity of the American political system are the beneficiaries of such substantive campaigns. They are the important third parties in such debates. The Lincoln-Douglass, Kennedy-Nixon, Reagan-Carter and other debates in history gave voters a priceless opportunity to exercise their most important obligation in American life — to vote for and choose leaders who deserve to represent the best views for a better America.

Voting is an emotional act. Most voters never actually meet and get to fully know a candidate for national office, but voting for our nation's leaders has an intimate quality to it. It is the creation of a personal relationship at an impersonal level. Voting is an expression of trust and solidarity. It is an intellectual union formed by common values. Supporting a candidate who shares a voter's value system and policy objectives creates a bond deeper than admiring an athlete or movie star, themselves public figures. The bond is based on something more personal than pure entertainment — it is a relationship built on trust that delegates to the elected official the right to vote in Congress on behalf of the people represented.

A campaign, like a successful life, needs a philosophy of priorities, values and goals to serve as a means of identity. In 1994, the Republican Party platform is the Contract with America (see Appendix I). Contracts are obligations, legal commitments, really, that obligate one contractual party to another. In election terms, the citizen's vote is exchanged for a leader's policy commitment. The Contract sets out specific measures that address the policy hopes and dreams of millions of Americans fed up with Congressional scandals, high taxes and overspending. The Contract becomes a crucial component of the Nethercutt campaign philosophy.

Nethercutt uses the phrase, "The government is too big and it spends too much." Foley's theme is, "Don't waste your vote on an unknown and send the Speakership to Georgia (the state of the next likely Speaker, Newt Gingrich, if the Republicans win in 1994)."

The ten provisions of the Contract with America define the nation's value system in a direct and personal way. The Contract contains ten Congressional policy objectives that have millions of supporters because the policy goals are consistent with the fundamental philosophy of most voters. It is a political rallying point that connects supportive candidates with voters. And it personally connects the voter with the policy. The means for affirming the policy and the voter is the candidate who supports the connection, and in this political year, it is the Republican candidates who connect. The Contract is masterful political art in 1994.

Foley is a respectful campaigner and debater, but his team is ruthless. In October, flush with campaign contributions, the Foley campaign launches a media blitz that raises questions about Nethercutt and his fitness for office. "We don't know who Nethercutt REALLY is," says one mail piece, suggesting that he and his policy positions are unknown and therefore dangerous. It is an incumbent message: trust what you know (the Speaker) — don't gamble on an unknown.

But the Foley camp has a problem with pushing the trust issue too far. Washington State voters have passed a term limits ballot measure in a prior election. It puts a six-year term limit on Congressmen. Tom Foley is a plaintiff in a lawsuit to overturn the term limits measure and thereby thwart the will of the voters. It is not a wise strategy for him in the election climate of 1994, and he pays a steep price for it.

Campaigns usually produce opportunities that turn an election for one candidate of the other. The Foley lawsuit against term limits offers Nethercutt a pivotal opportunity to raise the trust issue against Foley.[16] A new slogan appears: "Tom Foley is suing his own voters just to keep his job!" The trust and goodwill Foley has built up over thirty years is suddenly disappearing. Nethercutt is the beneficiary if he can show the voters he is worthy of their vote. The only hope for Foley is to rely on his Speakership and his ability to cast doubt on Nethercutt's abilities and knowledge, which may be why Foley agrees to so many debates.

Eight more debates, all televised, are held throughout October and into early November 1994. The polls are tightening. The race is deemed dead-even. Nethercutt makes no fatal mistakes or utterances in the debates. No scandals or hidden embarrassments emerge. This is now a race about issues and substance. Nethercutt has not withered under the glare of national Sunday interview shows. He survives tough questions by ABC's Sam Donaldson and George Will. The electorate is divided, but fully engaged. Both candidates appear before large and enthusiastic groups of supporters.

Nethercutt holds a "Natural Resources Rally" in late October, including a two-mile long caravan of logging trucks, farm vehicles and honking cars and trucks that runs right through the center of downtown Spokane. The backdrop for his rally speech to farm families and small-town, rural voters is a huge American flag that measures 20' by 40', a symbol for what many believe to be a referendum on the country's post-election direction, and the question of whether all things are still possible in the United States. This is a patriotic moment for regular citizens who believe in the power of the individual. It is a warning statement to the Foley campaign and a reassurance to hopeful Nethercutt supporters.

The final debate is held five days before Election Day, on Thursday, November 3, before the largest Spokane Rotary Club, at

Spokane's Ridpath Hotel at noon. The Rotary debate is notable because it is Foley's last chance to publicly and personally salvage his Speakership and preserve his legacy. The debate is covered by CNN, PBS and many other prominent foreign and domestic news outlets. By now the candidates have confronted each other repeatedly and debated largely the same issues and answered the same questions as a matter of record. But two things are different. For the first time in nine debates, Nethercutt wins the coin toss and elects to make the last closing statement. For the first time in nine debates, Foley's voice level is noticeably louder and he seems less convincing in his answers. Perhaps he is aware that he must exhort the crowd not to do what they are being asked to do — replace the Speaker. Nethercutt delivers the best of his closing arguments for a change in leaders — hopeful, smooth, thoughtful, respectful and reasonable — all the elements necessary for any challenger. Final applause erupts for both candidates.

Advertising in campaigns is essential to victory. Conveyance of a message to persuade voters is an art form. Awards are given to campaign advertising experts for masterful political commercials each election cycle. The ads must be visually attractive, of high visual and audio quality, and convey a clear message — not mixed or multiple messages. Messages are usually driven by polling data, but sometimes a clever ad is produced that conveys a warm feeling or an emotional enticement to a viewer.

The Nethercutts have an all-American family — two parents, two children, accessible and genuine. They also have a handsome Golden Retriever dog named Chestnut. Blond coat, big head and paws, lovable and energetic, this dog becomes a star of the campaign and helps Nethercutt blunt the negative advertising flooding the airwaves from the Foley camp. What becomes known as the "Chestnut ad" becomes Nethercutt's secret weapon.

Americans generally hate negative ads, even though they are effective weapons for a candidate. In the tense closing days of the campaign, the Chestnut ad defuses the negativity that pervades the airwaves and brings a smile to viewers who believe that anyone who has a dog that lovable can't be as bad as the commercials say he is. A Larry McCarthy masterpiece, the ad works. To the majority of voters, Nethercutt is "Every Man" with solid qualities worthy of a vote.

It is Election Day, November 8, 1994. All campaign literature has been dropped on doorsteps. No radio or television ads are running. All door-belling has ceased. There are no more debates. All across the nation, Americans of all races, religions, economic status and occupations exercise the precious right to vote, to choose freely public officials, to elect the leaders who by their decisions will make a critical difference in their lives, and set national policy. Voting is a valuable gift of a democratic society. It is a right for which Americans have fought and died. Its value to democracy and representative government is priceless. The 26th Amendment, adopted July 1, 1971, standardized the voting age at eighteen.

Election Day for Speaker Thomas S. Foley must be a moment of relief — that the race is nearly over, that he has competed well, that he has a very good chance to win and retire eventually — and on his own terms. For Nethercutt, the day is one of satisfaction for having been thrust into a sophisticated world of high-stakes politics against a top-flight opponent and survived. And so has his family survived with their dignity and integrity intact.

Election nights for candidates are a mixture of relief and letdown. There is the relief that the campaign pace has finally stopped, allowing the candidates to return to some sense of normalcy. Campaign schedules are brutally abnormal. The letdown derives from the energy transfer between supporter and candidate.

Campaigns are buoyant for candidates. Supporters assure that buoyancy by boosting spirits and voicing acceptance: They literally raise the endorphin levels of candidates. Supporters are encouraging and affirming, enthusiastic and reassuring. They are the lifeblood of a campaign.

Foley's victory venue is the Ridpath Hotel. Nethercutt's is the Spokane Convention Center. After dinner with a small group of friends, the Nethercutts make their way to a private room just off the Center's ballroom where a large crowd has gathered, anticipating victory. Music plays and food and beverages are served at both victory-watch locations against a backdrop of banners and balloons hanging from the walls and ceilings of each ballroom, where crowds are overflowing. The two campaigns have exchanged telephone numbers for the traditional congratulatory phone call when the race is declared over and a winner determined. Nethercutt supporters from every corner of the 5th District attend the Spokane victory party. Buttons are passed out saying "We Made History — 1860-1994," symbolizing an expectation of victory that would chronicle only the second time in history that a sitting Speaker of the House would be defeated, the first being the defeat of the 27th Speaker of the House, William Pennington, a Republican from New Jersey in 1860.

As the returns come in, it is evident that this race will be tight, extremely tight. As the totals ebb and flow, the crowds at each location shout cheers of support or groans of disappointment when a new total is reported. The Nethercutt lead holds on — 1,000, 2,000, 3,000 votes ahead, but not enough to declare victory. The race has not been called. Both candidates hold television interviews, cautious in their predictions. Nethercutt goes to the podium amid cheers and shouts. His supporters want a declaration of victory. Out of respect for Foley, he says he's glad to have a lead, but cannot declare victory. There is no phone call of concession from Tom Foley on election night.

It is 1 a.m. No victor is declared, but the small Nethercutt lead holds, for now. The victory celebrations close down, and the candidates go home. The decision to concede is Foley's alone. He is behind by some 3,000 votes. Most ballots are counted.

At 9 a.m., Nethercutt goes to his downtown Spokane campaign headquarters. It is teeming with anxious supporters. They know that Foley will either concede the election or demand a recount. At 11 a.m., Nethercutt is told that Foley is on the line. He takes Foley's call in a small side office. At the door he sees the anxious faces of the friends who have propelled him to this critical moment with their contributions, support, prayers and energy. He will never forget this moment, nor the reassuring smile of his wife, Mary Beth, who makes this brave journey by his side. Nor will he ever forget Foley's words: "George, I want to congratulate you on your victory. I will not contest the election."

As he thanks Foley for his kind words and hangs up the phone, the surrounding crowd bursts into cheers and applause. George Nethercutt has won the election — he has beaten the Speaker of the House. He embraces Mary Beth and meets the press. He says, "I wish there could be two winners today. I want to thank Mr. Foley for his service to our District and our country. I am very sad for him, but very happy for myself. I will do my best to represent the 5th District." He knows, too, that the Republicans have captured the majority in the House, so even had he won the election, Tom Foley would have relinquished the Speaker's Chair.

After private moments of tears and private prayers of thanksgiving, the Nethercutts escape outside for a walk around the building. It is a sweet, private moment never to be forgotten. As one journey ends, another begins for this candidate, soon to be Congressman.

In the 1994 elections, 5th District voters cast more votes than any of the eight other Congressional Districts in Washington State. A total of 216,131 votes are cast. Foley receives 106,074 votes; Nethercutt receives 110, 057 votes, a razor-thin margin of 3,983 votes.

This election is perhaps the kind of political opportunity envisioned by the Founding Fathers 218 years before as they devised a system of representative government that offers all Americans the opportunity to succeed and to lead. It is replicated in elections in the United States every election cycle — an opportunity that must always be preserved.

POSTSCRIPT

Many tangible legacies remain from Mr. Nethercutt's service as Washington's Fifth Congressional District Representative in Congress. One is the George NethercuttFoundation (see www.nethercuttfoundation.org), which continues a tradition of leadership and statesmanship begun by its namesake, the author of this book. Another is the George R. Nethercutt Reading Room in  the Foley Library at Spokane's Gonzaga University, where 200 boxes of documents, mementos and artifacts of ten years of public service — including his desk — are preserved for future scholars. Yet another is the Nethercutt-authored House Resolution 211, which names the Federal building in Spokane as the Thomas S.

Foley United States Courthouse and its entrance as the Walter F. Horan Plaza (the 106th Congress makes it law in 1999). Both Foley and Horan served the people of eastern Washington in Congress with honor and distinction, Horan for twenty-two years before being defeated by Foley in 1964, and Foley for thirty years (1964-1994).

CHAPTER 13

NEW CENTURY

We the People Move It, We the People Know

Lew centuries, like the start of every new year, offer new beginnings for both people and countries. The dawn of a new century is a time to reflect, analyze, take stock and develop a blueprint for the future. Early in the new millennium, the United States survives the disruptive challenge of a president in crisis; its economy is prosperous and economic indicators are positive; the Republican Congress and Democratic President are functioning effectively; there is relative peace in the world. The United Nations designates the year 2000 as the International Year for the Culture of Peace. Its aim is to establish and celebrate peace in the world. The Dow Jones Industrial Average exceeds 11,700 points, signaling American-led world prosperity. Worldwide population reaches 6.5 billion people. The largest continental increases occur in Africa.

The New Year is a staging opportunity for an emerging popular genre of music — rap — plus a continuation of pleasing, unremarkable musical hits such as Faith Hill's "Breathe," and the rising popularity of Latin music. Rap music (hip hop music), led initially by popular artists Eminem and Gnarls Barkley, has roots dating to the 1970s with scores of familiar black artists and performers.

229

The Message, by Grandmaster Flash and the Furious Five (1982), the first hip-hop act to be inducted into the Rock and Roll Hall of Fame, tells of the struggles and frustrations of living in a ghetto. The Library of Congress selects it as the first hip-hop recording for the National Recording Registry. The 2002 listing declares the song historically and culturally important.

Broken glass everywhere
People pissing on the stairs, you know they just
Don't care
I can't take the smell, I can't take the noise
Got no money to move out, I guess I got no choice
Rats in the front room, roaches in the back
Junkies in the alley with a baseball bat
I tried to get away, but I couldn't get far
'Cause the man with the tow-truck repossessed my car

CHORUS
Don't push me, 'cause I'm close to the edge
I'm trying not to lose my head
It's like a jungle sometimes, it makes me wonder
How I keep from going under

Ed Fletcher/Grandmaster Melle Mel/Bobby Robinson
"The Message"
1982

In 2000, rap music is free-verse poetry and social commentary contained within a pounding musical rhythm. It carries an "R" rating. While music can act as a statement on society, rap/hip hop music of the new century is filled with lyrics that offend traditional senses. Straining the sensibilities of free speech, most rap lyrics represent angry declarations about traditional society and the reality of ghetto life, reflecting a refuge for the different and the unconventional. This is music for the young, unintended for wide distribution. Monotone in range, confrontational in tone, it nevertheless attracts legions of listeners. Eminem's CD, the "Marshall Mathers LP" released in 2000, is the biggest selling hip hop album in American history, selling 1.8 million copies in its first week.

Obscenities, insults and threats to others, demeaning comments about women, police, figures of authority and other social commentary unrestricted by social norms are the hallmarks of such music. Because it is unrestrained by convention and illustrates anti-establishment talent, it is a music genre easy to emulate and copy. It reflects a society's and a generation's entitlement approach to the new century, a stiff-arm to authority figures and an embrace of "me-ism." Individual pleasure, no matter how odd in appearance or offensive in practice, is central to "me-ism." Abuse is at the heart of the message — abuse of women, language and manners. A new generation gap develops to wide commercial success, spawning a new dress code (grunge) driven by ethnicity and threats of violence, and the emergence of the new sport of "Ultimate Fighting."

On the conventional side of American society, a new presidential election campaign develops. Vice President Albert Gore is the Democratic frontrunner in 2000, seeking to continue the policies of President Clinton. Environmentalism and social progress are cornerstones of his campaign. From Texas, a familiar surname emerges to represent the Republican Party for executive authority — George W. Bush. Now a second-term Governor of Texas, Bush possesses all the qualities Republicans expect in a national leader: charm, executive experience, conservative philosophy and fund-raising ability. The eldest son of the 41st President, Bush seems somehow politically different from his father: He is down-home and straight-talking. Like Gore, he is Ivy-league educated and born of family wealth. Unlike Gore, he is a political product of state politics, a relative outsider to Washington, D.C., and federal policies. Bush is positioned to offer a "real-world" view of issues facing America in 2000.

Presidential elections are never uncontested. Election year 2000 sees a contest in both political parties for the presidential nomination. Former Democratic United States Senator Bill Bradley of New Jersey opposes Gore. Emerging from a large field of Republican candidates in 1999-2000, Senator John McCain of Arizona is the main challenger to Bush. Attracting a growing block of independent voters, McCain is less conservative than Bush, who calls himself a "compassionate conservative." The intellectual Bradley, a former pro basketball star, poses a strong challenge to Gore, who finds it politically necessary to separate himself from the Clinton scandals that plagued the Clinton administration and were an anchor-weight to Gore himself. After the national conventions have ended in early fall 2000, the stage is set for a Bush-Gore election contest to be 43rd President of the United States.

Presidential political campaigns usually try to find music to accompany their candidate at rallies and other campaign events in order to set a theme to music and summarize a preferred vision of a candidate. In 2000, the Gore campaign chooses "Let the Day Begin" by Call.

Here's to the babies in a brand new world
Here's to the beauty of the stars
Here's to the travelers on the open road
Here's to the dreamers in the bars

CHORUS
Here's to you my little loves with blessings from above
Now let the day begin

Michael Been
"Let the Day Begin"
1989

The Bush campaign chooses "We the People," a song written and performed by country star Billy Ray Cyrus.

The farmers rise up every morning at five
The truckers drive them eighteen-wheelers all night
The factory workers they build it with pride
Twenty four seven down the assembly line
In every city, in every town
Somebody's gotta make the world go round

CHORUS
We the people move it, we the people know
We the people we run the country

We the people prove it we're the heart and soul
We the people we run the country

Billy Ray Cyrus
"We the People"
2000

The Bush-Gore campaign offers a contrast in styles, political philosophy and message against a backdrop of the Clinton presidency and its relationship with a Republican Congress. The presidential campaign is notable for the running mates chosen by the candidates: Gore chooses a moderate United States Senator of political independence, Connecticut Senator Joseph Lieberman, the first-ever vice-presidential candidate of Jewish faith. Bush chooses former Wyoming Congressman, Secretary of Defense and businessman Richard Cheney, who served under the presidency of Bush's father. Both candidates for Vice President reflect perceived added value: Lieberman for the attraction of independent, New England and Jewish voters; Cheney for his Western connections and the wide experience in federal government and national leadership lacking in the Bush profile.

The Bush-Gore campaign is the most expensive in United States election history — an estimated $200 million each is spent by the candidates' campaign organizations. Bush rejects limitations on fund-raising and opts not to receive available federal funds; Gore elects to receive federal funds and limit his outside fund-raising. Various interest groups purchase television and radio time to run advertisements for or against each candidate. Campaign finance laws notwithstanding, total expenditures by the campaigns, including amounts spent for and on behalf of the candidates through interest groups, state political organizations and private individuals, are estimated to approach $1 billion. Presidential politics in the new century is more dependent on money than ever before.

On Election Day, November 7, 2000, Bush wins twenty-nine states (including Florida) to Gore's twenty-one; Bush receives 271 electoral votes to Gore's 266; Gore receives 50,999,897 votes (48.38%) to Bush's 50, 456,002 (47.8%), a winning margin of 543, 895 votes out of 101,455,899 cast. Because under the United States Constitution (Article II, Section 1) the institution for electing the President and Vice President of the United States is the Electoral College, rather than a strict popular vote, Bush is eventually declared the winner. Gore initially concedes the election, usually a signal that the election has been decided. But he quickly, and surprisingly, withdraws his concession in light of evidence of possible voter irregularities in Florida, whose twenty-five electoral votes are enough to swing the election to Gore. The separation of votes between the candidates in Florida is eventually 537 out of 5,825,043 cast, and it is Florida that ultimately determines the election outcome of 2000.

The election system in the United States is a fundamental part of American democracy, and its integrity is the foundation of trust in the institutions of government. The integrity of that election system becomes an issue of importance to American voters in 2000 after the polls close on November 7. Claims of voter irregularities in Florida, which decides the next President of the United States, create a Constitutional crisis. As soon as November 8 dawns, lawyers and legal teams of volunteers for both candidates flock to Florida to wage a second campaign in an election too close to call, but which hangs in the balance. At the start of a bitter "round two" in the legal fight for election victory, the leadership of the U.S. government is unsettled. The fight will be carried all the way to the

U.S. Supreme Court and will involve all three branches of the federal government.

Article II, Section 1, Clause 2 of the Constitution provides that states determine how presidential electors are chosen. In Florida, as in other states, electors are obligated to vote for the presidential candidate who receives the most popular votes, and that candidate receives the state's allotted electoral votes. The candidate who receives 270 electoral votes becomes President of the United States. Because the respective electoral votes of Bush and Gore are both under 270, Florida's allocation of twenty-five electoral votes will determine the election winner; without Florida's votes, neither candidate will reach 270. Because the vote totals are so close in Florida, under state law, a recount is ordered. Three days after the election, Bush's vote margin shrinks to 327. Since Florida law authorizes a candidate to request specific county recounts by hand, instead of automation, Gore seeks a manual recount in four specific counties, reliable Democratic counties that might yield him more votes in an effort to close the 327 vote gap. Gore fails to request recounts of traditionally Republican counties. It is a tactical mistake that creates the basis for a constitutional challenge.

Citing statutory deadline requirements for election certification, Florida's Republican Secretary of State, who receives election certifications in all of Florida's sixty-seven counties while four are conducting manual recounts, certifies the election in favor of Bush on November 26, 2000. Lawsuits and counter lawsuits ensue, and thirty-one days after the November 7 election, the Florida Supreme Court orders a statewide manual recount. Accepting the Bush appeal of that decision, the United States Supreme Court orders a stay of the Florida ruling on December 9, and agrees to hear oral arguments on the appeal on December 11, 2000.

Courtrooms are not usually the place for high drama, but the oral arguments in the United States Supreme Court on December 11 are worthy of any television drama or cinematic high moment. This author is there, surrounded by the illuminati of the Nation's Capital, celebrities in government, Members of Congress and Senators and press personalities. The Supreme Court is a sanctuary of decorum and tradition. Unfamiliar to most politicians and newsmakers, it is a venue under the strict control of nine Justices serving a life term, ostensibly caring little for politics and publicity, and caring deeply for the letter of the law and the dispensation of justice in a free society. They control the atmosphere. Their dialogue is with the parties' lawyers, not each other and not the audience. They are fully in charge, able to interrupt the advocates at will, articulately making points and expecting direct clarification of the nuances of the legal theories that bring the parties to this Court.

Less than a day later, the Supreme Court ends the legal drama of the 2000 Presidential election by the issuance of its ruling that using different recounting standards in the four Florida recount counties amounts to a violation of the Equal Protection Clause of the Constitution under the 14th Amendment. The 14th Amendment provides that no state shall deny to any person the equal protection of the laws. The Court also finds that December 12 is the deadline for all recounts established by Florida Courts for completing recounts, and that the Florida Supreme Court acts contrary to the intent of the Florida legislature in this matter. By a slim majority (five to four), the Supreme Court stops the recount and declares the election final, resulting in the award of Florida's twenty-five electoral votes to Bush, thereby assuring his election as President of the United States.

The decision is not without controversy. Democrats aggrieved by the Court's rulings charge judicial politics. Political activists decry the decision as un-American, corrupt and unlawful. Republicans breathe a sigh of relief that Bush prevails, citing corruption in the selective Florida recount effort. The nation is exposed to a new ballot phenomenon, the "hanging chad," the tiny, rectangular perforated piece of material punched through a ballot, but remaining attached to the ballot itself. Workers at the manual recount stations in Florida seek to determine the intent of a ballot containing a hanging chad. The unequal protection of the law referred to by the Supreme Court is the uncertainty in Florida of how to draw a legal, electoral conclusion from the hanging nature of such chads.

Bush is sworn in as the 43rd President on January 20, 2001. Other than John Quincy Adams, son of President John Adams, George W. Bush is the only person in United States history to follow his father as President. The controversy surrounding his final election victory does not abate. Bumper stickers are printed that say "He's not my president." Despite the controversy, most Americans accept the election outcome and the Supreme Court's legal decision that settles the election. The integrity of Bush's victory continues to be questioned for the next four years. But while the political opponents and critics of Bush plot for revenge in the 2004 election, opponents much more deadly plot against the United States and the western world.

President Bush's domestic agenda is economically aggressive. With a Republican House and Senate, he is able to usher through Congress a $1.35 trillion tax cut over ten years, one of the largest in American history. His commitment to improving national education results in a major overhaul titled the "No Child Left Behind Act," legislation designed to improve educational performance in all fifty states and formally signed into law in 2002 with bipartisan support.

While visiting an elementary school classroom in Florida on September 11, 2001, President Bush receives horrifying news of three terrorist attacks that will change his presidency and the sensibilities of the rest of the world. The World Trade Center Towers (referred to as the Twin Towers) in New York City are destroyed as two hijacked commercial airliners intentionally fly into the buildings. Nearly 3,000 lives are lost in three crash locations: New York City, the Pentagon in Washington, D.C., and Shanksville, Pennsylvania. The events are a coordinated effort of a Middle East terrorist organization *al Qa'ida* (Arabic for "the base"), also commonly referred to as Al-Qaeda.

Hijacking four commercial airliners, nineteen Arab terrorists under the direction of Osama bin Laden, leader of Al-Qaeda, commit suicide by crashing the planes, killing civilians from ninety different countries. Only the third time the United States has been attacked on American soil (the other two — Pearl Harbor in 1941 and World Trade Center in 1993), the September 11 attacks (referred to as 9-11) shock the world and bring forth an outpouring of sorrow and sympathy for "9-11" victims and their families.[17]

Members of every generation remember where they were when they first heard the news of a world-altering event years after it happens. Examples in the 20th century include V-E Day, the John F. Kennedy assassination and the moon landing. The terrorist attacks of 9-11 become the first of such events for the 21st century. Country singer Alan Jackson, distraught over the violence and heartbreak of the September 11 attacks, speaks for this generation when he asks, "Where Were You (When the World Stopped Turning?)"

Where were you when the world
stopped turning that September day
Were you in the yard with your wife and children
Working on some stage in LA
Did you stand there in shock at the sight of
That black smoke rising against that blue sky
Did you shout out in anger
In fear for your neighbor
Or did you just sit down and cry

Did you weep for the children
Who lost their dear loved ones
And pray for the ones who didn't know
Did you rejoice for the people who walked from the rubble
And sob for the ones left below

Did you burst out with pride
For the red white and blue
The heroes who died just doing what they do
Did you look up to heaven for some kind of answer
And look at yourself and what really matters

I'm just a singer of simple songs
I'm not a real political man
I watch CNN but I'm not sure I can tell you
The difference in Iraq and Iran
But I know Jesus and I talk to God
And I remember this from when I was young

Faith, hope and love are some good things he gave us
And the greatest is love

Where were you when the world
stopped turning that September day
Teaching a class full of innocent children
Driving down some cold interstate
Did you feel guilty 'cause you're a survivor
In a crowded room did you feel alone
Did you call up your mother and tell her you love her
Did you dust off that bible at home
Did you open your eyes and hope it never happened
Close your eyes and not go to sleep
Did you notice the sunset the first time in ages
Speak with some stranger on the street
Did you lay down at night and think of tomorrow
Go out and buy you a gun
Did you turn off that violent old movie you're watching
And turn on "I Love Lucy" reruns
Did you go to a church and hold hands with some stranger
Stand in line and give your own blood
Did you just stay home and cling tight to your family
Thank God you had somebody to love

I'm just a singer of simple songs
I'm not a real political man
I watch CNN but I'm not sure I can tell you
The difference in Iraq and Iran
But I know Jesus and I talk to God
And I remember this from when I was young

Faith, hope and love are some good things he gave us
And the greatest is love

I'm just a singer of simple songs
I'm not a real political man
I watch CNN but I'm not sure I can tell you
The difference in Iraq and Iran
But I know Jesus and I talk to God
And I remember this from when I was young
Faith hope and love are some good things he gave us
And the greatest is love

and the greatest is love
and the greatest is love

Where were you when the world
stopped turning that September day.

Alan Jackson
"Where Were You (When the World Stopped Turning?)"
2001

President Bush defines the attacks as a global threat to freedom by Islamic extremists. Identifying Osama bin Laden and Al Qaeda as the responsible parties, he orders the American government to full alert. Declaring a "War on Terrorism," Bush marshals American resources to prevent further attacks and destroy the terrorist network responsible for the attacks. The Taliban regime is a repressive, Pashtun fundamentalist, religious governing movement that had ruled Afghanistan since 1966. Noting bin Laden's ties to the Taliban in Afghanistan and his ten-year campaign to drive the

Soviet Union from Afghanistan (1978-1988), President Bush orchestrates an attack on Afghanistan on October 7, 2001, consisting of a North Atlantic Treaty Organization (NATO) coalition of United States-led forces, to unseat the Taliban regime. Appropriate as a NATO mission (a treaty recognition that an attack on one NATO nation is an attack on all), the attack removes the Taliban leadership, and more than twenty million Afghans are liberated from a Taliban regime that oppresses women and decries western culture. It is but one step forward in the "Global War on Terrorism," and the American government will be called upon to bolster its defenses in the post-9-11 world.

President Bush forms the Department of Homeland Security (DHS) in 2002, to prevent attacks and protect Americans — on the land, on the sea and in the air. It is the largest government reorganization in American history. The DHS becomes the third-largest Cabinet department, incorporating twenty-two federal agencies, including Customs, Coast Guard and Secret Service, with a combined workforce of more than 200,000 employees.

For Congress, political opponents and others holding bitterness from the 2000 election, the 9-11 attacks signal a coming-together of all Americans, a setting aside of political differences and a collective effort to work with other Americans and the people of other countries to defend against an emboldened enemy of freedom — international terrorist networks. The attacks set in motion a renewed pride in America and a realization of the fragility of freedom. Country music artist Lee Greenwood composed and performed a 1980s song that unified Americans in the aftermath of the 1991 Gulf War. It is resurrected in 2001 around a common theme: pride in the United States.

If tomorrow all the things were gone,
I'd worked for all my life.
And I had to start again,
With just my children and my wife.
I'd thank my lucky stars,
To be livin' here today.
'Cause the flag still stands for freedom,
And they can't take that away.

CHORUS
And I'm proud to be an American,
Where at least I know I'm free.
And I won't forget the men who died,
Who gave that right to me.
And I gladly stand up,
Next to you and defend her still today.
'Cause there ain't no doubt I love this land,
God bless the USA.

Lee Greenwood
"God Bless the USA"
1984

In the aftermath of the 9-11 attacks, with the Wall Street symbols of the Twin Towers smoldering, the American economy falters, but President Bush's approval rating soars to ninety percent, largely on the toughness with which he pursues retribution for the lives lost on September 11 and the steps he takes to reassure Americans that his Administration will protect American lives.

Protection of the homeland becomes an almost singular focus for Bush. It is an issue that will define him and his presidency; it will lead him to take military steps that will, in turn, lead others to condemn his presidency. In the name of pursuing terrorism, Bush defines a new approach to American foreign policy that becomes known as the Bush Doctrine, the idea of "Preemptive War."

After the attacks of September 11, 2001, Iraq's dictatorial leader, Saddam Hussein, continues to refuse to abide by United Nations resolutions dating back to the 1990s calling for Iraq to permit inspections for weapons of mass destruction. As the Bush Administration steps up efforts to root out terrorism in the Middle East, Iraq becomes a battleground of resistance to international order and a continuing threat to the existence of Israel. Saddam Hussein rules Iraq with threats and intimidation, and fear tactics designed to frighten his Middle East neighbors and the world at large with his claims of military might and willingness to use deadly military resources.[18]

Bush sees Iraq as a potential resource for terrorism. He proposes to depose Hussein. In a speech at the United States Military Academy at West Point, New York, on June 1, 2002, President Bush outlines his Doctrine of Preemptive War, a policy that permits a nation to take military action to prevent an imminent attack by another nation, instead of waiting to react to such an attack. He appears before the United Nations on September 12, 2002, to urge enforcement of more than a dozen prior U.N. Resolutions against Iraq, resolutions that affirm worldwide mobilization against the internationally unlawful conduct of Saddam Hussein's Iraq. When no conforming response is issued by Iraq, and in light of Iraq's daily anti-aircraft aggression against American patrol aircraft, Bush pursues bipartisan legislation in Congress to authorize his Administration to take first-strike steps against Iraq and remove the threat of military action by Saddam Hussein.[19]

House Joint Resolution 114, introduced by Speaker Dennis Hastert and Democratic Leader Richard Gephardt, and a nearly identical Senate Joint Resolution 45, sponsored by Democratic Leader Tom Daschle and Republican Leader Trent Lott, are introduced in the Congress in early October 2002. The House passes H.J.Res 114 on October 10, 2002, by a vote of 296-133, and the Senate passes it a day later by a vote of 77-23. Signed into law on October 16, 2002, the Resolution authorizes President Bush to pursue a diplomatic solution to the stalemate in Iraq, but also authorizes him to defend the national security of the United States against the threat of Iraq and enforce the existing U.N. resolutions against Iraq. It is authorization for war and the commitment of American military forces as part of a coalition including five other nations (Britain, Australia, Denmark, Poland and Spain). It leads to the removal of Saddam Hussein as ruler of Iraq in forty-two days (March 20-May 1, 2003) and occurs with surprisingly swift military action with a minimum of lost American soldiers. But it exacts a massive federal expense and leads to worldwide criticism of the Bush Administration when no weapons of mass destruction are found in Iraq. It leads further to the realization of the complexities of establishing freedom and a suitable style of democracy in the Middle East.

After the major ground offensive concludes, a United States Senate committee organizes to look into the quality of America's pre-war intelligence concerning Iraqi weapons of mass destruction (WMD) — the main trigger point for the war. The 500-plus page report identifies years of numerous failures in the intelligence-gathering and analysis process. The report finds that these failures led to the creation of inaccurate materials that misled both government policymakers and the American public. Fighting the Iraq war leads to the loss of over 4,500 American soldiers and results in thousands of Americans wounded, plus numerous Iraqi casualties. The prolonged aftermath of the fall of Hussein illustrates the difficulties for any American President in sustaining a long war. Americans do not instinctively support war, especially as the United States historically rejects foreign occupations or territorial expansion by force. The modern United States is quick to come to the aid of the oppressed (World War II, Korea, Vietnam, Bosnia, Kuwait, Afghanistan, Iraq) but is loathe to mount a sustained, long-term war and suffer the death that wars produce.

Bush's final legacy will likely be tarnished by the invasion of Iraq and the implementation of peacekeeping forces there, but history could also conclude that American efforts there liberated an oppressed people and fostered democracy in a region not used to elected representative government. The Bush domestic priorities of education improvement, homeland security, economic growth, record-setting AIDS relief, confirmation of two superbly qualified Supreme Court Justices, passing a prescription drug provision for senior citizens under Medicare, a convincing second-term victory in 2004 and a personally scandal-free eight years as President will likely be subservient to criticism of his Iraq War record. Bush's failure to control federal spending violates his commitment to fiscal responsibility. The twin issues of unpopular war and overspending will severely impact Republican majorities in Congress and lead to a return to Democratic control of Congress in 2006.

As with many of his predecessors, Bush's second term leads to his exit from office with low approval ratings and a weak national economy, for which he is blamed. This shift in public opinion illustrates the political impossibility of successfully leading a nation of more than 300 million people in a complex and dangerous world linked by a telecommunications network with the potential for shaping issues and influencing trends, despite the best intentions of outstanding and principled American leaders. Too, American politics and politicians are increasingly partisan. Overtures are made, on both sides, to "reach across the aisle," yet majority Members drive the agenda and remind minority Members, "We won." The American presidency is now so influential an office and so heavy a responsibility that no modern president can make forceful decisions without consequences. Doing so can lead to the message illustrated in a top musical hit of 2008, by the musical group Coldplay, and a memorable line from the song, "Viva la Vida," and make us wonder: "Oh, who would ever want to be king?"

I used to rule the world
Seas would rise when I gave the word
Now in the morning I sleep alone
Sweep the streets I used to own
I used to roll the dice
Feel the fear in my enemy's eyes
Listen as the crowd would sing
"Now the old king is dead! Long live the king!"

Guy Berryman/Jonathan Buckland/
Will Champion/Christopher Martin
"Viva La Vida"
2008

CHAPTER 14

THE WAY AHEAD

America! America! God Shed His Grace on Thee

Amerian politics, like American government, is more complex than ever in the 21st century. The 44th President, the first man of African heritage to occupy the nation's highest office, ascends to the presidency through a combination of intellect, campaign cash, careful election strategy and the desire of Americans for something new in presidential leadership. A United States Senator from Illinois, Barack Obama, is the candidate for the Democrats. He offers "Hope" and "Change," two powerful nouns in any election year where economic troubles lurk and incumbent leaders struggle. His campaign effectively demonizes the 43rd President and enumerates failed Republican policies. With fewer than three years as a Senator, Obama mounts a campaign that subtly emphasizes his racial profile and craftily outpaces the political talents of his chief Democratic rival, the United States Senator from New York (and former First Lady), Hillary Rodham Clinton. Minority voters and young, college-aged voters connect with the Obama slogan, "This is our time." The Obama campaign offers tremendous emotion, but few specifics.

Obama's opponent is seventy-one year old Republican Senator from Arizona, John McCain. Selectively conservative and proudly independent, McCain is less-beloved by Republican and

Independent voters than he was in 2000, when he opposed George W. Bush for the Republican presidential nomination. Recognizing the 2008 political reality of "first, win the nomination," McCain veers right to prove his conservative *bona fides*. He shows his independent quality by choosing a female as his running mate, Alaska's popular, but little known, governor, Sarah Palin.

Successful presidential campaigns are largely driven by energy of the candidate and his supporters but sometimes by the opposition's lack of energy. In 2008, the energy is all Democratic. Uninspired by the McCain campaign, some Republicans vote for Obama, intrigued by the historic nature of the race, disillusioned by the Bush team and record, and not entirely convinced that the inexperienced and unsophisticated Governor Palin is a worthy potential successor to the aged cancer-survivor McCain. The Obama campaign raises an estimated $1 billion, overwhelming the McCain campaign with get-out-the-vote efforts and abundant television advertising, and in the process, setting campaign fund-raising records.

Obama's campaign effectively uses cutting-edge technologies — e-mail, Twitter, text messaging, cell phones and Blackberries — to engage younger voters, college students and young professionals to create a massive network of advocates for change, get-out-the-vote and fund-raising efforts. The campaign is nearly flawless in its appeal to the "newness" and novelty of American voters taking a chance on a different kind of candidate — young, of mixed racial background and pleasing personality, a rising star with appeal to liberal and independent voters, and attractive to some Republicans disillusioned by more than a decade of conservative-like policies in a changing world. While the 2008 election is not a landslide, it is a convincing victory for Obama at a time when America's international reputation is tarnished. It is also a historic election, engendering the justifiable pride of black Americans, solidifying Democratic majorities in the United States House and Senate and inspiring people of other nations to respect the free choice of American voters. The Democratic Party will hold the presidency and both houses of Congress for the first time in fourteen years.

The year 2008 is also historic for three less lofty and more sobering reasons:

1. Foreign affairs are more dangerous, with the frightful reality of a turbulent Middle East and an unpredictable North Korea, both areas of the world with violent and aggressive anti-American tendencies.
2. The domestic and world economies teeter on the brink of massive national indebtedness and calamity and are slow to recover.
3. Americans, particularly college students, are more ignorant about history, economics, public policy and government than ever before.

Many argue that the third reason is the most internal and systemic and therefore the most consequential. In 2008, the Intercollegiate Studies Institute (ISI) issues a report by its National Civics Literacy Board titled, "Our Failing Heritage: Americans Fail a Basic Test on Their History and Institutions." In 2006 and 2007, ISI tests 14,000 college freshmen and seniors from fifty prominent colleges and universities on sixty-five multiple-choice questions covering basic topics concerning American government, economics, history and institutions. The average student scores are 51.4% for freshmen and 54.2% for seniors — failing grades in any case. The 2008 test of 2,508 American adults results in even worse average scores of 49%, failing grades all around.

In 2008, the Pew Center tests some 5,200 random adults nationally who declare themselves regular readers of books, magazines and newspapers. They are asked the following three questions:

1. Which political party controls the United States House of Representatives (2008)?
2. Who is the United States Secretary of State (2008)?
3. Who is the Prime Minister of Great Britain?

Only eighteen percent get all three answers right (Democrats, Condoleezza Rice, Gordon Brown). Let's re-state that: Eighty-two percent get it wrong.

Who can ignore the popular "Jaywalking" segments on "The Jay Leno Show," where Jay ventures out on the streets of Los Angeles with a microphone to ask random guests simple questions like, "Why do we celebrate July 4th?" or "What's the name of our National Anthem?" The wrong answers embarrass us as Americans and make us shake our heads in disbelief, or outrage. Do you know the answers? (The Fourth of July is America's Independence Day. The title of our national anthem is "The Star Spangled Banner.")

Famous author and historian David McCullough (author of *John Adams, 1776, Truman* and *Path Between the Seas,* among others) tells the story of returning to his *alma mater,* Yale University, to engage a group of students in a seminar. After asking the ice-breaker question "Who can tell me who George C. Marshall was?" (Marshall led the Allied victory in World War II), Mr. McCullough is dismayed that only a handful knows and is further dismayed when a student inquires if Marshall wasn't the man who invented "martial law!" McCullough describes today's college students as "cut flowers" — fresh and bright but without roots.

In a speech in Seattle, Washington, on September 14, 2009, retired U.S. Supreme Court Justice Sandra Day O'Connor, the first woman in American history to be appointed to the Supreme Court, asserted that as public schools have abandoned teaching civics and history, the public is ignorant of government, and young people are disengaged from civic life. Concluding that public schools were initially founded to engender a "civic mission" in students, Justice O'Connor lamented that only about a third of the public can name the three branches of government and America's school system is largely failing to adequately teach civics and history.

The sad and sobering reality is that more and more Americans, especially college students, are failing to learn the lessons of history. They are lacking in the knowledge of our country's roots and are unaware of how the American government really works. As a result, our nation suffers from ignorance about the correctness of public policy decisions, the conformance of policies to accepted Constitutional authority, and the qualities that make for principled national leaders. Another startling finding of the 2008 ISI study is that elected officials score lower than the general public on the civic knowledge test.

Just as the United States dares to compete in a sophisticated global economy, it faces the complicated problems of a dangerous world with a population that doesn't know its own story — and, worse, public officials who know less about America's heritage than the average citizen.

The year 2009 sees government takeovers of certain banking and automobile industry companies, and major changes are proposed to the private health insurance industry as 2010 dawns. The likelihood of a federal law conditioning citizenship on purchase of a health insurance policy looms. Public debt of the United States exceeds $12 trillion, increasing at more than $3.9 billion each day.

With a U.S. population of 307 million, each American's share of the national debt is just under $40,000. America's international stature comes into question as President Obama stresses a policy of international parity among nations, not American "exceptionalism." As more Americans are ignorant about our national history, the importance of U.S. foreign policy and economic integrity comes clearly into view.

A CHALLENGE FOR EDUCATORS

Knowing About Our Country Makes Us All Better Americans

This book has been about American roots — and how we can grow them deeper. All of American society can be participants in the cultivation of American heritage.

Because American public and private education systems are responsible for teaching our children, every grade school, middle school and high school and college should be expected to emphasize the teaching of fundamental civics and do so using primary documents. For example, teaching students about the major conflicts throughout American history gives them an appreciation for why Americans have fought and died to protect the United States. Knowing about our economic system will help students understand why the free enterprise system has helped the United States grow economic strength.

Until the 1960s, it was commonplace in some American public school districts to give each high school graduate a copy of the U.S. Constitution. One such benefactor in Spokane, Washington, was prominent newspaper publisher W. H. Cowles, who, for many years during his life, presented a copy of the Constitution to each graduate with the inscription:

This book, The Constitution of the United States — Its Sources and Its Application — is presented to you, in the hope that it will give you a better understanding and appreciation of your great heritage as a citizen of the United States of America.

In the preface to that book are the following words, written by former Vermont Congressman Samuel B. Pettengill in 1945. They are as true today as they were then:

In this era of world-wide social and political change, it behooves us, as never before, to know the fundamentals of our Constitution which, in times of stress as well as in peace, has provided the American people with a more enduring and practical government, and a greater degree of prosperity than any other people have ever had.

Every high school graduate should be able to pass a test like the Immigrant Citizenship Test before receiving a diploma. Every college graduate should have the requisite knowledge to be able to pass such a test before receiving a college diploma.

Naturalized citizens of the United States are arguably more civically literate than natural-born citizens. They must study for and pass the citizenship exam before becoming a United States citizen. Expecting high school and college passage of the same or similar exam should not be burdensome to graduates. If they are properly learning civics in school, the test should be a breeze. If not, they are civically under-educated and that condition should be unacceptable in modern American society. The civics issue is embraceable by both major political parties, because it is a winning issue with the public. When a student fails a citizenship test, that student fails at being a citizen. There is no more fundamental failure of our educational system, or our society, than this.

Teachers and professors should be expected to be the best civics education resources in America.

Senate Bill 659, a measure sponsored by U.S. Senator Lamar Alexander of Tennessee, and cosponsored by the late Senator Edward M. Kennedy of Massachusetts and Senator Robert C. Byrd of West Virginia, in the 111th Congress (2009-2010), is designed to improve the teaching and learning of American history and civics. This bill, and others like it, mandates the teaching of teachers so that civics education is institutionalized in the core of our nation's education system.

Too often, bright young students, eager to know America's story, are not exposed to the principles of constitutional democracy and its rich history in any meaningful or exciting way. Without a strategy to help teachers and educational institutions understand the importance and long-range value of such teaching, subsequent generations will be clueless about what makes America great. This book, using primary documents, sources and songs, is an example of the multi-media support materials on the shelf and ready to be employed in this effort. Teachers can learn technologically exciting ways to teach citizenship lessons to today's generation of tech-savvy students that will inspire them to learn basic American history. With the ingenuity that exists in the hearts of thousands of hard-working American teachers, surely there are thousands of good ideas available in the education establishment for creatively addressing the problem of citizen and student civics under-education.

The ISI study mentioned in this book targets colleges and universities as the best resources for the proper civics education of every college student. If our nation is to be serious about civics and citizenship training, colleges and universities must be prepared to take greater responsibility for fully educating America's young people about fundamental foundations of student education — understanding America's great story. Thomas Jefferson, the founder of the University of Virginia, believed that an educated citizenry would "recognize and thwart tyranny."

Candidates for political office should expect to be held accountable for their commitment to civics education, but also advocate for increased emphasis on civics education.

As a former Congressman, I know the role Members of Congress can play in advocating for an American public that understands American history and founding principles. While in office, I started a program called the STAR Program (Students Taking Action and Responsibility), an essay contest whereby students would write an essay answer to a question I would pose about public policy and government. The winning students would receive an all-expenses-paid trip to Washington, D.C. to meet public officials and learn about the operations of government, thereby giving them an opportunity to gain civic literacy. Americans who are civically engaged and educated make for more informed voters and citizens. Elected officials who make important decisions about public policy should know our country's basic principles and history and convey their importance to their constituents. Any candidate for Congress who doesn't understand this history has no business running for or serving in this important office. Those who have the privilege of serving should undertake creative efforts like the STAR Program to encourage student and citizen involvement in the operations of the American system of government. Doing so would be a gift to the citizen and the public official, and help perpetuate the positive legacy of America that it so richly deserves.

Why is this book important? Why is the subject matter important? Because just living in America doesn't make us all good

Americans. Knowing about our country means knowing about US. The American story is OUR story. It is a history worth knowing and preserving — to really know America and our dramatic and dynamic history is to love it. Knowing how our country works and the systems that drive the government makes us all better judges of our leaders and their values. We can know how much they love the freedoms so dramatically fought for over generations — and their commitments to do the will of the people.

Knowing about our country makes us all better Americans. The point needs to be made here that being a better American is, in fact, a good thing. No American should ever be ashamed of being one. While we may disagree with some actions taken by our government on our behalf, that is all the more reason to assert our Americanism and speak out, organize and vote, armed with the knowledge and authority of a sound education.

This book is but a snapshot of the principles and history that every American should know. It is a bare minimum of information about us. The American story is noteworthy. It is worth singing about.

Close your eyes, repeat the inspiring words of our national anthem, and reflect on what you now know about the stories and songs of our nation. My hope is that there is, now, a new birth of freedom within you and a greater appreciation for it. What America is to become is being written by your life. Make your life a good song, for some day, others may be singing it.

Let freedom sing!

ENDNOTES

1. In 1215, King John of England agrees to the distribution of handwritten copies of the *Magna Carta* throughout the kingdom, binding himself, his heirs and successors, to the principles of liberty and individual rights that will span centuries and give rise to colonial freedom. The subject of intense negotiations and compromises between barons of the times and their king, the *Magna Carta* secures personal rights and liberties, requires lawful judgments against individuals for trespasses, and assures that laws are upheld and personal rights and justices are protected. Interestingly, these rights apply mostly to the privileged.

2. The Coercive Acts called for the closing of Boston's port, requiring colonists to furnish British troops with barracks and supplies, no trials for British officials, colonial charter annulments and eliminating colonies in Massachusetts and Connecticut.

3. Hopkinson is a Member of Congress from Pennsylvania, a lawyer who argues the famous constitutional case of *McCulloch v. Maryland* before the U.S. Supreme Court (see p. 29). That case stands for the proposition that state action cannot impede a valid federal exercise of constitutional authority. The U.S. Constitution grants Congress implied powers to implement the Constitution's express powers so that the federal government can function efficiently.

4. The Federalist Papers were eighty-five articles written by James Madison, Alexander Hamilton and John Jay, and published in 1787 advocating ratification of the Constitution. No. 78 is Hamilton's explanation of the judiciary under the Constitution.

5. The original U.S. flag, sewn by Philadelphia upholsterer Betsy Ross in June 1776, had thirteen stars and stripes. On June 14, 1777, the Continental Congress adopted the National Flag Resolution. Under the Flag Act of 1794, the American flag had fifteen stars and stripes, recognizing the addition of Vermont in 1791 and Kentucky in 1792 as states.

6. The case stands for the proposition that state action cannot impede a valid exercise of constitutional authority. The federal government has implied powers which allow the federal system to work efficiently. Maryland wants to tax the First Bank. The Supreme Court says "no" — states cannot tax the federal government.

7. Statement to John Holmes by Thomas Jefferson at Monticello, April 22, 1820.

8. A caisson is a vehicle that carries a cannon.

9. "The Congress shall have power to lay and collect taxes, duties, imports and excises, to pay the debts and provide for the common defense and general welfare of the United States; but all duties, imposts and excises shall be uniform throughout the United States."

10. Amending the Constitution takes Congressional action and subsequent ratification by two-thirds of the state legislatures.

11. Amendment XVIII prohibited the manufacture, sale, transportation, and import or export thereof within the states.

12. The animated cartoon, "Der Fuehrer's Face," wins an Academy Award for Walt Disney Studios in 1943. However, because of its propagandistic nature, and the fact that Donald Duck appears as a Nazi, Disney keeps the film out of general circulation after the war. It isn't until 2004 that the cartoon receives its official video release on a DVD of Walt Disney Treasures.

13. V-E Day — Victory in Europe Day — May 8, 1945; V-J Day — Victory Over Japan Day — August 15, 1945

14. Carter begins his presidency with a sixty-six percent approval rating, which falls to a thirty-one percent approval rating at the time of the 1980 election. He becomes the first president since Herbert Hoover — in 1932 — to lose a reelection bid.

15. Whitewater is a controversial Arkansas real estate deal involving Bill and Hillary Clinton that failed in the 1970s and 1980s.

16. In Nethercutt's 2000 reelection bid, citing a change of heart and commitment to completing unfinished business on behalf of the 5th District, he breaks a self-imposed six-year term limit, but is overwhelmingly reelected. He learns a powerful lesson about answering hypothetical debate questions.

17. As a lesson from the World Trade Center evacuation, post 9-11 commercial building codes are modified across the country to increase the fire resistance of elevator shafts. It is believed many more people would have made it out alive had they been allowed to use the elevators instead of being forced to use the stairwells many dozens of stories above the street.

18. Congress is regularly briefed in 2002 about circumstances in Iraq, including U.S. military demonstrations of preparations for soldier protection against Iraqi use of chemical weapons.

19. Iraqi anti-aircraft gunfire is usually a daily occurrence as Iraqi ground forces fire at U.S. jets patrolling the no-fly zone over Iraq.

ACKNOWLEDGMENTS

T his book is the product of much collaboration and the association of many indispensable contributors. My family has been the vital component directly involved on a continuous basis since the genesis of my idea for a book to facilitate more civics education in America and a plan to accomplish that education. My wife, Mary Beth, endured the reading of many manuscript drafts and contributed essential creative thought and good judgments about content, style and word choice. She offered the format for blending music and history in order to enliven historical records in order to attract a wide audience hungry for essential American history. As with everything in my life, she remains always by my side with advice, encouraging words and abiding love. This is her project, too, for I could not have completed it without her.

Daughter Meredith helped perfect the creative idea for the connection of music to history. An accomplished pianist as a young girl, she contributed another valuable set of eyes to see and ears to listen to the heartbeat of this project. Son Elliott brought to bear a young man's modern perspective on music content and the generational appeal of a book containing American history and commentary about the state of America's development over two centuries, and offered winning marketing strategies. For their love, support and constructive comments, I remain forever grateful, and they will forever remain in my Last Will and Testament.

Tom McArthur was the perfect co-author for this project. A history lover and, more importantly, a fine human being who deeply loves our country, Tom offered a former newsman's perspective and a modern creative side to writing and incorporating music. I knew Tom could write creatively and uniquely relate to history and government. As a historian, supporter of the Nethercutt Foundation and participant with the students the Foundation serves, he added style and substance to this book. His thoughtful additions to content and his abiding good cheer and pleasant nature made working with him rewarding.

Product appearance and dissemination are highly important to any successful publication. Dave Demers of Spokane's Marquette Books spotted the appeal of this book early-on and handled its publication with unselfish professionalism and advice to perfect its content and layout, offering respectful suggestions for improvements. The designer of the dust jacket, Jayne Floyd of JF Design in Spokane, patiently provided her outstanding artistic and marketing advice in order to assure the book's brand and appeal. Her friendship and design experience made working with her a joy. Tom Read, owner of American Christian Network in Spokane and a conglomerate of other radio stations, provided me unfettered access to the airwaves to discuss American civics, *In Tune With America*, political commentary, and the Nethercutt Foundation, among other things, and for his friendship and broad media experience, I am eternally grateful.

My friend Kent Adams of KAYU television in Spokane, Washington, offered media support and the creative idea of bringing the content of the book to the public through the medium of television, and spurred the idea of the "U.S. History by the Minute" series that contains excerpts from the book and has received acclaim from its viewing audience. Not only is he supportive of the Nethercutt Foundation, Kent has gone far beyond a business relationship in promoting the need for civics education for all Americans and has contributed ideas and encouragement to circulate the idea behind the book and television series on a national level.

Mark J. Estren, former executive producer for CBS and ABE News and "The Nightly Business Report" on PBS and music reviewer for the *Washington Post*, provided an unbiased review of the manuscript and thoughtful advice. One of the brightest and most creative people I know, and someone whose judgment I trust, Mark always provided solid recommendations and counsel on the book with good humor and sensitivity, using his vast media experience to help guide the project to publication and distribution. I have been grateful for his cordial manner and genuine enthusiasm and support.

Kristina Sabestinas, Executive Director of the George Nethercutt Foundation, has provided unflappable assistance to the connection of the book project with the Nethercutt Foundation. Her predecessor, Shelly O'Quinn, helped launch the book idea and served the students of the Foundation with passion and efficiency.

Because this project focuses on education, former teacher and dear family friend Kim Johnson was a vital supporter who read and re-read the manuscript to assure grammatical correctness and strength of content. Her valuable teaching experience and expertise helped improve the book and establish a foundation for development of curricula appropriate for schools so that civics education can be fun and interesting for students and teachers alike. Former college friend and president of the National Association of Independent colleges and Universities (NAICU), David L. Warren, provided constructive counsel on national education policy and civics education strategies.

The encouragement I received from friends and family over the months of research and writing devoted to this book has been heartwarming and sustaining. Washington, D.C., media expert Larry McCarthy, who developed winning commercials for my political campaigns, has been y friend, supporter and adviser since 1994. James Moore of Brightline Media, gave me support and advice on all things media, and has provided Web site support to the Nethercutt Foundation without reservation. Two directors of the Nethercutt Foundation, Rich Kuhling and Shaun Cross of Spokane, offered constructive advice and thoughtful recommendations regarding the Foundation and are both readers of the first order.

Of particular importance has been the help of my trusted assistant, Katie Gernes, who has always offered and provided encouragement for this project, the Foundation, my family, the Foundation students and consistent good advice since I have known her. She is a gem who helps manage my business life with grace and efficiency.

Writing a book about our country is different than writing articles, speeches or commentaries on political issues of the day. It requires precision of thought for such a long project and an examination of one's deep feelings about the United States and all the heroic figures who have preceded my generation. This book in particular required that I set aside my natural political persuasions in order to look objectively at presidents, leaders and circumstances that have contributed to the development of America and to appreciate where we've been as a nation, where we are and where we might be headed. After reviewing all 44 presidential inaugural addresses, countless books, articles and documents of history, I have not strayed from my undying respect for America's story, but am bolstered by the experience of history, that our nation is best served by realizing that we are "one nation, under God, with liberty and justice for all." If we ever forget these simple, great principles of governing a civilized society, may Heaven help us.

SAMPLE IMMIGRANT CITIZENSHIP TEST QUESTIONS

1. What are the colors of our flag?
2. How many stars are there in our flag?
3. What color are the stars on our flag?
4. What do the stars on the flag mean?
5. How many stripes are there in the flag?
6. What color are the stripes?
7. What do the stripes on the flag mean?
8. How many states are there in the Union?
9. What is the 4th of July?
10. What is the date of Independence Day?
11. Independence from whom?
12. What country did we fight during the Revolutionary War?
13. Who was the first President of the United States?
14. Who is the President of the United States today?
15. Who is the vice-president of the United States today?
16. Who elects the President of the United States?
17. Who becomes President of the United States if the President should die?
18. For how long do we elect the President?
19. What is the Constitution?
20. Can the Constitution be changed?
21. What do we call a change to the Constitution?
22. How many changes or amendments are there to the Constitution?

23. How many branches are there in our government?
24. What are the three branches of our government?
25. What is the legislative branch of our government?
26. Who makes the laws in the United States?
27. What is the Congress?
28. What are the duties of Congress?
29. Who elects the Congress?
30. How many senators are there in Congress?
31. Can you name the two senators from your state?
32. For how long do we elect each senator?
33. How many representatives are there in Congress?
34. For how long do we elect the representatives?
35. What is the executive branch of our government?
36. What is the judiciary branch of our government?
37. What are the duties of the Supreme Court?
38. What is the supreme court law of the United States?
39. What is the Bill of Rights?
40. What is the capital of your state?
41. Who is the current governor of your state?
42. Who becomes President of the United States if the President and the vice-president should die?
43. Who is the Chief Justice of the Supreme Court?
44. Can you name thirteen original states?
45. Who said, "Give me liberty or give me death."?
46. Which countries were our enemies during World War II?
47. What are the 49th and 50th states of the Union?
48. How many terms can the President serve?
49. Who was Martin Luther King, Jr.?
50. Who is the head of your local government?

Answers are available at <http://usgovinfo.about.com/blinstst.htm>.

UNITED STATES CONSTITUTION

We the People of the United States, in Order to form a more perfect Union, establish Justice, insure domestic Tranquility, provide for the common defence, promote the general Welfare, and secure the Blessings of Liberty to ourselves and our Posterity, do ordain and establish this Constitution for the United States of America.

Article 1.

Section 1
All legislative Powers herein granted shall be vested in a Congress of the United States, which shall consist of a Senate and House of Representatives.

Section 2
The House of Representatives shall be composed of Members chosen every second Year by the People of the several States, and the Electors in each State shall have the Qualifications requisite for Electors of the most numerous Branch of the State Legislature.

No Person shall be a Representative who shall not have attained to the Age of twenty five Years, and been seven Years a Citizen of the United States, and who shall not, when elected, be an Inhabitant of that State in which he shall be chosen.

Representatives and direct Taxes shall be apportioned among the several States which may be included within this Union, according to their respective Numbers, which shall be determined by adding to the whole Number of free Persons, including those bound to Service for a Term of Years, and excluding Indians not taxed, three fifths of all other Persons.

The actual Enumeration shall be made within three Years after the first Meeting of the Congress of the United States, and within every subsequent Term of ten Years, in such Manner as they shall by Law direct. The Number of Representatives shall not exceed one for every thirty Thousand, but each State shall have at Least one Representative; and until such enumeration shall be made, the State of New Hampshire shall be entitled to choose three, Massachusetts eight, Rhode Island and Providence Plantations one, Connecticut five, New York six, New

Jersey four, Pennsylvania eight, Delaware one, Maryland six, Virginia ten, North Carolina five, South Carolina five and Georgia three.

When vacancies happen in the Representation from any State, the Executive Authority thereof shall issue Writs of Election to fill such Vacancies.

The House of Representatives shall choose their Speaker and other Officers; and shall have the sole Power of Impeachment.

Section 3

The Senate of the United States shall be composed of two Senators from each State, chosen by the Legislature thereof, for six Years; and each Senator shall have one Vote.

Immediately after they shall be assembled in Consequence of the first Election, they shall be divided as equally as may be into three Classes. The Seats of the Senators of the first Class shall be vacated at the Expiration of the second Year, of the second Class at the Expiration of the fourth Year, and of the third Class at the Expiration of the sixth Year, so that one third may be chosen every second Year; and if Vacancies happen by Resignation, or otherwise, during the Recess of the Legislature of any State, the Executive thereof may make temporary Appointments until the next Meeting of the Legislature, which shall then fill such Vacancies.

No person shall be a Senator who shall not have attained to the Age of thirty Years,

and been nine Years a Citizen of the United States, and who shall not, when elected, be an Inhabitant of that State for which he shall be chosen.

The Vice President of the United States shall be President of the Senate, but shall have no Vote, unless they be equally divided.

The Senate shall choose their other Officers, and also a President pro tempore, in the absence of the Vice President, or when he shall exercise the Office of President of the United States.

The Senate shall have the sole Power to try all Impeachments. When sitting for that Purpose, they shall be on Oath or Affirmation. When the President of the United States is tried, the Chief Justice shall preside: And no Person shall be convicted without the Concurrence of two thirds of the Members present.

Judgment in Cases of Impeachment shall not extend further than to removal from Office, and disqualification to hold and enjoy any Office of honor, Trust or Profit under the United States: but the Party convicted shall nevertheless be liable and subject to Indictment, Trial, Judgment and Punishment, according to Law.

Section 4

The Times, Places and Manner of holding Elections for Senators and Representatives, shall be prescribed in each State by the Legislature thereof; but the Congress may at any time by Law make or alter such Regulations, except as to the Place of Choosing Senators.

The Congress shall assemble at least once in every Year, and such Meeting shall be on the first Monday in December, unless they shall by Law appoint a different Day.

Section 5
Each House shall be the Judge of the Elections, Returns and Qualifications of its own Members, and a Majority of each shall constitute a Quorum to do Business; but a smaller number may adjourn from day to day, and may be authorized to compel the Attendance of absent Members, in such Manner, and under such Penalties as each House may provide.

Each House may determine the Rules of its Proceedings, punish its Members for disorderly Behavior, and, with the Concurrence of two-thirds, expel a Member.

Each House shall keep a Journal of its Proceedings, and from time to time publish the same, excepting such Parts as may in their Judgment require Secrecy; and the Yeas and Nays of the Members of either House on any question shall, at the Desire of one fifth of those Present, be entered on the Journal.

Neither House, during the Session of Congress, shall, without the Consent of the other, adjourn for more than three days, nor to any other Place than that in which the two Houses shall be sitting.

Section 6
The Senators and Representatives shall receive a Compensation for their Services, to be ascertained by Law, and paid out of the Treasury of the United States. They shall in all Cases, except Treason, Felony and Breach of the Peace, be privileged from Arrest during their Attendance at the Session of their respective Houses, and in going to and returning from the same; and for any Speech or Debate in either House, they shall not be questioned in any other Place.

No Senator or Representative shall, during the Time for which he was elected, be appointed to any civil Office under the Authority of the United States which shall have been created, or the Emoluments whereof shall have been increased during such time; and no Person holding any Office under the United States, shall be a Member of either House during his Continuance in Office.

Section 7
All bills for raising Revenue shall originate in the House of Representatives; but the Senate may propose or concur with Amendments as on other Bills.

Every Bill which shall have passed the House of Representatives and the Senate, shall, before it become a Law, be presented to the President of the United States; If he approve he shall sign it, but if not he shall return it, with his Objections to that House in which it shall have originated, who shall enter the Objections at large on their Journal, and proceed to reconsider it. If after such Reconsideration two thirds of that House shall agree to pass the Bill, it shall be sent, together with the Objections, to the other House, by which it shall likewise be reconsidered, and if approved by two thirds of that House, it shall become a Law. But in all such Cases the Votes of both Houses shall be determined by Yeas and Nays, and the Names of the Persons voting for and against the Bill shall be entered on the Journal of each House respectively. If any Bill shall not be returned by the President within ten Days (Sundays excepted) after it shall have been presented to him, the Same shall be a Law, in like Manner as if he had signed it, unless the Congress by their Adjournment prevent its Return, in which Case it shall not be a Law.

Every Order, Resolution, or Vote to which the Concurrence of the Senate and House of Representatives may be necessary (except on a question of Adjournment) shall be presented to the President of the United States; and before the Same shall take Effect, shall be approved by him, or being disapproved by him, shall be repassed by two thirds of the Senate and House of Representatives, according to the Rules and Limitations prescribed in the Case of a Bill.

Section 8

The Congress shall have Power To lay and collect Taxes, Duties, Imposts and Excises, to pay the Debts and provide for the common Defence and general Welfare of the United States; but all Duties, Imposts and Excises shall be uniform throughout the United States; To borrow money on the credit of the United States; To regulate Commerce with foreign Nations, and among the several States, and with the Indian Tribes; To establish an uniform Rule of Naturalization, and uniform Laws on the subject of Bankruptcies throughout the United States; To coin Money,

regulate the Value thereof, and of foreign Coin, and fix the Standard of Weights and Measures; To provide for the Punishment of counterfeiting the Securities and current Coin of the United States; To establish Post Offices and Post Roads; To promote the Progress of Science and useful Arts, by securing for limited Times to Authors and Inventors the exclusive Right to their respective Writings and Discoveries; To constitute Tribunals inferior to the supreme Court; To define and punish Piracies and Felonies committed on the high Seas, and Offenses against the Law of Nations; To declare War, grant Letters of Marque and Reprisal, and make Rules concerning Captures on Land and Water; To raise and support Armies, but no Appropriation of Money to that Use shall be for a longer Term than two Years; To provide and maintain a Navy; To make Rules for the Government and Regulation of the land and naval Forces; To provide for calling forth the Militia to execute the Laws of the Union, suppress Insurrections and repel Invasions; To provide for organizing, arming, and disciplining the Militia, and for governing such Part of them as may be employed in the Service of the United States, reserving to the States respectively, the Appointment of the Officers, and the Authority of training the Militia according to the discipline prescribed by Congress; To exercise exclusive Legislation in all Cases whatsoever, over such District (not exceeding ten Miles square) as may, by Cession of particular States, and the acceptance of Congress, become the Seat of the Government of the United States, and to exercise like Authority over all Places purchased by the Consent of the

Legislature of the State in which the Same shall be, for the Erection of Forts, Magazines, Arsenals, dock-Yards, and other needful Buildings; And To make all Laws which shall be necessary and proper for carrying into Execution the foregoing Powers, and all other Powers vested by this Constitution in the Government of the United States, or in any Department or Officer thereof.

Section 9

The Migration or Importation of such Persons as any of the States now existing shall think proper to admit, shall not be prohibited by the Congress prior to the Year one thousand eight hundred and eight, but a tax or duty may be imposed on such Importation, not exceeding ten dollars for each Person.

The privilege of the Writ of Habeas Corpus shall not be suspended, unless when in Cases of Rebellion or Invasion the public Safety may require it. No Bill of Attainder or ex post facto Law shall be passed. No capitation, or other direct, Tax shall be laid, unless in Proportion to the Census or Enumeration herein before directed to be taken. No Tax or Duty shall be laid on Articles exported from any State. No Preference shall be given by any Regulation of Commerce or Revenue to the Ports of one State over those of another: nor shall Vessels bound to, or from, one State, be obliged to enter, clear, or pay Duties in another. No Money shall be drawn from the Treasury, but in Consequence of Appropriations made by Law; and a regular Statement and Account of the Receipts and Expenditures of all public Money shall be published from time to time. No Title of Nobility shall be granted by the United States: And no Person holding any Office of Profit or Trust under them, shall, without the Consent of the Congress, accept of any present, Emolument, Office, or Title, of any kind whatever, from any King, Prince or foreign State.

Section 10

No State shall enter into any Treaty, Alliance, or Confederation; grant Letters of Marque and Reprisal; coin Money; emit Bills of Credit; make any Thing but gold and silver Coin a Tender in Payment of Debts; pass any Bill of Attainder, ex post facto Law, or Law impairing the Obligation of Contracts, or grant any Title of Nobility.

No State shall, without the Consent of the Congress, lay any Imposts or Duties on Imports or Exports, except what may be absolutely necessary for executing its inspection Laws: and the net Produce of all Duties and Imposts, laid by any State on Imports or Exports, shall be for the Use of the Treasury of the United States; and all such Laws shall be subject to the Revision and Control of the Congress.

No State shall, without the Consent of Congress, lay any duty of Tonnage, keep Troops, or Ships of War in time of Peace, enter into any Agreement or Compact with another State, or with a foreign Power, or engage in War, unless actually invaded, or in such imminent Danger as will not admit of delay.

Article 2.

Section 1

The executive Power shall be vested in a President of the United States of America. He shall hold his Office during the Term of four Years, and, together with the Vice-President chosen for the same Term, be elected, as follows:

Each State shall appoint, in such Manner as the Legislature thereof may direct, a Number of Electors, equal to the whole Number of Senators and Representatives to which the State may be entitled in the Congress: but no Senator or Representative, or Person holding an Office of Trust or Profit under the United States, shall be appointed an Elector.

The Electors shall meet in their respective States, and vote by Ballot for two persons, of whom one at least shall not lie an Inhabitant of the same State with themselves. And they shall make a List of all the Persons voted for, and of the Number of Votes for each; which List they shall sign and certify, and transmit sealed to the Seat of the Government of the United States, directed to the President of the Senate. The President of the Senate shall, in the Presence of the Senate and House of Representatives, open all the Certificates, and the Votes shall then be counted. The Person having the greatest Number of Votes shall be the President, if such Number be a Majority of the whole Number of Electors appointed; and if there be more than one who have such Majority, and have an equal Number of Votes, then the House of Representatives shall immediately choose by Ballot one of them

for President; and if no Person have a Majority, then from the five highest on the List the said House shall in like Manner choose the President. But in choosing the President, the Votes shall be taken by States, the Representation from each State having one Vote; a quorum for this Purpose shall consist of a Member or Members from two-thirds of the States, and a Majority of all the States shall be necessary to a Choice. In every Case, after the Choice of the President, the Person having the greatest Number of Votes of the Electors shall be the Vice President. But if there should remain two or more who have equal Votes, the Senate shall choose from them by Ballot the Vice-President.

The Congress may determine the Time of choosing the Electors, and the Day on which they shall give their Votes; which Day shall be the same throughout the United States.

No person except a natural born Citizen, or a Citizen of the United States, at the time of the Adoption of this Constitution, shall be eligible to the Office of President; neither shall any Person be eligible to that Office who shall not have attained to the Age of thirty-five Years, and been fourteen Years a Resident within the United States.

In Case of the Removal of the President from Office, or of his Death, Resignation, or Inability to discharge the Powers and Duties of the said Office, the same shall devolve on the Vice President, and the Congress may by Law provide for the Case of Removal, Death, Resignation or Inability, both of the President and Vice

President, declaring what Officer shall then act as President, and such Officer shall act accordingly, until the Disability be removed, or a President shall be elected.

The President shall, at stated Times, receive for his Services, a Compensation, which shall neither be increased nor diminished during the Period for which he shall have been elected, and he shall not receive within that Period any other Emolument from the United States, or any of them.

Before he enter on the Execution of his Office, he shall take the following Oath or Affirmation:

"I do solemnly swear (or affirm) that I will faithfully execute the Office of President of the United States, and will to the best of my Ability, preserve, protect and defend the Constitution of the United States."

Section 2

The President shall be Commander in Chief of the Army and Navy of the United States, and of the Militia of the several States, when called into the actual Service of the United States; he may require the Opinion, in writing, of the principal Officer in each of the executive Departments, upon any subject relating to the Duties of their respective Offices, and he shall have Power to Grant Reprieves and Pardons for Offenses against the United States, except in Cases of Impeachment.

He shall have Power, by and with the Advice and Consent of the Senate, to make Treaties, provided two thirds of the Senators present concur; and he shall nominate, and by and with the Advice and Consent of the Senate, shall appoint Ambassadors, other public Ministers and Consuls, Judges of the supreme Court, and all other Officers of the United States, whose Appointments are not herein otherwise provided for, and which shall be established by Law: but the Congress may by Law vest the Appointment of such inferior Officers, as they think proper, in the President alone, in the Courts of Law, or in the Heads of Departments.

The President shall have Power to fill up all Vacancies that may happen during the Recess of the Senate, by granting Commissions which shall expire at the End of their next Session.

Section 3 He shall from time to time give to the Congress Information of the State of the Union, and recommend to their Consideration such Measures as he shall judge necessary and expedient; he may, on extraordinary Occasions, convene both Houses, or either of them, and in Case of Disagreement between them, with Respect to the Time of Adjournment, he may adjourn them to such Time as he shall think proper; he shall receive Ambassadors and other public Ministers; he shall take Care that the Laws be faithfully executed, and shall Commission all the Officers of the United States.

Section 4

The President, Vice President and all civil Officers of the United States, shall be removed from Office on Impeachment for, and Conviction of, Treason, Bribery, or other high Crimes and Misdemeanors.

Article 3.

Section 1

The judicial Power of the United States, shall be vested in one supreme Court, and in such inferior Courts as the Congress may from time to time ordain and establish. The Judges, both of the supreme and inferior Courts, shall hold their Offices during good Behavior, and shall, at stated Times, receive for their Services a Compensation which shall not be diminished during their Continuance in Office.

Section 2

The judicial Power shall extend to all Cases, in Law and Equity, arising under this Constitution, the Laws of the United States, and Treaties made, or which shall be made, under their Authority; to all Cases affecting Ambassadors, other public Ministers and Consuls; to all Cases of admiralty and maritime Jurisdiction; to Controversies to which the United States shall be a Party; to Controversies between two or more States; between a State and Citizens of another State; between Citizens of different States; between Citizens of the same State claiming Lands under Grants of different States, and between a State, or the Citizens thereof, and foreign States, Citizens or Subjects.

In all Cases affecting Ambassadors, other public Ministers and Consuls, and those in which a State shall be Party, the supreme Court shall have original Jurisdiction. In all the other Cases before mentioned, the supreme Court shall have appellate Jurisdiction, both as to Law and Fact, with

such Exceptions, and under such Regulations as the Congress shall make.

The Trial of all Crimes, except in Cases of Impeachment, shall be by Jury; and such Trial shall be held in the State where the said Crimes shall have been committed; but when not committed within any State, the Trial shall be at such Place or Places as the Congress may by Law have directed.

Section 3

Treason against the United States, shall consist only in levying War against them, or in adhering to their Enemies, giving them Aid and Comfort. No Person shall be convicted of Treason unless on the Testimony of two Witnesses to the same overt Act, or on Confession in open Court.

The Congress shall have power to declare the Punishment of Treason, but no Attainder of Treason shall work Corruption of Blood, or Forfeiture except during the Life of the Person attainted.

Article 4.

Section 1

Full Faith and Credit shall be given in each State to the public Acts, Records, and judicial Proceedings of every other State. And the Congress may by general Laws prescribe the Manner in which such Acts, Records and Proceedings shall be proved, and the Effect thereof.

Section 2

The Citizens of each State shall be entitled to all Privileges and Immunities
of Citizens in the several States.

A Person charged in any State with Treason, Felony, or other Crime, who shall flee from Justice, and be found in another State, shall on demand of the executive Authority of the State from which he fled, be delivered up, to be removed to the State having Jurisdiction of the Crime.

No Person held to Service or Labour in one State, under the Laws thereof, escaping into another, shall, in Consequence of any Law or Regulation therein, be discharged from such Service or Labour, But shall be delivered up on Claim of the Party to whom such Service or Labour may be due.

Section 3

New States may be admitted by the Congress into this Union; but no new States shall be formed or erected within the Jurisdiction of any other State; nor any State be formed by the Junction of two or more States, or parts of States, without the Consent of the Legislatures of the States concerned as well as of the Congress.

The Congress shall have Power to dispose of and make all needful Rules and Regulations respecting the Territory or other Property belonging to the United States; and nothing in this Constitution shall be so construed as to Prejudice any Claims of the United States, or of any particular State.

Section 4

The United States shall guarantee to every State in this Union a Republican Form of Government, and shall protect each of them against Invasion; and on Application

of the Legislature, or of the Executive (when the Legislature cannot be convened) against domestic Violence.

Article 5.

The Congress, whenever two thirds of both Houses shall deem it necessary, shall propose Amendments to this Constitution, or, on the Application of the Legislatures of two thirds of the several States, shall call a Convention for proposing Amendments, which, in either Case, shall be valid to all Intents and Purposes, as part of this Constitution, when ratified by the Legislatures of three fourths of the several States, or by Conventions in three fourths thereof, as the one or the other Mode of Ratification may be proposed by the Congress; Provided that no Amendment which may be made prior to the Year One thousand eight hundred and eight shall in any Manner affect the first and fourth Clauses in the Ninth Section of the first Article; and that no State, without its Consent, shall be deprived of its equal Suffrage in the Senate.

Article 6.

All Debts contracted and Engagements entered into, before the Adoption of this Constitution, shall be as valid against the United States under this Constitution, as under the Confederation.

This Constitution, and the Laws of the United States which shall be made in Pursuance thereof; and all Treaties made, or which shall be made, under the Authority of the United States, shall be the supreme Law of the Land; and the Judges in every State shall be bound thereby, any Thing in the Constitution or Laws of any State to the Contrary notwithstanding.

The Senators and Representatives before mentioned, and the Members of the several State Legislatures, and all executive and judicial Officers, both of the United States and of the several States, shall be bound by Oath or Affirmation, to support this Constitution; but no religious Test shall ever be required as a Qualification to any Office or public Trust under the United States.

Article 7.

The Ratification of the Conventions of nine States, shall be sufficient for the Establishment of this Constitution between the States so ratifying the Same.

Done in Convention by the Unanimous Consent of the States present the Seventeenth Day of September in the Year of our Lord one thousand seven hundred and Eighty seven and of the Independence of the United States of America the Twelfth. In Witness whereof We have hereunto subscribed our Names. George Washington - President and deputy from Virginia - New Hampshire - John Langdon, Nicholas Gilman Massachusetts - Nathaniel Gorham, Rufus King Connecticut - William Samuel Johnson, Roger Sherman New York - Alexander Hamilton New Jersey - William Livingston, David Brearley, William Paterson, Jonathan Dayton Pennsylvania - Benjamin Franklin, Thomas Mifflin,

Robert Morris, George Clymer, Thomas Fitzsimons, Jared Ingersoll, James Wilson, Gouvernour Morris Delaware - George Read, Gunning Bedford Jr., John Dickinson, Richard Bassett, Jacob Broom Maryland - James McHenry, Daniel of St Thomas Jenifer, Daniel Carroll Virginia - John Blair, James Madison Jr. North Carolina - William Blount, Richard Dobbs Spaight, Hugh Williamson South Carolina - John Rutledge, Charles Cotesworth Pinckney, Charles Pinckney, Pierce Butler Georgia - William Few, Abraham Baldwin Attest: William Jackson, Secretary

Amendments

Amendment 1
Congress shall make no law respecting an establishment of religion, or prohibiting the free exercise thereof; or abridging the freedom of speech, or of the press; or the right of the people peaceably to assemble, and to petition the Government for a redress of grievances.

Amendment 2
A well regulated Militia, being necessary to the security of a free State, the right of the people to keep and bear Arms, shall not be infringed.

Amendment 3
No Soldier shall, in time of peace be quartered in any house, without the consent of the Owner, nor in time of war, but in a manner to be prescribed by law.

Amendment 4
The right of the people to be secure in their persons, houses, papers, and effects, against unreasonable searches and

seizures, shall not be violated, and no Warrants shall issue, but upon probable cause, supported by Oath or affirmation, and particularly describing the place to be searched, and the persons or things to be seized.

Amendment 5

No person shall be held to answer for a capital, or otherwise infamous crime, unless on a presentment or indictment of a Grand Jury, except in cases arising in the land or naval forces, or in the Militia, when in actual service in time of War or public danger; nor shall any person be subject for the same offense to be twice put in jeopardy of life or limb; nor shall be compelled in any criminal case to be a witness against himself, nor be deprived of life, liberty, or property, without due process of law; nor shall private property be taken for public use, without just compensation.

Amendment 6

In all criminal prosecutions, the accused shall enjoy the right to a speedy and public trial, by an impartial jury of the State and district wherein the crime shall have been committed, which district shall have been previously ascertained by law, and to be informed of the nature and cause of the accusation; to be confronted with the witnesses against him; to have compulsory process for obtaining witnesses in his favor, and to have the Assistance of Counsel for his defence.

Amendment 7

In Suits at common law, where the value in controversy shall exceed twenty dollars, the right of trial by jury shall be preserved,

and no fact tried by a jury, shall be otherwise re-examined in any Court of the United States, than according to the rules of the common law.

Amendment 8

Excessive bail shall not be required, nor excessive fines imposed, nor cruel and unusual punishments inflicted.

Amendment 9

The enumeration in the Constitution, of certain rights, shall not be construed to deny or disparage others retained by the people.

Amendment 10

The powers not delegated to the United States by the Constitution, nor prohibited by it to the States, are reserved to the States respectively, or to the people.

Amendment 11

The Judicial power of the United States shall not be construed to extend to any suit in law or equity, commenced or prosecuted against one of the United States by Citizens of another State, or by Citizens or Subjects of any Foreign State.

Amendment 12

The Electors shall meet in their respective states, and vote by ballot for President and Vice-President, one of whom, at least, shall not be an inhabitant of the same state with themselves; they shall name in their ballots the person voted for as President, and in distinct ballots the person voted for as Vice-President, and they shall make distinct lists of all persons voted for as President, and of all persons voted for as Vice-President and of the number of votes for each, which lists they shall sign and certify, and transmit sealed to the seat of the government of the United States, directed to the President of the Senate;

The President of the Senate shall, in the presence of the Senate and House of Representatives, open all the certificates and the votes shall then be counted;

The person having the greatest Number of votes for President, shall be the President, if such number be a majority of the whole number of Electors appointed; and if no person have such majority, then from the persons having the highest numbers not exceeding three on the list of those voted for as President, the House of Representatives shall choose immediately, by ballot, the President. But in choosing the President, the votes shall be taken by states, the representation from each state having one vote; a quorum for this purpose shall consist of a member or members from two-thirds of the states, and a majority of all the states shall be necessary to a choice. And if the House of Representatives shall not choose a President whenever the right of choice shall devolve upon them, before the fourth day of March next following, then the Vice-President shall act as President, as in the case of the death or other constitutional disability of the President.

The person having the greatest number of votes as Vice-President, shall be the Vice-President, if such number be a majority of the whole number of Electors appointed, and if no person have a majority, then from the two highest numbers on the list,

the Senate shall choose the Vice-President; a quorum for the purpose shall consist of two-thirds of the whole number of Senators, and a majority of the whole number shall be necessary to a choice. But no person constitutionally ineligible to the office of President shall be eligible to that of Vice-President of the United States.

Amendment 13

1. Neither slavery nor involuntary servitude, except as a punishment for crime whereof the party shall have been duly convicted, shall exist within the United States, or any place subject to their jurisdiction.

2. Congress shall have power to enforce this article by appropriate legislation.

Amendment 14

1. All persons born or naturalized in the United States, and subject to the jurisdiction thereof, are citizens of the United States and of the State wherein they reside. No State shall make or enforce any law which shall abridge the privileges or immunities of citizens of the United States; nor shall any State deprive any person of life, liberty, or property, without due process of law; nor deny to any person within its jurisdiction the equal protection of the laws.

2. Representatives shall be apportioned among the several States according to their respective numbers, counting the whole number of persons in each State, excluding Indians not taxed. But when the right to vote at any election for the choice of electors for President and Vice-President

of the United States, Representatives in Congress, the Executive and Judicial officers of a State, or the members of the Legislature thereof, is denied to any of the male inhabitants of such State, being twenty-one years of age, and citizens of the United States, or in any way abridged, except for participation in rebellion, or other crime, the basis of representation therein shall be reduced in the proportion which the number of such male citizens shall bear to the whole number of male citizens twenty-one years of age in such State.

3. No person shall be a Senator or Representative in Congress, or elector of President and Vice-President, or hold any office, civil or military, under the United States, or under any State, who, having previously taken an oath, as a member of Congress, or as an officer of the United States, or as a member of any State legislature, or as an executive or judicial officer of any State, to support the Constitution of the United States, shall have engaged in insurrection or rebellion against the same, or given aid or comfort to the enemies thereof. But Congress may by a vote of two-thirds of each House, remove such disability.

4. The validity of the public debt of the United States, authorized by law, including debts incurred for payment of pensions and bounties for services in suppressing insurrection or rebellion, shall not be questioned. But neither the United States nor any State shall assume or pay any debt or obligation incurred in aid of insurrection or rebellion against the United States, or any claim for the loss or emancipation of any slave; but all such debts, obligations and claims shall be held illegal and void.

5. The Congress shall have power to enforce, by appropriate legislation, the provisions of this article.

Amendment 15

1. The right of citizens of the United States to vote shall not be denied or abridged by the United States or by any State on account of race, color, or previous condition of servitude.

2. The Congress shall have power to enforce this article by appropriate legislation.

Amendment 16

The Congress shall have power to lay and collect taxes on incomes, from whatever source derived, without apportionment among the several States, and without regard to any census or enumeration.

Amendment 17

The Senate of the United States shall be composed of two Senators from each State, elected by the people thereof, for six years; and each Senator shall have one vote. The electors in each State shall have the qualifications requisite for electors of the most numerous branch of the State legislatures.

When vacancies happen in the representation of any State in the Senate, the executive authority of such State shall issue writs of election to fill such vacancies: Provided, That the legislature of any State may empower the executive thereof to make temporary appointments until the people fill the vacancies by election as the legislature may direct.

This amendment shall not be so construed as to affect the election or term of any Senator chosen before it becomes valid as part of the Constitution.

Amendment 18

1. After one year from the ratification of this article the manufacture, sale, or transportation of intoxicating liquors within, the importation thereof into, or the exportation thereof from the United States and all territory subject to the jurisdiction thereof for beverage purposes is hereby prohibited.

2. The Congress and the several States shall have concurrent power to enforce this article by appropriate legislation.

3. This article shall be inoperative unless it shall have been ratified as an amendment to the Constitution by the legislatures of the several States, as provided in the Constitution, within seven years from the date of the submission hereof to the States by the Congress.

Amendment 19

The right of citizens of the United States to vote shall not be denied or abridged by the United States or by any State on account of sex.

Congress shall have power to enforce this article by appropriate legislation.

Amendment 20

1. The terms of the President and Vice President shall end at noon on the 20th day of January, and the terms of Senators and Representatives at noon on the 3d day of January, of the years in which such terms would have ended if this article had not been ratified; and the terms of their successors shall then begin.

2. The Congress shall assemble at least once in every year, and such meeting shall begin at noon on the 3d day of January, unless they shall by law appoint a different day.

3. If, at the time fixed for the beginning of the term of the President, the President elect shall have died, the Vice President elect shall become President. If a President shall not have been chosen before the time fixed for the beginning of his term, or if the President elect shall have failed to qualify, then the Vice President elect shall act as President until a President shall have qualified; and the Congress may by law provide for the case wherein neither a President elect nor a Vice President elect shall have qualified, declaring who shall then act as President, or the manner in which one who is to act shall be selected, and such person shall act accordingly until a President or Vice President shall have qualified.

4. The Congress may by law provide for the case of the death of any of the persons from whom the House of Representatives may choose a President whenever the right of choice shall have devolved upon them, and for the case of the death of any of the persons from whom the Senate may

choose a Vice President whenever the right of choice shall have devolved upon them.

5. Sections 1 and 2 shall take effect on the 15th day of October following the ratification of this article.

6. This article shall be inoperative unless it shall have been ratified as an amendment to the Constitution by the legislatures of three-fourths of the several States within seven years from the date of its submission.

Amendment 21
1. The eighteenth article of amendment to the Constitution of the United States is hereby repealed.

2. The transportation or importation into any State, Territory, or possession of the United States for delivery or use therein of intoxicating liquors, in violation of the laws thereof, is hereby prohibited.

3. The article shall be inoperative unless it shall have been ratified as an amendment to the Constitution by conventions in the several States, as provided in the Constitution, within seven years from the date of the submission hereof to the States by the Congress.

Amendment 22
1. No person shall be elected to the office of the President more than twice, and no person who has held the office of President, or acted as President, for more than two years of a term to which some other person was elected President shall be elected to the office of the President more than once. But this Article shall not apply to any person holding the office of President, when this Article was proposed by the Congress, and shall not prevent any person who may be holding the office of President, or acting as President, during the term within which this Article becomes operative from holding the office of President or acting as President during the remainder of such term.

2. This article shall be inoperative unless it shall have been ratified as an amendment to the Constitution by the legislatures of three-fourths of the several States within seven years from the date of its submission to the States by the Congress.

Amendment 23
1. The District constituting the seat of Government of the United States shall appoint in such manner as the Congress may direct: A number of electors of President and Vice President equal to the whole number of Senators and Representatives in Congress to which the District would be entitled if it were a State, but in no event more than the least populous State; they shall be in addition to those appointed by the States, but they shall be considered, for the purposes of the election of President and Vice President, to be electors appointed by a State; and they shall meet in the District and perform such duties as provided by the twelfth article of amendment.

2. The Congress shall have power to enforce this article by appropriate legislation.

Amendment 24

1. The right of citizens of the United States to vote in any primary or other election for President or Vice President, for electors for President or Vice President, or for Senator or Representative in Congress, shall not be denied or abridged by the United States or any State by reason of failure to pay any poll tax or other tax.

2. The Congress shall have power to enforce this article by appropriate legislation.

Amendment 25

1. In case of the removal of the President from office or of his death or resignation, the Vice President shall become President.

2. Whenever there is a vacancy in the office of the Vice President, the President shall nominate a Vice President who shall take office upon confirmation by a majority vote of both Houses of Congress.

3. Whenever the President transmits to the President pro tempore of the Senate and the Speaker of the House of Representatives his written declaration that he is unable to discharge the powers and duties of his office, and until he transmits to them a written declaration to the contrary, such powers and duties shall be discharged by the Vice President as Acting President.

4. Whenever the Vice President and a majority of either the principal officers of the executive departments or of such other body as Congress may by law provide, transmit to the President pro tempore of the Senate and the Speaker of the House of Representatives their written declaration that the President is unable to discharge the powers and duties of his office, the Vice President shall immediately assume the powers and duties of the office as Acting President.

Thereafter, when the President transmits to the President pro tempore of the Senate and the Speaker of the House of Representatives his written declaration that no inability exists, he shall resume the powers and duties of his office unless the Vice President and a majority of either the principal officers of the executive department or of such other body as Congress may by law provide, transmit within four days to the President pro tempore of the Senate and the Speaker of the House of Representatives their written declaration that the President is unable to discharge the powers and duties of his office. Thereupon Congress shall decide the issue, assembling within forty eight hours for that purpose if not in session. If the Congress, within twenty one days after receipt of the latter written declaration, or, if Congress is not in session, within twenty one days after Congress is required to assemble, determines by two thirds vote of both Houses that the President is unable to discharge the powers and duties of his office, the Vice President shall continue to discharge the same as Acting President; otherwise, the President shall resume the powers and duties of his office.

Amendment 26

1. The right of citizens of the United States, who are eighteen years of age or

older, to vote shall not be denied or abridged by the United States or by any State on account of age.

2. The Congress shall have power to enforce this article by appropriate legislation.

Amendment 27

No law, varying the compensation for the services of the Senators and Representatives, shall take effect, until an election of Representatives shall have intervened.

APPENDIX C

DECLARATION OF INDEPENDENCE

IN CONGRESS, JULY 4, 1776
The unanimous Declaration of the thirteen united States of America

When in the Course of human events it becomes necessary for one people to dissolve the political bands which have connected them with another and to assume among the powers of the earth, the separate and equal station to which the Laws of Nature and of Nature's God entitle them, a decent respect to the opinions of mankind requires that they should declare the causes which impel them to the separation.

We hold these truths to be self-evident, that all men are created equal, that they are endowed by their Creator with certain unalienable Rights, that among these are Life, Liberty and the pursuit of Happiness. — That to secure these rights, Governments are instituted among Men, deriving their just powers from the consent of the governed, — That whenever any Form of Government becomes destructive of these ends, it is the Right of the People to alter or to abolish it, and to institute new Government, laying its foundation on such principles and organizing its powers in such form, as to them shall seem most likely to effect their Safety and Happiness. Prudence, indeed, will dictate that Governments long established should not be changed for light and transient causes; and accordingly all experience hath shewn that mankind are more disposed to suffer, while evils are sufferable than to right themselves by abolishing the forms to which they are accustomed. But when a long train of abuses and usurpations, pursuing invariably the same Object evinces a design to reduce them under absolute Despotism, it is their right, it is their duty, to throw off such Government, and to provide new Guards for their future security. — Such has been the patient sufferance of these Colonies; and such is now the necessity which constrains them to alter their former Systems of Government. The history of the present King of Great Britain is a history of repeated injuries and usurpations, all having in direct object the establishment of an absolute Tyranny over these States. To prove this, let Facts be submitted to a candid world.

He has refused his Assent to Laws, the most wholesome and necessary for the public good.

He has forbidden his Governors to pass Laws of immediate and pressing importance, unless suspended in their operation till his Assent should be obtained; and when so suspended, he has utterly neglected to attend to them.

He has refused to pass other Laws for the accommodation of large districts of people, unless those people would relinquish the right of Representation in the Legislature, a right inestimable to them and formidable to tyrants only.

He has called together legislative bodies at places unusual, uncomfortable, and distant from the depository of their Public Records, for the sole purpose of fatiguing them into compliance with his measures.

He has dissolved Representative Houses repeatedly, for opposing with manly firmness his invasions on the rights of the people.

He has refused for a long time, after such dissolutions, to cause others to be elected, whereby the Legislative Powers, incapable of Annihilation, have returned to the People at large for their exercise; the State remaining in the mean time exposed to all the dangers of invasion from without, and convulsions within.

He has endeavoured to prevent the population of these States; for that purpose obstructing the Laws for Naturalization of Foreigners; refusing to pass others to encourage their migrations hither, and raising the conditions of new Appropriations of Lands.

He has obstructed the Administration of Justice by refusing his Assent to Laws for establishing Judiciary Powers.

He has made Judges dependent on his Will alone for the tenure of their offices, and the amount and payment of their salaries.

He has erected a multitude of New Offices, and sent hither swarms of

Officers to harass our people and eat out their substance.

He has kept among us, in times of peace, Standing Armies without the Consent of our legislatures.

He has affected to render the Military independent of and superior to the Civil Power.

He has combined with others to subject us to a jurisdiction foreign to our constitution, and unacknowledged by our laws; giving his Assent to their Acts of pretended Legislation:

For quartering large bodies of armed troops among us:

For protecting them, by a mock Trial from punishment for any Murders which they should commit on the Inhabitants of these States:

For cutting off our Trade with all parts of the world:

For imposing Taxes on us without our Consent:

For depriving us in many cases, of the benefit of Trial by Jury:

For transporting us beyond Seas to be tried for pretended offences:

For abolishing the free System of English Laws in a neighbouring Province, establishing therein an Arbitrary government, and enlarging its Boundaries so as to render it at once an example and fit instrument for introducing the same absolute rule into these Colonies

For taking away our Charters, abolishing our most valuable Laws and altering fundamentally the Forms of our Governments:

For suspending our own Legislatures, and declaring themselves invested with power to legislate for us in all cases whatsoever.

He has abdicated Government here, by declaring us out of his Protection and waging War against us.

He has plundered our seas, ravaged our coasts, burnt our towns, and destroyed the lives of our people.

He is at this time transporting large Armies of foreign Mercenaries to compleat the works of death, desolation, and tyranny, already begun with circumstances of Cruelty & Perfidy scarcely paralleled in the most barbarous ages, and totally unworthy the Head of a civilized nation.

He has constrained our fellow Citizens taken Captive on the high Seas to bear

Arms against their Country, to become the executioners of their friends and Brethren, or to fall themselves by their Hands.

He has excited domestic insurrections amongst us, and has endeavoured to bring on the inhabitants of our frontiers, the merciless Indian Savages whose known rule of warfare, is an undistinguished destruction of all ages, sexes and conditions.

In every stage of these Oppressions We have Petitioned for Redress in the most humble terms: Our repeated Petitions have been answered only by repeated injury. A Prince, whose character is thus marked by every act which may define a Tyrant, is unfit to be the ruler of a free people.

Nor have We been wanting in attentions to our British brethren. We have warned them from time to time of attempts by their legislature to extend an unwarrantable jurisdiction over us. We have reminded them of the circumstances of our emigration and settlement here. We have appealed to their native justice and magnanimity, and we have conjured them by the ties of our common kindred to disavow these usurpations, which would inevitably interrupt our connections and correspondence. They too have been deaf to the voice of justice and of consanguinity. We must,

therefore, acquiesce in the necessity, which denounces our Separation, and hold them, as we hold the rest of mankind, Enemies in War, in Peace Friends.

We, therefore, the Representatives of the united States of America, in General Congress, Assembled, appealing to the Supreme Judge of the world for the rectitude of our intentions, do, in the Name, and by Authority of the good People of these Colonies, solemnly publish and declare, That these united Colonies are, and of Right ought to be Free and Independent States, that they are Absolved from all Allegiance to the British Crown, and that all political connection between them and the State of Great Britain, is and ought to be totally dissolved; and that as Free and Independent States, they have full Power to levy War, conclude Peace, contract Alliances, establish Commerce, and to do all other Acts and Things which Independent States may of right do. — And for the support of this Declaration, with a firm reliance on the protection of Divine Providence, we mutually pledge to each other our Lives, our Fortunes, and our sacred Honor.

— John Hancock

New Hampshire:
Josiah Bartlett, William Whipple,
Matthew Thornton

Massachusetts:
John Hancock, Samuel Adams, John
Adams, Robert Treat Paine, Elbridge
Gerry

Rhode Island:
Stephen Hopkins, William Ellery

Connecticut:
Roger Sherman, Samuel Huntington,
William Williams, Oliver Wolcott

New York:
William Floyd, Philip Livingston,
Francis Lewis, Lewis Morris

New Jersey:
Richard Stockton, John
Witherspoon, Francis Hopkinson,
John Hart, Abraham Clark

Pennsylvania:
Robert Morris, Benjamin Rush,
Benjamin Franklin, John Morton,

George Clymer, James Smith,
George Taylor, James Wilson,
George Ross

Delaware:
Caesar Rodney, George Read,
Thomas McKean

Maryland:
Samuel Chase, William Paca,
Thomas Stone, Charles Carroll of
Carrollton

Virginia:
George Wythe, Richard Henry Lee,
Thomas Jefferson, Benjamin
Harrison, Thomas Nelson, Jr.,
Francis Lightfoot Lee, Carter Braxton

North Carolina:
William Hooper, Joseph Hewes, John
Penn

South Carolina:
Edward Rutledge, Thomas Heyward,
Jr., Thomas Lynch, Jr., Arthur
Middleton

Georgia:
Button Gwinnett, Lyman Hall,
George Walton

APPENDIX D

MAGNA CARTA

(The *Magna Carta* was originally written in Latin. This translation was taken from G. R. C. Davis, *Magna Carta*, Revised Edition, British Library, 1989.)

JOHN, by the grace of God King of England, Lord of Ireland, Duke of Normandy and Aquitaine, and Count of Anjou, to his archbishops, bishops, abbots, earls, barons, justices, foresters, sheriffs, stewards, servants, and to all his officials and loyal subjects, Greeting.

KNOW THAT BEFORE GOD, for the health of our soul and those of our ancestors and heirs, to the honour of God, the exaltation of the holy Church, and the better ordering of our kingdom, at the advice of our reverend fathers Stephen, archbishop of Canterbury, primate of all England, and cardinal of the holy Roman Church, Henry archbishop of Dublin, William bishop of London, Peter bishop of Winchester, Jocelin bishop of Bath and Glastonbury, Hugh bishop of Lincoln, Walter Bishop of Worcester, William bishop of Coventry, Benedict bishop of Rochester, Master Pandulf subdeacon and member of the papal household, Brother Aymeric master of the knighthood of the Temple in England, William Marshal earl of Pembroke, William earl of Salisbury, William earl of Warren, William earl of Arundel, Alan de Galloway constable of Scotland, Warin Fitz Gerald, Peter Fitz Herbert, Hubert de Burgh seneschal of Poitou, Hugh de Neville, Matthew Fitz Herbert, Thomas Basset, Alan Basset, Philip Daubeny, Robert de Roppeley, John Marshal, John Fitz Hugh, and other loyal subjects:

(1) FIRST, THAT WE HAVE GRANTED TO GOD, and by this present charter have confirmed for us and our heirs in perpetuity, that the English Church shall be free, and shall have its rights undiminished, and its liberties unimpaired. That we wish this so to be observed, appears from the fact that of our own free will, before the outbreak of the present dispute between us and our barons, we granted and confirmed by charter the freedom of the Church's elections - a right reckoned to be of the

greatest necessity and importance to it - and caused this to be confirmed by Pope Innocent III. This freedom we shall observe ourselves, and desire to be observed in good faith by our heirs in perpetuity.

TO ALL FREE MEN OF OUR KINGDOM we have also granted, for us and our heirs for ever, all the liberties written out below, to have and to keep for them and their heirs, of us and our heirs:

(2) If any earl, baron, or other person that holds lands directly of the Crown, for military service, shall die, and at his death his heir shall be of full age and owe a 'relief', the heir shall have his inheritance on payment of the ancient scale of 'relief'. That is to say, the heir or heirs of an earl shall pay £100 for the entire earl's barony, the heir or heirs of a knight l00s. at most for the entire knight's 'fee', and any man that owes less shall pay less, in accordance with the ancient usage of 'fees'

(3) But if the heir of such a person is under age and a ward, when he comes of age he shall have his inheritance without 'relief' or fine.

(4) The guardian of the land of an heir who is under age shall take from it only reasonable revenues, customary dues, and feudal services. He shall do this without destruction or damage to men or property. If we have given the guardianship of the land to a sheriff, or to any person answerable to us for the revenues, and he commits destruction or damage, we will exact compensation from him, and the land shall be entrusted to two worthy and prudent men of the same 'fee', who shall be answerable to us for the revenues, or to the person to whom we have assigned them. If we have given or sold to anyone the guardianship of such land, and he causes destruction or damage, he shall lose the guardianship of it, and it shall be handed over to two worthy and prudent men of the same 'fee', who shall be similarly answerable to us.

(5) For so long as a guardian has guardianship of such land, he shall maintain the houses, parks, fish preserves, ponds, mills, and everything else pertaining to it, from the revenues of the land itself. When the heir comes of age, he shall restore the whole land to him, stocked with plough teams and such implements of husbandry as the season demands and the revenues from the land can reasonably bear.

(6) Heirs may be given in marriage, but not to someone of lower social standing. Before a marriage takes place, it shall be' made known to the heir's next-of-kin.

(7) At her husband's death, a widow may have her marriage portion and inheritance at once and without trouble. She shall pay nothing for her dower, marriage portion, or any inheritance that she and her husband held jointly on the day of his death. She may remain in her husband's house for forty days after his death, and within this period her dower shall be assigned to her.

(8) No widow shall be compelled to marry, so long as she wishes to remain without a husband. But she must give security that

she will not marry without royal consent, if she holds her lands of the Crown, or without the consent of whatever other lord she may hold them of.

(9) Neither we nor our officials will seize any land or rent in payment of a debt, so long as the debtor has movable goods sufficient to discharge the debt. A debtor's sureties shall not be distrained upon so long as the debtor himself can discharge his debt. If, for lack of means, the debtor is unable to discharge his debt, his sureties shall be answerable for it. If they so desire, they may have the debtor's lands and rents until they have received satisfaction for the debt that they paid for him, unless the debtor can show that he has settled his obligations to them.

(10) If anyone who has borrowed a sum of money from Jews dies before the debt has been repaid, his heir shall pay no interest on the debt for so long as he remains under age, irrespective of whom he holds his lands. If such a debt falls into the hands of the Crown, it will take nothing except the principal sum specified in the bond.

(11) If a man dies owing money to Jews, his wife may have her dower and pay nothing towards the debt from it. If he leaves children that are under age, their needs may also be provided for on a scale appropriate to the size of his holding of lands. The debt is to be paid out of the residue, reserving the service due to his feudal lords. Debts owed to persons other than Jews are to be dealt with similarly.

(12) No 'scutage' or 'aid' may be levied in our kingdom without its general consent, unless it is for the ransom of our person, to make our eldest son a knight, and (once) to marry our eldest daughter. For these purposes ouly a reasonable 'aid' may be levied. 'Aids' from the city of London are to be treated similarly.

(13) The city of London shall enjoy all its ancient liberties and free customs, both by land and by water. We also will and grant that all other cities, boroughs, towns, and ports shall enjoy all their liberties and free customs.

(14) To obtain the general consent of the realm for the assessment of an 'aid' - except in the three cases specified above - or a 'scutage', we will cause the archbishops, bishops, abbots, earls, and greater barons to be summoned individually by letter. To those who hold lands directly of us we will cause a general summons to be issued, through the sheriffs and other officials, to come together on a fixed day (of which at least forty days notice shall be given) and at a fixed place. In all letters of summons, the cause of the summons will be stated. When a summons has been issued, the business appointed for the day shall go forward in accordance with the resolution of those present, even if not all those who were summoned have appeared.

(15) In future we will allow no one to levy an 'aid' from his free men, except to ransom his person, to make his eldest son a knight, and (once) to marry his eldest daughter. For these purposes only a reasonable 'aid' may be levied.

(16) No man shall be forced to perform more service for a knight's 'fee', or other free holding of land, than is due from it.

(17) Ordinary lawsuits shall not follow the royal court around, but shall be held in a fixed place.

(18) Inquests of novel disseisin, mort d'ancestor, and darrein presentment shall be taken only in their proper county court. We ourselves, or in our absence abroad our chief justice, will send two justices to each county four times a year, and these justices, with four knights of the county elected by the county itself, shall hold the assizes in the county court, on the day and in the place where the court meets.

(19) If any assizes cannot be taken on the day of the county court, as many knights and freeholders shall afterwards remain behind, of those who have attended the court, as will suffice for the administration of justice, having regard to the volume of business to be done.

(20) For a trivial offence, a free man shall be fined only in proportion to the degree of his offence, and for a serious offence correspondingly, but not so heavily as to deprive him of his livelihood. In the same way, a merchant shall be spared his merchandise, and a husbandman the implements of his husbandry, if they fall upon the mercy of a royal court. None of these fines shall be imposed except by the assessment on oath of reputable men of the neighbourhood.

(21) Earls and barons shall be fined only by their equals, and in proportion to the gravity of their offence.

(22) A fine imposed upon the lay property of a clerk in holy orders shall be assessed upon the same principles, without reference to the value of his ecclesiastical benefice.

(23) No town or person shall be forced to build bridges over rivers except those with an ancient obligation to do so.

(24) No sheriff, constable, coroners, or other royal officials are to hold lawsuits that should be held by the royal justices.

(25) Every county, hundred, wapentake, and tithing shall remain at its ancient rent, without increase, except the royal demesne manors.

(26) If at the death of a man who holds a lay 'fee' of the Crown, a sheriff or royal official produces royal letters patent of summons for a debt due to the Crown, it shall be lawful for them to seize and list movable goods found in the lay 'fee' of the dead man to the value of the debt, as assessed by worthy men. Nothing shall be removed until the whole debt is paid, when the residue shall be given over to the executors to carry out the dead man s will. If no debt is due to the Crown, all the movable goods shall be regarded as the property of the dead man, except the reasonable shares of his wife and children.

(27) If a free man dies intestate, his movable goods are to be distributed by his next-of-kin and friends, under the

supervision of the Church. The rights of his debtors are to be preserved.

(28) No constable or other royal official shall take corn or other movable goods from any man without immediate payment, unless the seller voluntarily offers postponement of this.

(29) No constable may compel a knight to pay money for castle-guard if the knight is willing to undertake the guard in person, or with reasonable excuse to supply some other fit man to do it. A knight taken or sent on military service shall be excused from castle-guard for the period of this servlce.

(30) No sheriff, royal official, or other person shall take horses or carts for transport from any free man, without his consent.

(31) Neither we nor any royal official will take wood for our castle, or for any other purpose, without the consent of the owner.

(32) We will not keep the lands of people convicted of felony in our hand for longer than a year and a day, after which they shall be returned to the lords of the `fees' concerned.

(33) All fish-weirs shall be removed from the Thames, the Medway, and throughout the whole of England, except on the sea coast.

(34) The writ called precipe shall not in future be issued to anyone in respect of any holding of land, if a free man could thereby be deprived of the right of trial in his own lord's court.

(35) There shall be standard measures of wine, ale, and corn (the London quarter), throughout the kingdom. There shall also be a standard width of dyed cloth, russett, and haberject, namely two ells within the selvedges. Weights are to be standardised similarly.

(36) In future nothing shall be paid or accepted for the issue of a writ of inquisition of life or limbs. It shall be given gratis, and not refused.

(37) If a man holds land of the Crown by `fee-farm', `socage', or `burgage', and also holds land of someone else for knight's service, we will not have guardianship of his heir, nor of the land that belongs to the other person's `fee', by virtue of the `fee-farm', `socage', or `burgage', unless the `fee-farm' owes knight's service. We will not have the guardianship of a man's heir, or of land that he holds of someone else, by reason of any small property that he may hold of the Crown for a service of knives, arrows, or the like.

(38) In future no official shall place a man on trial upon his own unsupported statement, without producing credible witnesses to the truth of it.

(39) No free man shall be seized or imprisoned, or stripped of his rights or possessions, or outlawed or exiled, or deprived of his standing in any other way, nor will we proceed with force against him, or send others to do so, except by the

lawful judgement of his equals or by the law of the land.

(40) To no one will we sell, to no one deny or delay right or justice.

(41) All merchants may enter or leave England unharmed and without fear, and may stay or travel within it, by land or water, for purposes of trade, free from all illegal exactions, in accordance with ancient and lawful customs. This, however, does not apply in time of war to merchants from a country that is at war with us. Any such merchants found in our country at the outbreak of war shall be detained without injury to their persons or property, until we or our chief justice have discovered how our own merchants are being treated in the country at war with us. If our own merchants are safe they shall be safe too.

(42) In future it shall be lawful for any man to leave and return to our kingdom unharmed and without fear, by land or water, preserving his allegiance to us, except in time of war, for some short period, for the common benefit of the realm. People that have been imprisoned or outlawed in accordance with the law of the land, people from a country that is at war with us, and merchants - who shall be dealt with as stated above - are excepted from this provision.

(43) If a man holds lands of any `escheat' such as the `honour' of Wallingford, Nottingham, Boulogne, Lancaster, or of other `escheats' in our hand that are baronies, at his death his heir shall give us only the `relief' and service that he would

have made to the baron, had the barony been in the baron's hand. We will hold the `escheat' in the same manner as the baron held it.

(44) People who live outside the forest need not in future appear before the royal justices of the forest in answer to general summonses, unless they are actually involved in proceedings or are sureties for someone who has been seized for a forest offence.

(45) We will appoint as justices, constables, sheriffs, or other officials, only men that know the law of the realm and are minded to keep it well.

(46) All barons who have founded abbeys, and have charters of English kings or ancient tenure as evidence of this, may have guardianship of them when there is no abbot, as is their due.

(47) All forests that have been created in our reign shall at once be disafforested. River-banks that have been enclosed in our reign shall be treated similarly.

(48) All evil customs relating to forests and warrens, foresters, warreners, sheriffs and their servants, or river-banks and their wardens, are at once to be investigated in every county by twelve sworn knights of the county, and within forty days of their enquiry the evil customs are to be abolished completely and irrevocably. But we, or our chief justice if we are not in England, are first to be informed.

(49) We will at once return all hostages and charters delivered up to us by

Englishmen as security for peace or for loyal service.

(50) We will remove completely from their offices the kinsmen of Gerard de Athée, and in future they shall hold no offices in England. The people in question are Engelard de Cigogné', Peter, Guy, and Andrew de Chanceaux, Guy de Cigogné, Geoffrey de Martigny and his brothers, Philip Marc and his brothers, with Geoffrey his nephew, and all their followers.

(51) As soon as peace is restored, we will remove from the kingdom all the foreign knights, bowmen, their attendants, and the mercenaries that have come to it, to its harm, with horses and arms.

(52) To any man whom we have deprived or dispossessed of lands, castles, liberties, or rights, without the lawful judgement of his equals, we will at once restore these. In cases of dispute the matter shall be resolved by the judgement of the twenty-five barons referred to below in the clause for securing the peace (§ 61). In cases, however, where a man was deprived or dispossessed of something without the lawful judgement of his equals by our father King Henry or our brother King Richard, and it remains in our hands or is held by others under our warranty, we shall have respite for the period commonly allowed to Crusaders, unless a lawsuit had been begun, or an enquiry had been made at our order, before we took the Cross as a Crusader. On our return from the Crusade, or if we abandon it, we will at once render justice in full.

(53) We shall have similar respite in rendering justice in connexion with forests that are to be disafforested, or to remain forests, when these were first a-orested by our father Henry or our brother Richard; with the guardianship of lands in another person's `fee', when we have hitherto had this by virtue of a `fee' held of us for knight's service by a third party; and with abbeys founded in another person's `fee', in which the lord of the `fee' claims to own a right. On our return from the Crusade, or if we abandon it, we will at once do full justice to complaints about these matters.

(54) No one shall be arrested or imprisoned on the appeal of a woman for the death of any person except her husband.

(55) All fines that have been given to us unjustiy and against the law of the land, and all fines that we have exacted unjustly, shall be entirely remitted or the matter decided by a majority judgement of the twenty-five barons referred to below in the clause for securing the peace (§ 61) together with Stephen, archbishop of Canterbury, if he can be present, and such others as he wishes to bring with him. If the archbishop cannot be present, proceedings shall continue without him, provided that if any of the twenty-five barons has been involved in a similar suit himself, his judgement shall be set aside, and someone else chosen and sworn in his place, as a substitute for the single occasion, by the rest of the twenty-five.

(56) If we have deprived or dispossessed any Welshmen of lands, liberties, or anything else in England or in Wales,

without the lawful judgement of their equals, these are at once to be returned to them. A dispute on this point shall be determined in the Marches by the judgement of equals. English law shall apply to holdings of land in England, Welsh law to those in Wales, and the law of the Marches to those in the Marches. The Welsh shall treat us and ours in the same way.

(57) In cases where a Welshman was deprived or dispossessed of anything, without the lawful judgement of his equals, by our father King Henry or our brother King Richard, and it remains in our hands or is held by others under our warranty, we shall have respite for the period commonly allowed to Crusaders, unless a lawsuit had been begun, or an enquiry had been made at our order, before we took the Cross as a Crusader. But on our return from the Crusade, or if we abandon it, we will at once do full justice according to the laws of Wales and the said regions.

(58) We will at once return the son of Llywelyn, all Welsh hostages, and the charters delivered to us as security for the peace.

(59) With regard to the return of the sisters and hostages of Alexander, king of Scotland, his liberties and his rights, we will treat him in the same way as our other barons of England, unless it appears from the charters that we hold from his father William, formerly king of Scotland, that he should be treated otherwise. This matter

shall be resolved by the judgement of his equals in our court.

(60) All these customs and liberties that we have granted shall be observed in our kingdom in so far as concerns our own relations with our subjects. Let all men of our kingdom, whether clergy or laymen, observe them similarly in their relations with their own men.

(61) SINCE WE HAVE GRANTED ALL THESE THINGS for God, for the better ordering of our kingdom, and to allay the discord that has arisen between us and our barons, and since we desire that they shall be enjoyed in their entirety, with lasting strength, for ever, we give and grant to the barons the following security:

The barons shall elect twenty-five of their number to keep, and cause to be observed with all their might, the peace and liberties granted and confirmed to them by this charter.

If we, our chief justice, our officials, or any of our servants offend in any respect against any man, or transgress any of the articles of the peace or of this security, and the offence is made known to four of the said twenty-five barons, they shall come to us - or in our absence from the kingdom to the chief justice - to declare it and claim immediate redress. If we, or in our absence abroad the chief justice, make no redress within forty days, reckoning from the day on which the offence was declared to us or to him, the four barons shall refer the matter to the rest of the twenty-five barons, who may distrain upon and assail us in every way possible, with the support of the whole community of the land, by seizing our castles, lands, possessions, or anything else saving only our own person and those of the queen and our children, until they have secured such redress as they have determined upon. Having secured the redress, they may then resume their normal obedience to us.

Any man who so desires may take an oath to obey the commands of the twenty-five barons for the achievement of these ends, and to join with them in assailing us to the utmost of his power. We give public and free permission to take this oath to any man who so desires, and at no time will we prohibit any man from taking it. Indeed, we will compel any of our subjects who are unwilling to take it to swear it at our command.

If-one of the twenty-five barons dies or leaves the country, or is prevented in any other way from discharging his duties, the rest of them shall choose another baron in his place, at their discretion, who shall be duly sworn in as they were.

In the event of disagreement among the twenty-five barons on any matter referred to them for decision, the verdict of the majority present shall have the same validity as a unanimous verdict of the whole twenty-five, whether these were all present or some of those summoned were unwilling or unable to appear.

The twenty-five barons shall swear to obey all the above articles faithfully, and shall cause them to be obeyed by others to the best of their power.

We will not seek to procure from anyone, either by our own efforts or those of a third party, anything by which any part of these concessions or liberties might be revoked or diminished. Should such a thing be procured, it shall be null and void and we will at no time make use of it, either ourselves or through a third party.

(62) We have remitted and pardoned fully to all men any ill-will, hurt, or grudges that have arisen between us and our subjects, whether clergy or laymen, since the beginning of the dispute. We have in addition remitted fully, and for our own part have also pardoned, to all clergy and laymen any offences committed as a result of the said dispute between Easter in the sixteenth year of our reign (i.e. 1215) and the restoration of peace.

In addition we have caused letters patent to be made for the barons, bearing witness to this security and to the concessions set out above, over the seals of Stephen archbishop of Canterbury, Henry archbishop of Dublin, the other bishops named above, and Master Pandulf.

(63) IT IS ACCORDINGLY OUR WISH AND COMMAND that the English Church shall be free, and that men in our kingdom shall have and keep all these liberties, rights, and concessions, well and peaceably in their fulness and entirety for them and their heirs, of us and our heirs, in all things and all places for ever.

Both we and the barons have sworn that all this shall be observed in good faith and without deceit. Witness the abovementioned people and many others.

Given by our hand in the meadow that is called Runnymede, between Windsor and Staines, on the fifteenth day of June in the seventeenth year of our reign (i.e. 1215: the new regnal year began on 28 May).

.

MONROE DOCTRINE

From President James Monroe's seventh annual message to Congress, December 2, 1823:

At the proposal of the Russian Imperial Government, made through the minister of the Emperor residing here, a full power and instructions have been transmitted to the Minister of the United States at St. Petersburgh to arrange, by amicable negotiation, the respective rights and interests of the two nations on the northwest coast of this continent. A similar proposal has been made by His Imperial Majesty to the Government of Great Britain, which has likewise been acceded to. The Government of the United States has been desirous, by this friendly proceeding, of manifesting the great value which they have invariably attached to the friendship of the Emperor, and their solicitude to cultivate the best understanding with his Government. In the discussions to which this interest has given rise, and in the arrangements by which they may terminate the occasion has been judged proper for asserting, as a principle in which the rights and interests of the United States are involved, that the American continents, by the free and independent condition which they have assumed and maintain, are henceforth not to be considered as subjects for future colonization by any European powers....

It was stated at the commencement of the last session that a great effort was then making in Spain and Portugal, to improve the condition of the people of those countries, and that it appeared to be conducted with extraordinary moderation. It need scarcely be remarked, that the result has been, so far, very different from what was then anticipated. Of events in that quarter of the globe, with which we have so much intercourse, and from which we derive our origin, we have always been anxious and interested spectators. The citizens of the United States cherish sentiments the most friendly, in favor of the liberty and happiness of their fellow men on that side of the Atlantic. In the wars of the European powers, in matters relating to themselves, we have never taken any part, nor does it comport with our policy to do so. It is only when our rights are invaded, or seriously menaced, that we resent injuries, or make preparation for our defence. With the movements in this hemisphere, we are, of necessity, more immediately connected, and by causes which must be obvious to all enlightened and impartial observers. The political system of the allied powers is essentially different, in this respect, from that of America. This difference proceeds from that which exists in their respective governments. And to the defence of our own, which has been achieved by the loss of so much blood and treasure, and matured by the wisdom of their most enlightened citizens, and under which we have enjoyed unexampled felicity, this whole nation is devoted. We owe it, therefore, to candor, and to the amicable relations existing between the United States and those powers, to declare, that we should consider any attempt on their part to extend their system to any portion of this hemisphere, as dangerous to our peace and safety. With the existing colonies or dependencies of any European power we have not interfered, and shall not interfere. But with the governments who have declared their independence, and maintained it, and whose independence we have, on great consideration, and on just principles, acknowledged, we could not view any interposition for the purpose of oppressing them, or controlling, in any other manner, their destiny, by any European power in any other light than as the manifestation of an unfriendly disposition towards the United States. In the war between those new governments and Spain we declared our neutrality at the time of their

recognition, and to this we have adhered, and shall continue to adhere, provided no change shall occur, which, in the judgement of the competent authorities of this government, shall make a corresponding change, on the part of the United States, indispensable to their security.

The late events in Spain and Portugal, shew that Europe is still unsettled. Of this important fact, no stronger proof can be adduced than that the allied powers should have thought it proper, on any principle satisfactory to themselves, to have interposed, by force, in the internal concerns of Spain. To what extent such interposition may be carried, on the same principle, is a question, to which all independent powers, whose governments differ from theirs, are interested; even those most remote, and surely none more so than the United States. Our policy, in regard to Europe, which was adopted at an early stage of the wars which have so long agitated that quarter of the globe, nevertheless remains the same, which is, not to interfere in the internal concerns of any of its powers; to consider the government de facto as the legitimate government for us; to cultivate friendly relations with it, and to preserve those relations by a frank, firm, and manly policy; meeting, in all instances, the just claims of every power; submitting to injuries from none. But, in regard to these continents, circumstances are eminently and conspicuously different. It is impossible that the allied powers should extend their political system to any portion of either continent, without endangering our peace and happiness: nor can any one believe that our Southern Brethren, if left to themselves, would adopt it of their own accord. It is equally impossible, therefore, that we should behold such interposition, in any form, with indifference. If we look to the comparative strength and resources of Spain and those new governments, and their distance from each other, it must be obvious that she can never subdue them. It is still the true policy of the United States to leave the parties to themselves, in the hope that other powers will pursue the same course.

EMANCIPATION PROCLAMATION

The Emancipation Proclamation
January 1, 1863

By the President of the United States of America:

A Proclamation.

Whereas, on the twenty-second day of September, in the year of our Lord one thousand eight hundred and sixty-two, a proclamation was issued by the President of the United States, containing, among other things, the following, to wit:

"That on the first day of January, in the year of our Lord one thousand eight hundred and sixty-three, all persons held as slaves within any State or designated part of a State, the people whereof shall then be in rebellion against the United States, shall be then, thenceforward, and forever free; and the Executive Government of the United States, including the military and naval authority thereof, will recognize and maintain the freedom of such persons, and will do no act or acts to repress such persons, or any of them, in any efforts they may make for their actual freedom.

"That the Executive will, on the first day of January aforesaid, by proclamation, designate the States and parts of States, if any, in which the people thereof, respectively, shall then be in rebellion against the United States; and the fact that any State, or the people thereof, shall on that day be, in good faith, represented in the Congress of the United States by members chosen thereto at elections wherein a majority of the qualified voters of such State shall have participated, shall, in the absence of strong countervailing testimony, be deemed conclusive evidence that such State, and the people thereof, are not then in rebellion against the United States."

Now, therefore I, Abraham Lincoln, President of the United States, by virtue of the power in me vested as Commander-in-Chief, of the Army and Navy of the United States in time of actual armed rebellion against the authority and government of the United States, and as a fit and necessary war measure for suppressing said rebellion, do, on this first day of January, in the year of our Lord one thousand eight hundred and sixty-three, and in accordance with my purpose so to do publicly proclaimed for the full period of one hundred days, from the day first above mentioned, order and designate as the States and parts of States wherein the people thereof respectively, are this day in rebellion against the United States, the following, to wit:

Arkansas, Texas, Louisiana, (except the Parishes of St. Bernard, Plaquemines, Jefferson, St. John, St. Charles, St. James Ascension, Assumption, Terrebonne, Lafourche, St. Mary, St. Martin, and Orleans, including the City of New Orleans) Mississippi, Alabama, Florida, Georgia, South Carolina, North Carolina, and Virginia, (except the forty-eight counties designated as West Virginia, and also the counties of Berkley, Accomac, Northampton, Elizabeth City, York, Princess Ann, and Norfolk, including the cities of Norfolk and Portsmouth[)], and which excepted parts, are for the present, left precisely as if this proclamation were not issued.

And by virtue of the power, and for the purpose aforesaid, I do order and declare that all persons held as slaves within said designated States, and parts of States, are, and henceforward shall be free; and that the Executive government of the United States, including the military and naval authorities thereof, will recognize and maintain the freedom of said persons.

And I hereby enjoin upon the people so declared to be free to abstain from all violence, unless in necessary self-defence; and I recommend to them that, in all cases when allowed, they labor faithfully for reasonable wages.

And I further declare and make known, that such persons of suitable condition, will be received into the armed service of the United States to garrison forts, positions, stations, and other places, and to man vessels of all sorts in said service.

And upon this act, sincerely believed to be an act of justice, warranted by the Constitution, upon military necessity, I invoke the considerate judgment of mankind, and the gracious favor of Almighty God.

In witness whereof, I have hereunto set my hand and caused the seal of the United States to be affixed.

Done at the City of Washington, this first day of January, in the year of our Lord one thousand eight hundred and sixty three, and of the Independence of the United States of America the eighty-seventh.

By the President: ABRAHAM LINCOLN WILLIAM H. SEWARD, Secretary of State.

American Presidents

18th Century

    1. George Washington   2. John Adams

19th Century

3. Thomas Jefferson	15. James Buchanan
4. James Madison	16. Abraham Lincoln
5. James Monroe	17. Andrew Johnson
6. John Quincy Adams	18. Ulysses S. Grant
7. Andrew Jackson	19. Rutherford B. Hayes
8. Martin Van Buren	20. James Garfield
9. William Henry Harrison	21. Chester A. Arthur
10. John Tyler	22. Grover Cleveland
11. James K. Polk	23. Benjamin Harrison
12. Zachary Taylor	24. Grover Cleveland
13. Millard Fillmore	25. William McKinley
14. Franklin Pierce	

20th Century

26. Theodore Roosevelt	35. John F. Kennedy
27. William Howard Taft	36. Lyndon B. Johnson
28. Woodrow Wilson	37. Richard M. Nixon
29. Warren G. Harding	38. Gerald R. Ford
30. Calvin Coolidge	39. James Carter
31. Herbert Hoover	40. Ronald Reagan
32. Franklin D. Roosevelt	41. George H. W. Bush
33. Harry S. Truman	42. William J. Clinton
34. Dwight D. Eisenhower	

21st Century

    43. George W. Bush   44. Barack Obama

NORTH ATLANTIC
TREATY ORGANIZATION

The North Atlantic Treaty
Washington D.C. - 4 April 1949

The Parties to this Treaty reaffirm their faith in the purposes and principles of the Charter of the United Nations and their desire to live in peace with all peoples and all governments.

They are determined to safeguard the freedom, common heritage and civilisation of their peoples, founded on the principles of democracy, individual liberty and the rule of law. They seek to promote stability and well-being in the North Atlantic area.

They are resolved to unite their efforts for collective defence and for the preservation of peace and security. They therefore agree to this North Atlantic Treaty :

Article 1

The Parties undertake, as set forth in the Charter of the United Nations, to settle any international dispute in which they may be involved by peaceful means in such a manner that international peace and security and justice are not endangered, and to refrain in their international relations from the threat or use of force in any manner inconsistent with the purposes of the United Nations.

Article 2

The Parties will contribute toward the further development of peaceful and friendly international relations by strengthening their free institutions, by bringing about a better understanding of the principles upon which these institutions are founded, and by promoting conditions of stability and well-being. They will seek to eliminate conflict in their international economic policies and will encourage economic collaboration between any or all of them.

Article 3

In order more effectively to achieve the objectives of this Treaty, the Parties, separately and jointly, by means of continuous and effective self-help and mutual aid, will maintain and develop their individual and collective capacity to resist armed attack.

Article 4

The Parties will consult together whenever, in the opinion of any of them, the territorial integrity, political independence or security of any of the Parties is threatened.

Article 5

The Parties agree that an armed attack against one or more of them in Europe or North America shall be considered an attack against them all and consequently they agree that, if such an armed attack occurs, each of them, in exercise of the right of individual or collective self-defence recognised by Article 51 of the Charter of the United Nations, will assist the Party or Parties so attacked by taking forthwith, individually and in concert with the other Parties, such action as it deems necessary, including the use of armed force, to restore and maintain the security of the North Atlantic area.

Any such armed attack and all measures taken as a result thereof shall immediately be reported to the Security Council. Such measures shall be terminated when the Security Council has taken the measures necessary to restore and maintain international peace and security .

Article 6 (1)

For the purpose of Article 5, an armed attack on one or more of the Parties is deemed to include an armed attack:

on the territory of any of the Parties in Europe or North America, on the Algerian Departments of France (2), on the territory of or on the Islands under the jurisdiction of any of the Parties in the North Atlantic area north of the Tropic of Cancer; on the forces, vessels, or aircraft of any of the Parties, when in or over these territories or any other area in Europe in which occupation forces of any of the Parties were stationed on the date when the Treaty entered into force or the Mediterranean Sea or the North Atlantic area north of the Tropic of Cancer.

Article 7

This Treaty does not affect, and shall not be interpreted as affecting in any way the rights and obligations under the Charter of the Parties which are members of the United Nations, or the primary responsibility of the Security Council for the maintenance of international peace and security.

Article 8

Each Party declares that none of the international engagements now in force between it and any other of the Parties or any third State is in conflict with the provisions of this Treaty, and undertakes not to enter into any international engagement in conflict with this Treaty.

Article 9

The Parties hereby establish a Council, on which each of them shall be represented, to consider matters concerning the implementation of this Treaty. The Council shall be so organised as to be able to meet promptly at any time. The Council shall set up such subsidiary bodies as may be necessary; in particular it shall establish immediately a defence committee which shall recommend measures for the implementation of Articles 3 and 5.

Article 10

The Parties may, by unanimous agreement, invite any other European State in a position to further the principles of this Treaty and to contribute to the security of the North Atlantic area to accede to this Treaty. Any State so invited may become a Party to the Treaty by depositing its instrument of accession with the Government of the United States of America. The Government of the United States of America will inform each of the Parties of the deposit of each such instrument of accession.

Article 11

This Treaty shall be ratified and its provisions carried out by the Parties in accordance with their respective constitutional processes. The instruments of ratification shall be deposited as soon as possible with the Government of the United States of America, which will notify all the other signatories of each deposit. The Treaty shall enter into force between the States which have ratified it as soon as the ratifications of the majority of the signatories, including the ratifications of Belgium, Canada, France, Luxembourg, the Netherlands, the United Kingdom and the United States, have been deposited and

shall come into effect with respect to other States on the date of the deposit of their ratifications. (3)

Article 12

After the Treaty has been in force for ten years, or at any time thereafter, the Parties shall, if any of them so requests, consult together for the purpose of reviewing the Treaty, having regard for the factors then affecting peace and security in the North Atlantic area, including the development of universal as well as regional arrangements under the Charter of the United Nations for the maintenance of international peace and security.

Article 13

After the Treaty has been in force for twenty years, any Party may cease to be a Party one year after its notice of denunciation has been given to the Government of the United States of America, which will inform the Governments of the other Parties of the deposit of each notice of denunciation.

Article 14

This Treaty, of which the English and French texts are equally authentic, shall be deposited in the archives of the Government of the United States of America. Duly certified copies will be transmitted by that Government to the Governments of other signatories.

REPUBLICAN CONTRACT
WITH AMERICA

As Republican Members of the House of Representatives and as citizens seeking to join that body we propose not just to change its policies, but even more important, to restore the bonds of trust between the people and their elected representatives.

That is why, in this era of official evasion and posturing, we offer instead a detailed agenda for national renewal, a written commitment with no fine print.

This year's election offers the chance, after four decades of one-party control, to bring to the House a new majority that will transform the way Congress works. That historic change would be the end of government that is too big, too intrusive, and too easy with the public's money. It can be the beginning of a Congress that respects the values and shares the faith of the American family.

Like Lincoln, our first Republican president, we intend to act "with firmness in the right, as God gives us to see the right." To restore accountability to Congress. To end its cycle of scandal and disgrace. To make us all proud again of the way free people govern themselves.

On the first day of the 104th Congress, the new Republican majority will immediately pass the following major reforms, aimed at restoring the faith and trust of the American people in their government:

FIRST, require all laws that apply to the rest of the country also apply equally to the Congress;

SECOND, select a major, independent auditing firm to conduct a comprehensive audit of Congress for waste, fraud or abuse;

THIRD, cut the number of House committees, and cut committee staff by one-third;

FOURTH, limit the terms of all committee chairs;

FIFTH, ban the casting of proxy votes in committee;

SIXTH, require committee meetings to be open to the public;

SEVENTH, require a three-fifths majority vote to pass a tax increase;

EIGHTH, guarantee an honest accounting of our Federal Budget by implementing zero base-line budgeting.

Thereafter, within the first 100 days of the 104th Congress, we shall bring to the House Floor the following bills, each to be given full and open debate, each to be given a clear and fair vote and each to be immediately available this day for public inspection and scrutiny.

1. THE FISCAL RESPONSIBILITY ACT: A balanced budget/tax limitation amendment and a legislative line-item veto to restore fiscal responsibility to an out- of-control Congress, requiring them to live under the same budget constraints as families and businesses.

2. THE TAKING BACK OUR STREETS ACT: An anti-crime package including stronger truth-in- sentencing, "good faith" exclusionary rule exemptions, effective death penalty provisions, and cuts in social spending from this summer's "crime" bill to fund prison construction and additional law enforcement to keep people secure in their neighborhoods and kids safe in their schools.

3. THE PERSONAL RESPONSIBILITY ACT: Discourage illegitimacy and teen pregnancy by prohibiting welfare to minor mothers and denying increased AFDC for additional children while on welfare, cut spending for welfare programs, and enact a tough two-years-and-out provision with work requirements to promote individual responsibility.

4. THE FAMILY REINFORCEMENT ACT: Child support enforcement, tax incentives for adoption, strengthening rights of parents in their children's education, stronger child pornography laws, and an elderly dependent care tax credit to reinforce the central role of families in American society.

5. THE AMERICAN DREAM RESTORATION ACT: A S500 per child tax credit, begin repeal of the marriage tax penalty, and creation of American Dream Savings Accounts to provide middle class tax relief.

6. THE NATIONAL SECURITY RESTORATION ACT: No U.S. troops under U.N. command and restoration of the essential parts of our national security funding to strengthen our national defense and maintain our credibility around the world.

7. THE SENIOR CITIZENS FAIRNESS ACT: Raise the Social Security earnings limit which currently forces seniors out of the work force, repeal the 1993 tax hikes on Social Security benefits and provide tax incentives for private long-term care insurance to let Older Americans keep more of what they have earned over the years.

8. THE JOB CREATION AND WAGE ENHANCEMENT ACT: Small business incentives, capital gains cut and indexation, neutral cost recovery, risk assessment/cost-benefit analysis, strengthening the Regulatory Flexibility Act and unfunded mandate reform to create jobs and raise worker wages.

9. THE COMMON SENSE LEGAL REFORM ACT: "Loser pays" laws, reasonable limits on punitive damages and reform of product liability laws to stem the endless tide of litigation.

10. THE CITIZEN LEGISLATURE ACT: A first-ever vote on term limits to replace career politicians with citizen legislators.

Further, we will instruct the House Budget Committee to report to the floor and we will work to enact additional budget savings, beyond the budget cuts specifically included in the legislation described above, to ensure that the Federal budget deficit will be less than it would have been without the enactment of these bills.

Respecting the judgment of our fellow citizens as we seek their mandate for reform, we hereby pledge our names to this Contract with America.

INDEX TO SONGS

NAME INDEX

SUBJECT INDEX

V

W

About the Author

George R. Nethercutt, Jr. is founder and chairman of The George Nethercutt Foundation, a nonprofit, nonpartisan organization established to foster an understanding of government and public policies in young adults and create a new generation of principled leadership in America. He is an attorney and, from 1995 to 2005, represented Washington State's 5th Congressional District as a member of the U.S. House of Representatives.